D

Jane Austen's
NORTHANGER ABBEY

NORTHANGER ABBEY. Contains material originally published in magazine form as NORTHANGER ABBEY #1-5. First printing 2012. ISBN# 978-0-7851-6440-1. Published by MARVEL WORLDWIDE, INC., a subsidiary of MARVEL ENTERTAINMENT, LLC. OFFICE OF PUBLICATION: 135 West 50th Street, New York, NY 10020. Copyright © 2011 and 2012 Marvel Characters, Inc. All rights reserved. $14.99 per copy in the U.S. and $16.99 in Canada (GST #R127032852); Canadian Agreement #40668537. All characters featured in this issue and the distinctive names and likenesses thereof, and all related indicia are trademarks of Marvel Characters, Inc. No similarity between any of the names, characters, persons, and/or institutions in this magazine with those of any living or dead person or institution is intended, and any such similarity which may exist is purely coincidental. Printed in the U.S.A. ALAN FINE, EVP - Office of the President, Marvel Worldwid[...] - Print, Animation & Digital Divisions; JOE QUESADA, Chief Creative Officer; TOM BREVOORT, SV[...] N JAYATILLEKE, SVP & Associate Publisher, Publishing; [...].B. CEBULSKI, SVP of Creator & Content [...]ULLO, SVP of Brand Planning & Communications; JIM [...]'KEEFE, VP of Operations & Logistics; DA[...]ions Manager; ALEX MORALES, Publishing Operations Manager; STAN LEE, Chairman Emeritus. Fo[...] Niza Disla, Director of Marvel Partnerships, at ndisla@ marvel.com. For Marvel subscription inqu[...]2 by SHERIDAN BOOKS, INC., CHELSEA, MI, USA.

0 9 8 7 6 5 4 3 2 1

NORTHANGER ABBEY

BASED ON THE
NOVEL BY

Jane Austen

WRITER
Nancy Butler

ARTIST
Janet K. Lee

COLOR ARTIST
Nick Filardi

LETTERER
Jeff Eckleberry

ASSISTANT EDITORS
Rachel Pinnelas & Jon Moisan

EDITOR
Sana Amanat

Collection Editor: Mark D. Beazley • Assistant Editors: Nelson Ribeiro & Alex Starbuck
Editor, Special Projects: Jennifer Grünwald • Senior Editor, Special Projects: Jeff Youngquist
Senior Vice President of Sales: David Gabriel
SVP of Brand Planning & Communications: Michael Pasciullo
Book Design: Jeff Powell

Editor in Chief: Axel Alonso • Chief Creative Officer: Joe Quesada
Publisher: Dan Buckley • Executive Producer: Alan Fine

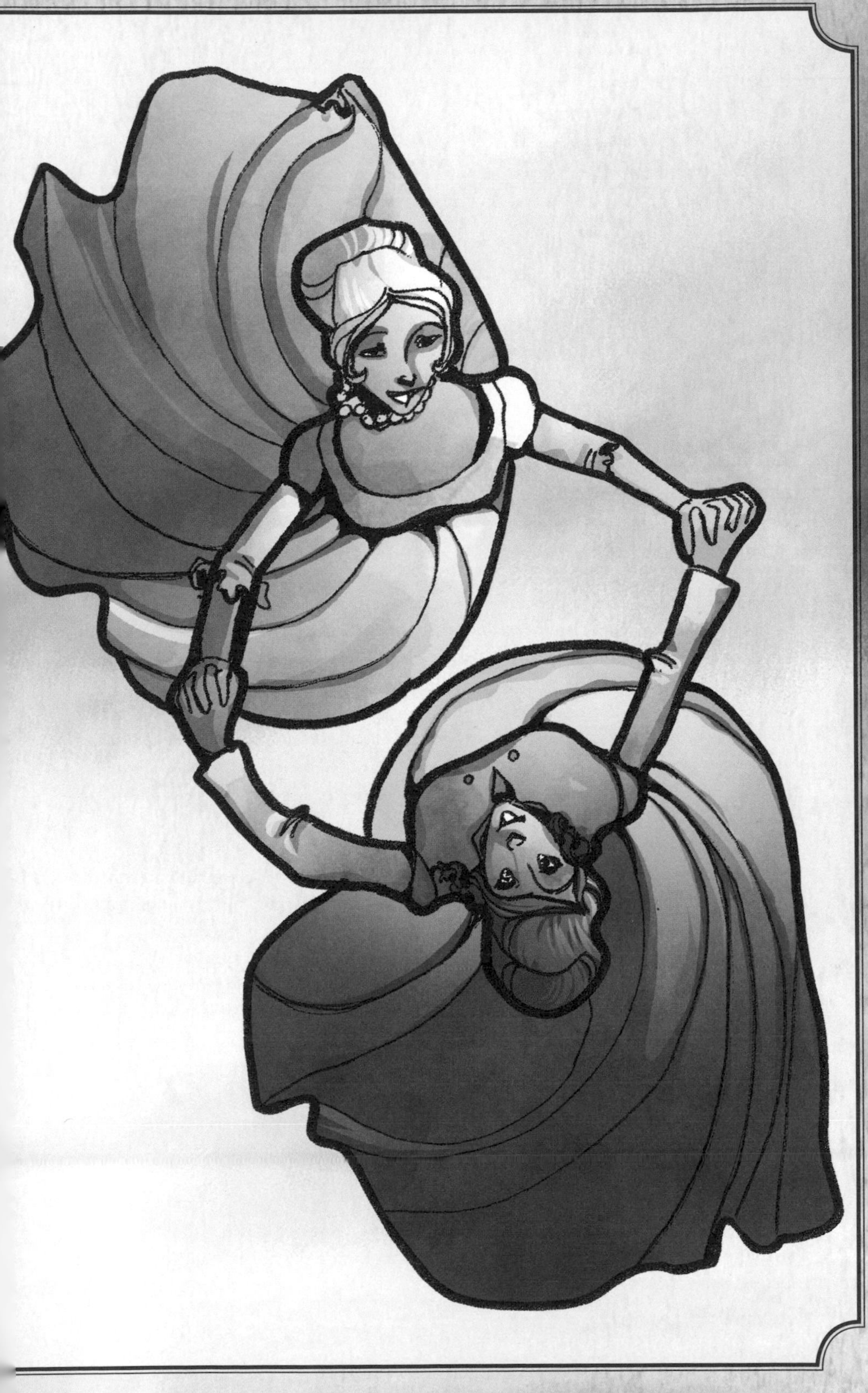

Introduction

Northanger Abbey is Jane Austen on steroids.

A writer who excelled at sly innuendo and who uttered her social criticism behind a silken, though frequently sheer, hanky, Austen never even bothers to raise the hanky here and subsequently pulls out all the stops. Austen has also removed much of the emotional underpinnings that grounded her other works, and with Northanger Abbey offers us blatant parody . . . of the dark Gothic novels so popular in her day . . . of young bucks with inflated egos . . . of encroaching, scheming females . . . and of crusty, demanding military officers who treat their children like their troops. (Scholars believe she initially intended this story for family entertainment, and it does have the same high level of lampooning humor—and "insider" jokes—as her teen-age effort, *The History of England*, also written for fireside amusement. She clearly possessed an iconoclastic nature at an early age; nothing was sacred when viewed by Jane's basilisk eye!)

As a result, Austen's usual supporting cast of upstarts, ne'er-do-wells, social climbers, toadeaters, and entrenched snobs has now morphed into a gallery of near-grotesques: Isabella preens endlessly, grinning fit to fracture her jaw; John Thorpe brags, boasts, and blithely mocks everyone he meets (including his own mother); and General Tilney gnashes his teeth, strides across the parlor, and whips his crop through the air like a… well, like a proper Gothic villain. Yet Austen handles every bit—nuanced or over the top—with an expert grip, grappling effortlessly with this farcical format and giving lie to the dire warnings of classical actors that "tragedy's easy; *comedy* is hard." Austen makes creating broad comedy seem as effortless as a Sunday stroll along the Royal Crescent.

Yet in the midst of this literary sideshow stands Austen's most understated and heartfelt hero. Catherine Morland may be the star of the story, but Henry Tilney shines as its emotional core. He is the sort of suitor most Regency young ladies dreamt about: good looking, comfortably off, old enough to be wise and socially adept, yet young enough to delight in teasing and witty banter. It is no wonder he fascinated Catherine, so often in the company of insufferable, boorish John Thorpe. But Henry Tilney would always appeal—as a "steady guy" with a twinkle in his eye—even were he not juxtaposed with a buffoon. Some critics claim Henry is patronizing, or even condescending to callow young Catherine, but I prefer to view him as bemused and even compelled by her artlessness. Yes, he occasionally schools her, but I never sense that he is using his superior intellect to put her down; rather it seems he wants to elevate her and allow her to make the most of her own gifts.

Oh, you lovers of Austen can have your dour Darcys, your noble Knightleys . . . I fear I am smitten with humble Henry. How can any woman resist a man who "understands muslins" *and* landscapes his own garden?

Austen, who is not above preaching, finds real grist for her mill here—using several exchanges in the book to defend the writers of novels. When *Northanger Abbey* was completed in 1799, these narrative tales were still considered lowbrow diversions by many in society, and even harmful to youthful sensibilities by some members of the clergy. Here, Austen stoutly defends her chosen genre: "It is only a novel," a hypothetical young lady says dismissively of the book she is reading, and then Catherine (in Austen's voice) adds, "or, in short, only some work in which the greatest powers of the mind are displayed, in which the most thorough knowledge of human nature, the happiest delineation of its varieties, the liveliest effusions of wit and humor, are conveyed to the world in the best-chosen language."

The book itself had an odd career. It is likely the third novel she worked on, but the first she completed and offered for publication. In 1803 she sold it for £10 to a London bookseller, Crosby & Co., who never published it. Austen (or her brother Henry) bought it back in 1816, for the same £10, the publisher never realizing that the author had by then written four successful novels. Henry had it published in 1817, after his sister's death, as part of a four-volume set.

This is the second Austen title I have worked on with illustrator Janet K. Lee—we first collaborated on Marvel's *Emma*—and once again she has found the perfect balance between period accuracy and her own distinctive style of illustration. Her evocations of Katherine's overwrought imaginings while visiting the Abbey are especially tasty—equal parts frightening and funny. And I must also applaud the appropriate "Gothicity" of Julian Totino Tedesco's beautiful, moody covers.

For myself, I enjoyed doing this adaptation immensely. A book I was only briefly acquainted with many years back has now become akin to a dear, cherished friend. I look forward to rereading it in the years ahead. Meanwhile, I shall have this Marvel volume to page through whenever I want to revisit Catherine and Henry . . . and Northanger Abbey.

Nancy Butler
August 2012

Nancy Butler, the author of 12 Signet Regencies and three Christmas novellas, was twice awarded the RITA by the Romance Writers of America; won two Reviewer's Choice Awards from *Romantic Times Magazine*; and was retired to the Hall of Fame by the New Jersey Romance Writers. Under her own name, Nancy Hajeski, she is the author of young adult nonfiction titles, such as *The Hammond Book of Presidents*, and *Hammond Undercover: Rocks and Minerals*, as well as the upcoming coffee table book, *Hollywood Fashion*. Butler lives in the Catskill Mountains beside a world-famous trout stream.

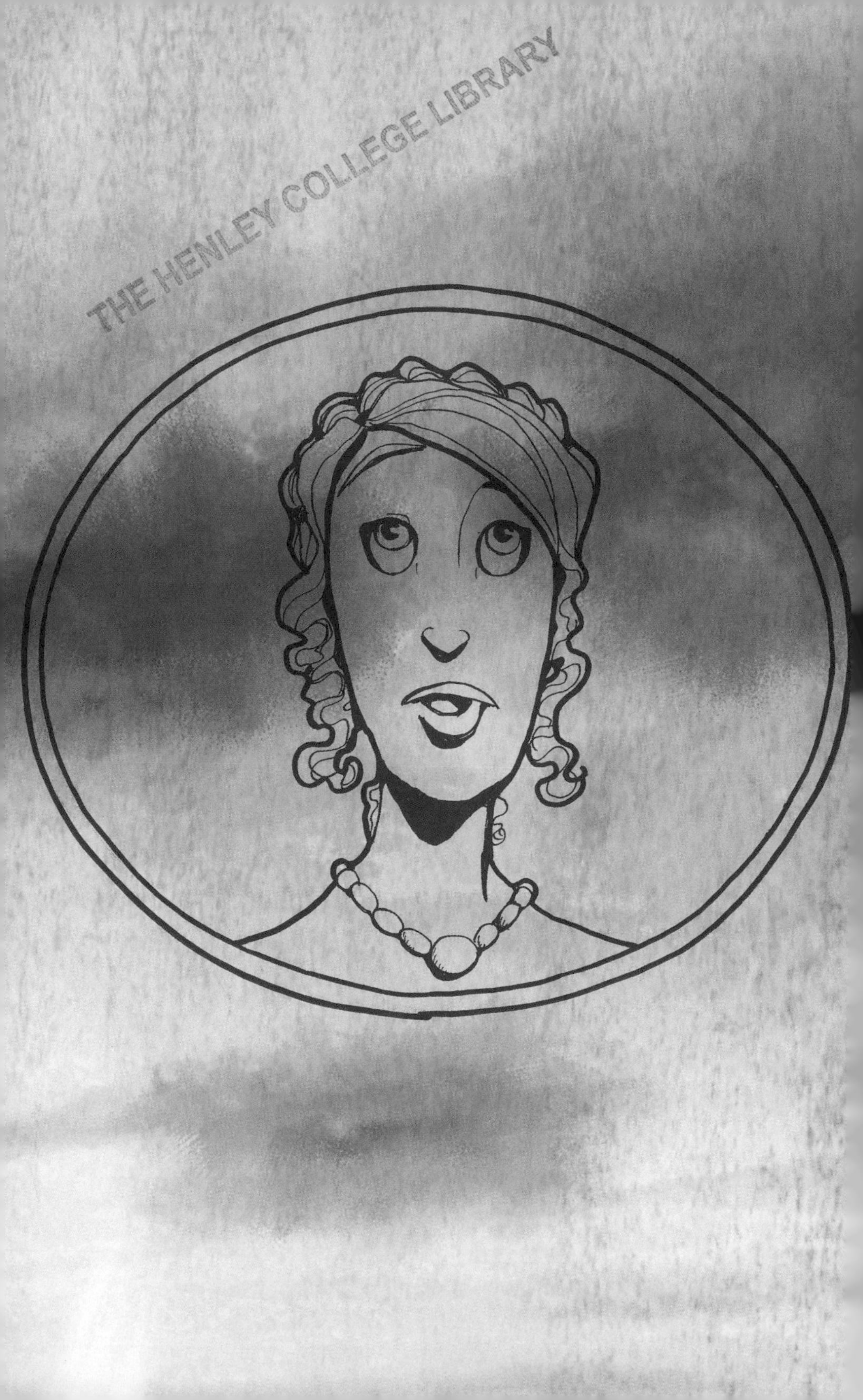

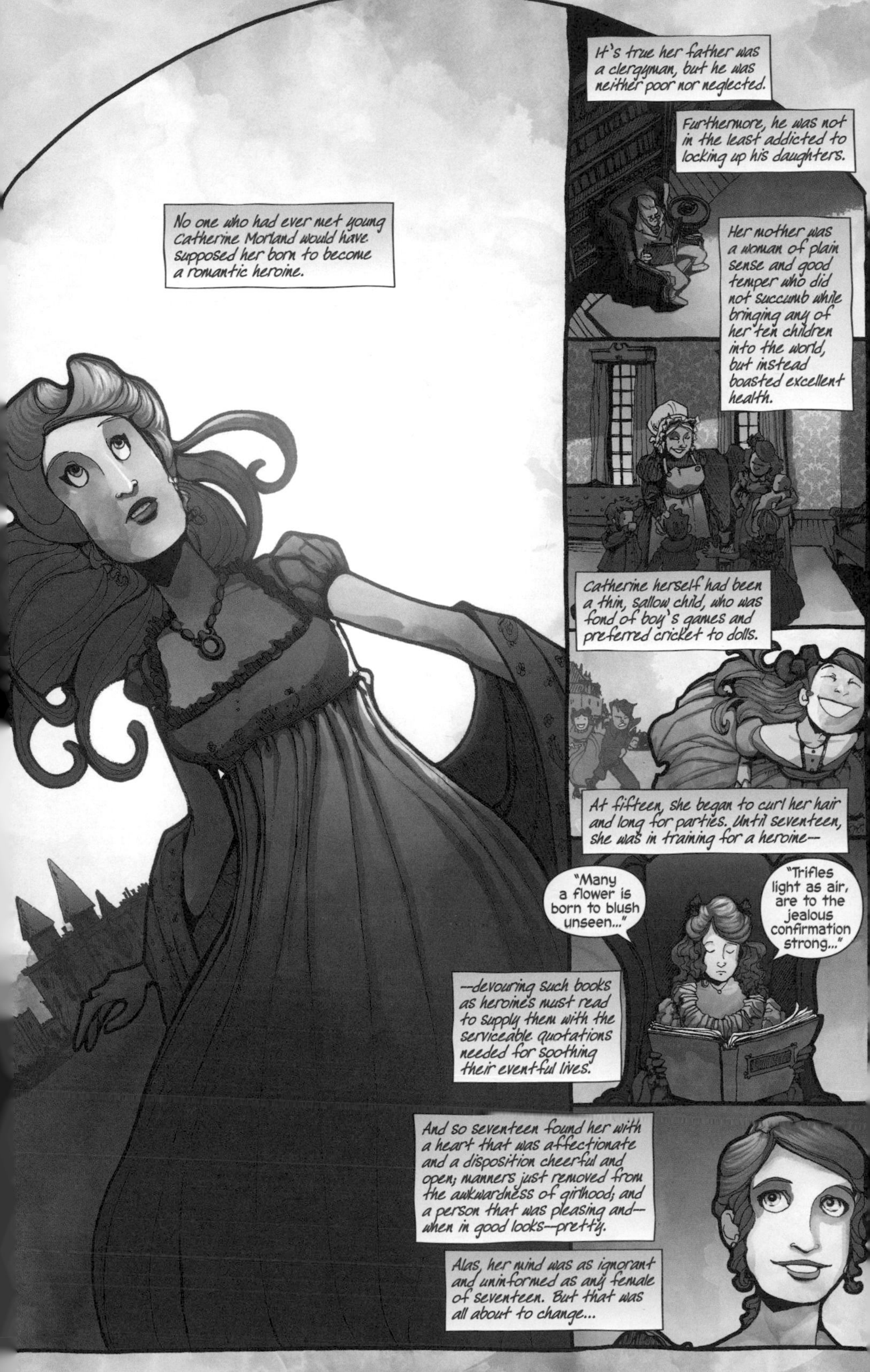
No one who had ever met young Catherine Morland would have supposed her born to become a romantic heroine.
It's true her father was a clergyman, but he was neither poor nor neglected.
Furthermore, he was not in the least addicted to locking up his daughters.
Her mother was a woman of plain sense and good temper who did not succumb while bringing any of her ten children into the world, but instead boasted excellent health.
Catherine herself had been a thin, sallow child, who was fond of boy's games and preferred cricket to dolls.
At fifteen, she began to curl her hair and long for parties. Until seventeen, she was in training for a heroine--
"Many a flower is born to blush unseen..."
"Trifles light as air, are to the jealous confirmation strong..."
--devouring such books as heroines must read to supply them with the serviceable quotations needed for soothing their eventful lives.
And so seventeen found her with a heart that was affectionate and a disposition cheerful and open; manners just removed from the awkwardness of girlhood; and a person that was pleasing and--when in good looks--pretty.
Alas, her mind was as ignorant and uninformed as any female of seventeen. But that was all about to change...

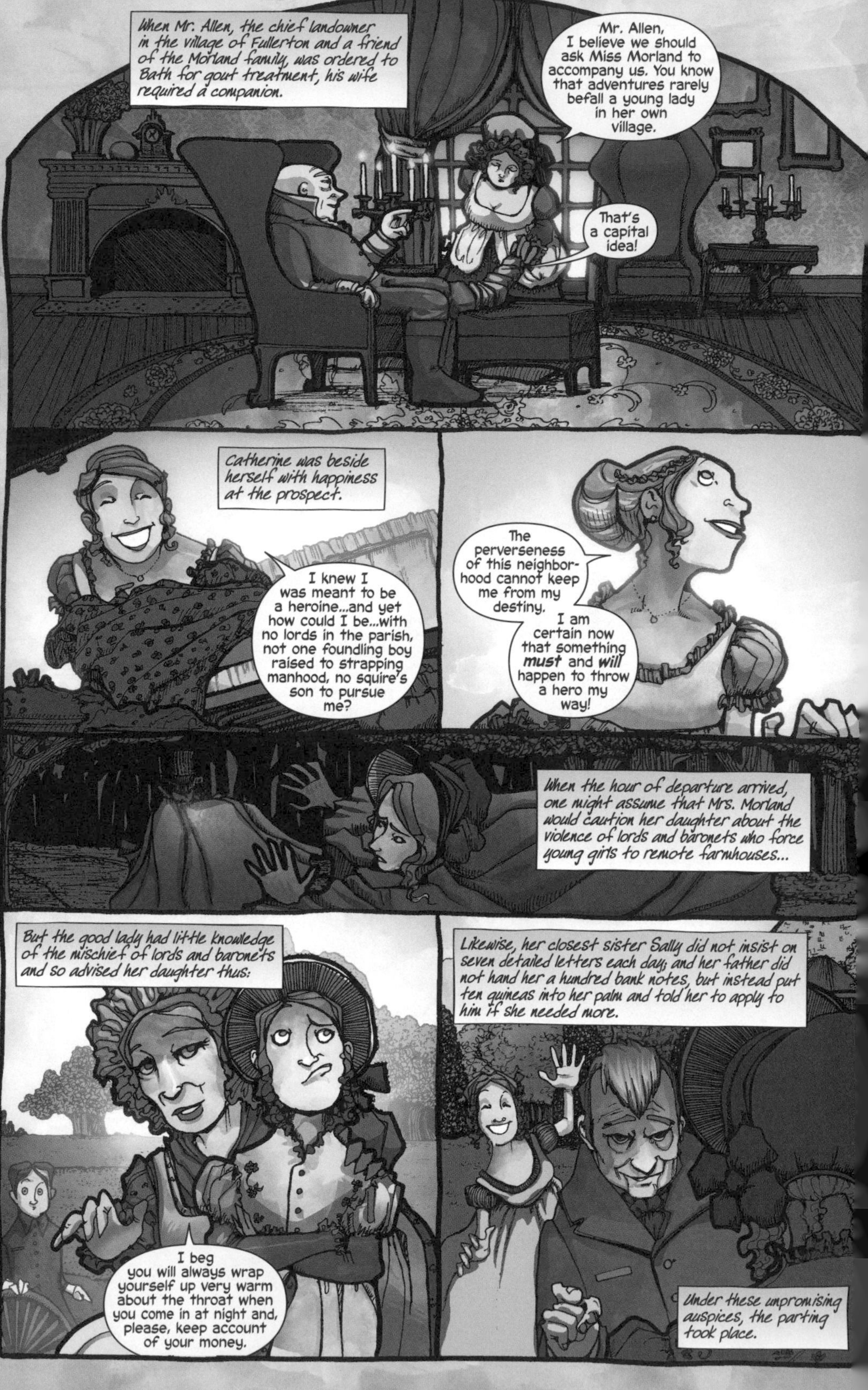
When Mr. Allen, the chief landowner in the village of Fullerton and a friend of the Morland family, was ordered to Bath for gout treatment, his wife required a companion.
Mr. Allen, I believe we should ask Miss Morland to accompany us. You know that adventures rarely befall a young lady in her own village.
That's a capital idea!
Catherine was beside herself with happiness at the prospect.
I knew I was meant to be a heroine...and yet how could I be...with no lords in the parish, not one foundling boy raised to strapping manhood, no squire's son to pursue me?
The perverseness of this neighborhood cannot keep me from my destiny.
I am certain now that something must and will happen to throw a hero my way!
When the hour of departure arrived, one might assume that Mrs. Morland would caution her daughter about the violence of lords and baronets who force young girls to remote farmhouses...
But the good lady had little knowledge of the mischief of lords and baronets and so advised her daughter thus:
I beg you will always wrap yourself up very warm about the throat when you come in at night and, please, keep account of your money.
Likewise, her closest sister Sally did not insist on seven detailed letters each day; and her father did not hand her a hundred bank notes, but instead put ten guineas into her palm and told her to apply to him if she needed more.
Under these unpromising auspices, the parting took place.

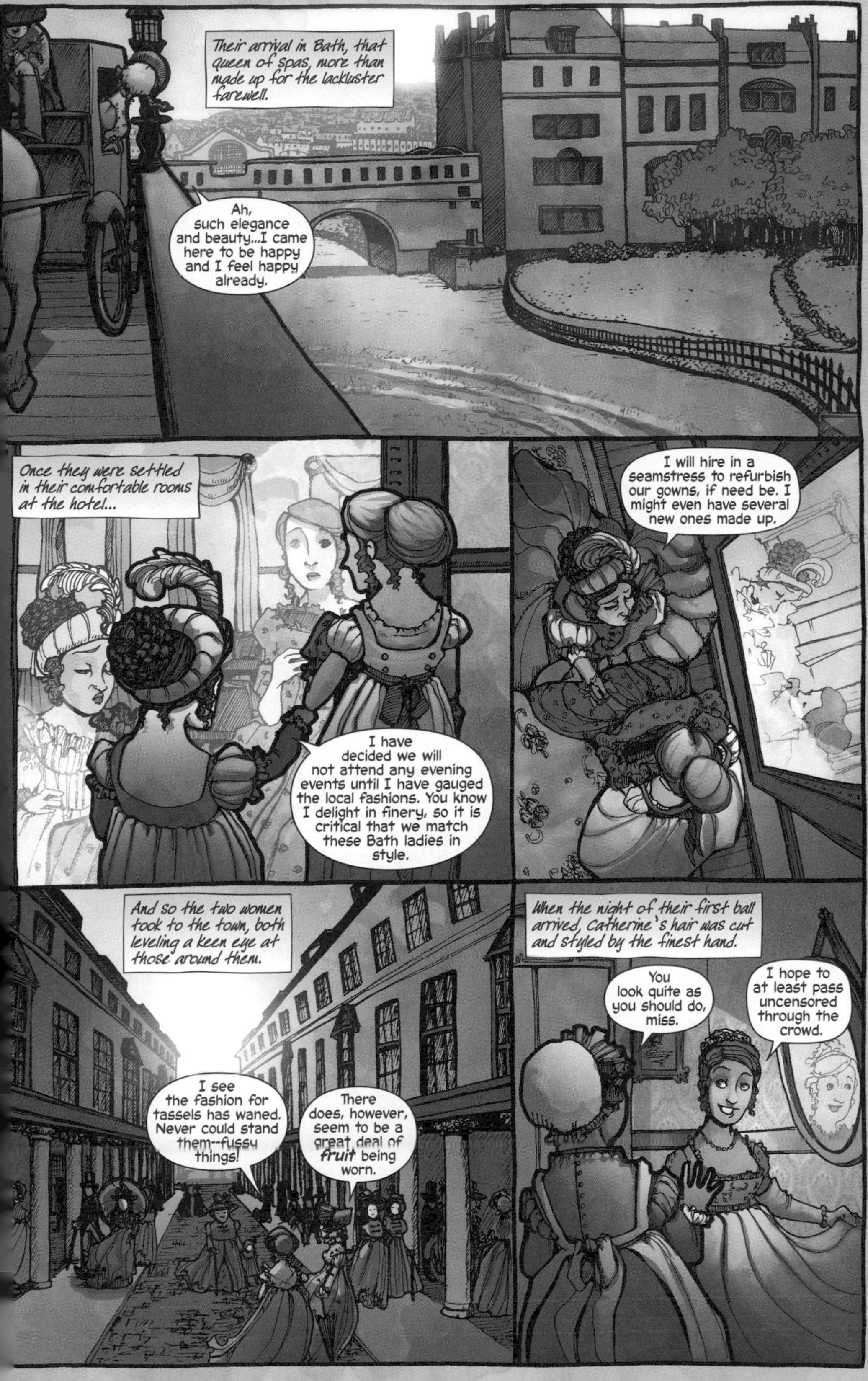
Their arrival in Bath, that queen of spas, more than made up for the lackluster farewell.
Ah, such elegance and beauty...I came here to be happy and I feel happy already.
Once they were settled in their comfortable rooms at the hotel...
I have decided we will not attend any evening events until I have gauged the local fashions. You know I delight in finery, so it is critical that we match these Bath ladies in style.
I will hire in a seamstress to refurbish our gowns, if need be. I might even have several new ones made up.
And so the two women took to the town, both leveling a keen eye at those around them.
I see the fashion for tassels has waned. Never could stand them--fussy things!
There does, however, seem to be a great deal of fruit being worn.
When the night of their first ball arrived, Catherine's hair was cut and styled by the finest hand.
You look quite as you should do, miss.
I hope to at least pass uncensored through the crowd.

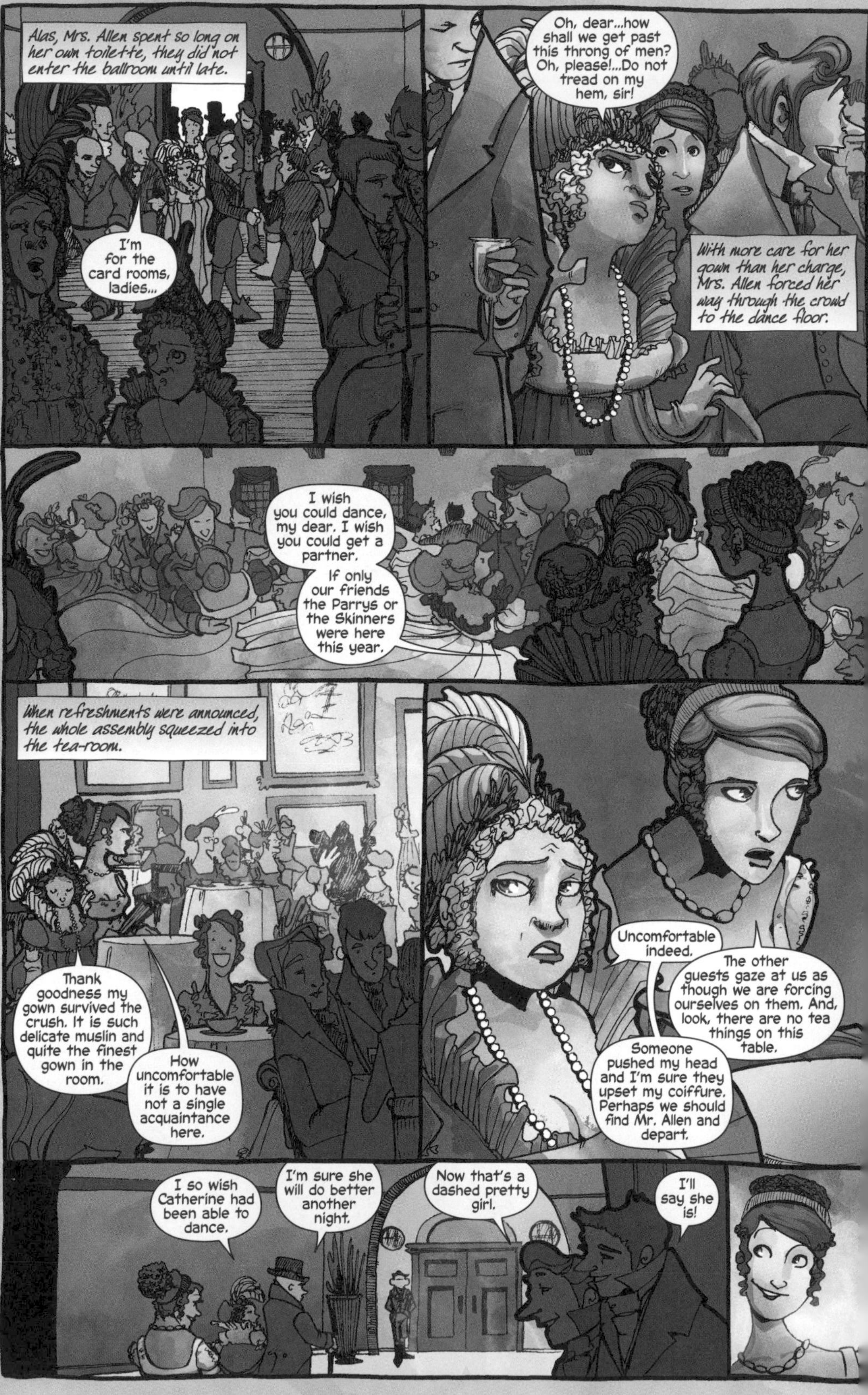

Alas, Mrs. Allen spent so long on her own toilette, they did not enter the ballroom until late.
I'm for the card rooms, ladies...
Oh, dear...how shall we get past this throng of men? Oh, please!...Do not tread on my hem, sir!
With more care for her gown than her charge, Mrs. Allen forced her way through the crowd to the dance floor.
I wish you could dance, my dear. I wish you could get a partner.
If only our friends the Parrys or the Skinners were here this year.
When refreshments were announced, the whole assembly squeezed into the tea-room.
Thank goodness my gown survived the crush. It is such delicate muslin and quite the finest gown in the room.
How uncomfortable it is to have not a single acquaintance here.
Uncomfortable indeed.
The other guests gaze at us as though we are forcing ourselves on them. And, look, there are no tea things on this table.
Someone pushed my head and I'm sure they upset my coiffure. Perhaps we should find Mr. Allen and depart.
I so wish Catherine had been able to dance.
I'm sure she will do better another night.
Now that's a dashed pretty girl.
I'll say she is!

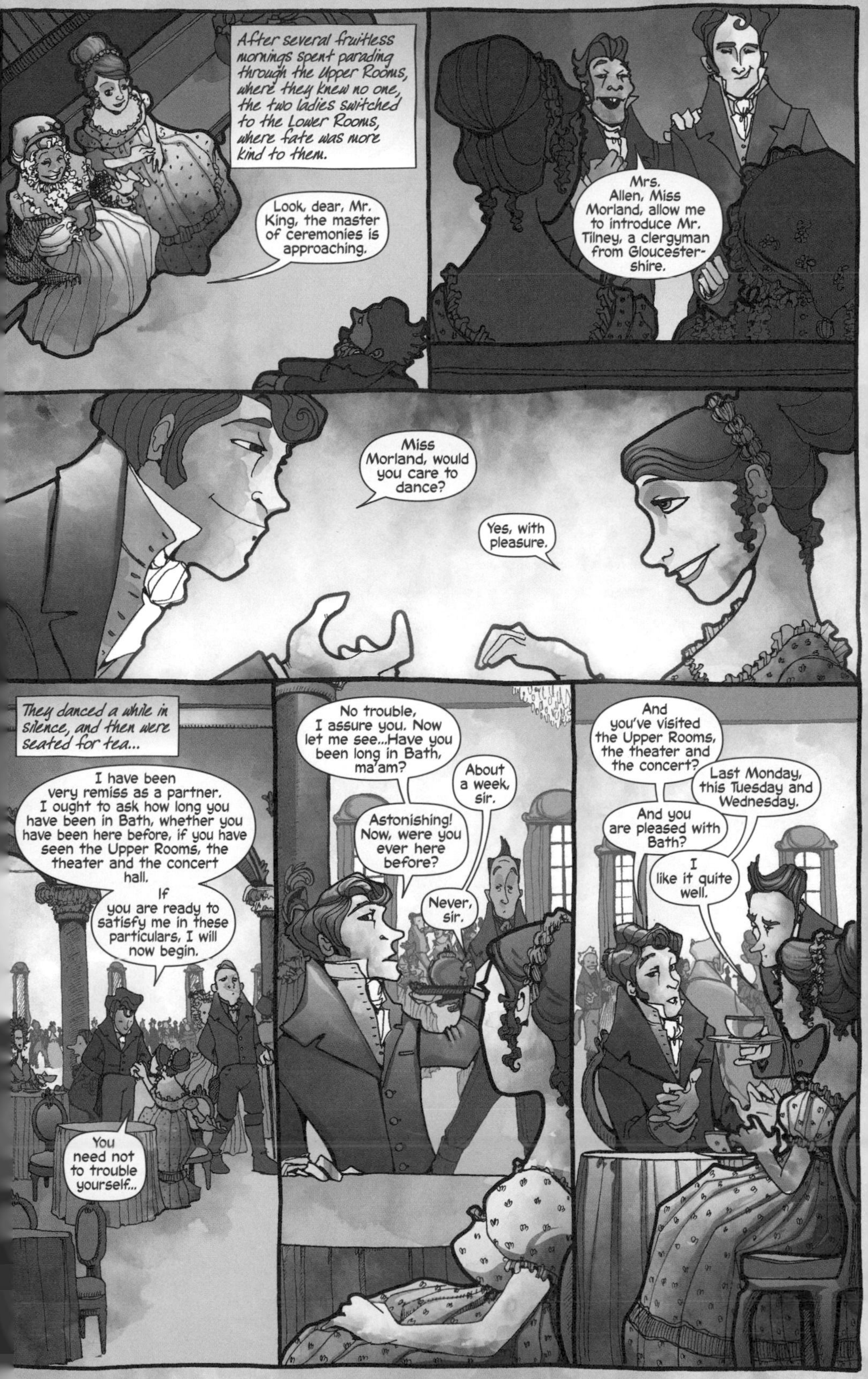
After several fruitless mornings spent parading through the Upper Rooms, where they knew no one, the two ladies switched to the Lower Rooms, where fate was more kind to them.
Look, dear, Mr. King, the master of ceremonies is approaching.
Mrs. Allen, Miss Morland, allow me to introduce Mr. Tilney, a clergyman from Gloucestershire.
Miss Morland, would you care to dance?
Yes, with pleasure.
They danced a while in silence, and then were seated for tea...
I have been very remiss as a partner. I ought to ask how long you have been in Bath, whether you have been here before, if you have seen the Upper Rooms, the theater and the concert hall.
If you are ready to satisfy me in these particulars, I will now begin.
You need not to trouble yourself...
No trouble, I assure you. Now let me see...Have you been long in Bath, ma'am?
About a week, sir.
Astonishing! Now, were you ever here before?
Never, sir.
And you've visited the Upper Rooms, the theater and the concert?
Last Monday, this Tuesday and Wednesday.
And you are pleased with Bath?
I like it quite well.

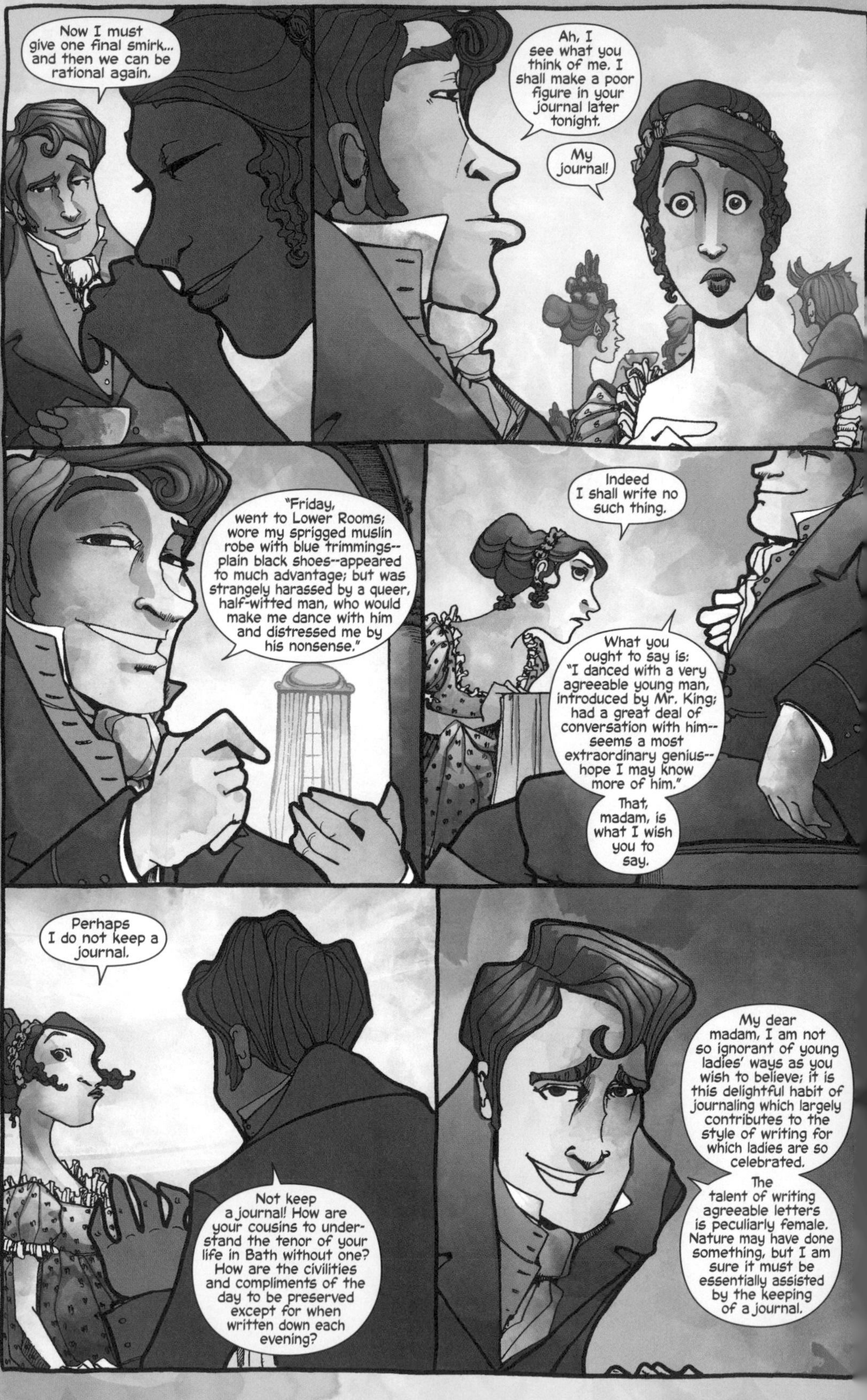
Now I must give one final smirk... and then we can be rational again.
Ah, I see what you think of me. I shall make a poor figure in your journal later tonight.
My journal!
"Friday, went to Lower Rooms; wore my sprigged muslin robe with blue trimmings--plain black shoes--appeared to much advantage; but was strangely harassed by a queer, half-witted man, who would make me dance with him and distressed me by his nonsense."
Indeed I shall write no such thing.
What you ought to say is: "I danced with a very agreeable young man, introduced by Mr. King; had a great deal of conversation with him--seems a most extraordinary genius--hope I may know more of him."
That, madam, is what I wish you to say.
Perhaps I do not keep a journal.
Not keep a journal! How are your cousins to understand the tenor of your life in Bath without one? How are the civilities and compliments of the day to be preserved except for when written down each evening?
My dear madam, I am not so ignorant of young ladies' ways as you wish to believe; it is this delightful habit of journaling which largely contributes to the style of writing for which ladies are so celebrated.
The talent of writing agreeable letters is peculiarly female. Nature may have done something, but I am sure it must be essentially assisted by the keeping of a journal.

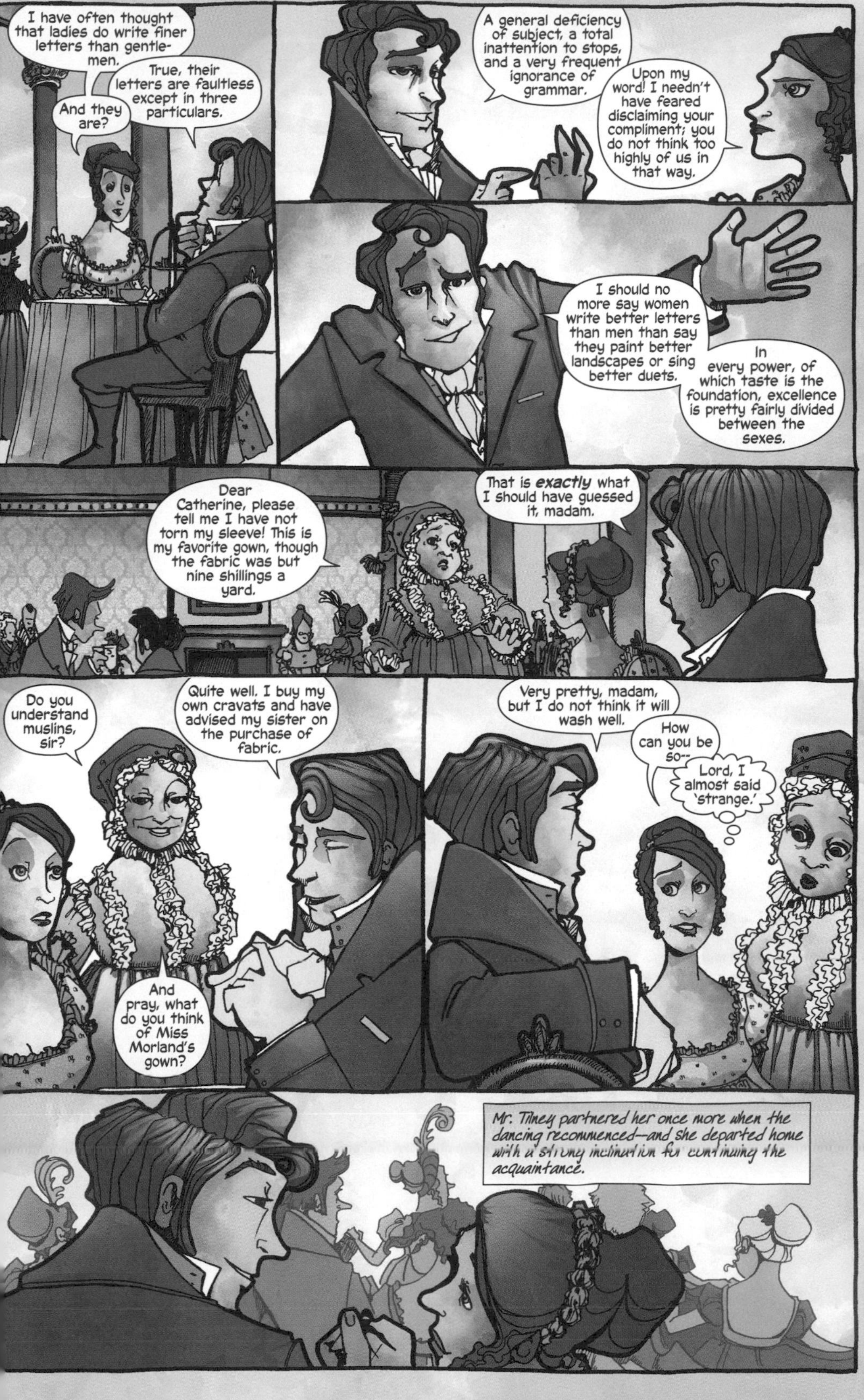

I have often thought that ladies do write finer letters than gentlemen.
And they are?
True, their letters are faultless except in three particulars.
A general deficiency of subject, a total inattention to stops, and a very frequent ignorance of grammar.
Upon my word! I needn't have feared disclaiming your compliment; you do not think too highly of us in that way.
I should no more say women write better letters than men than say they paint better landscapes or sing better duets.
In every power, of which taste is the foundation, excellence is pretty fairly divided between the sexes.
Dear Catherine, please tell me I have not torn my sleeve! This is my favorite gown, though the fabric was but nine shillings a yard.
That is *exactly* what I should have guessed it, madam.
Do you understand muslins, sir?
Quite well. I buy my own cravats and have advised my sister on the purchase of fabric.
And pray, what do you think of Miss Morland's gown?
Very pretty, madam, but I do not think it will wash well.
How can you be so--
Lord, I almost said 'strange.'
Mr. Tilney partnered her once more when the dancing recommenced—and she departed home with a strong inclination for continuing the acquaintance.

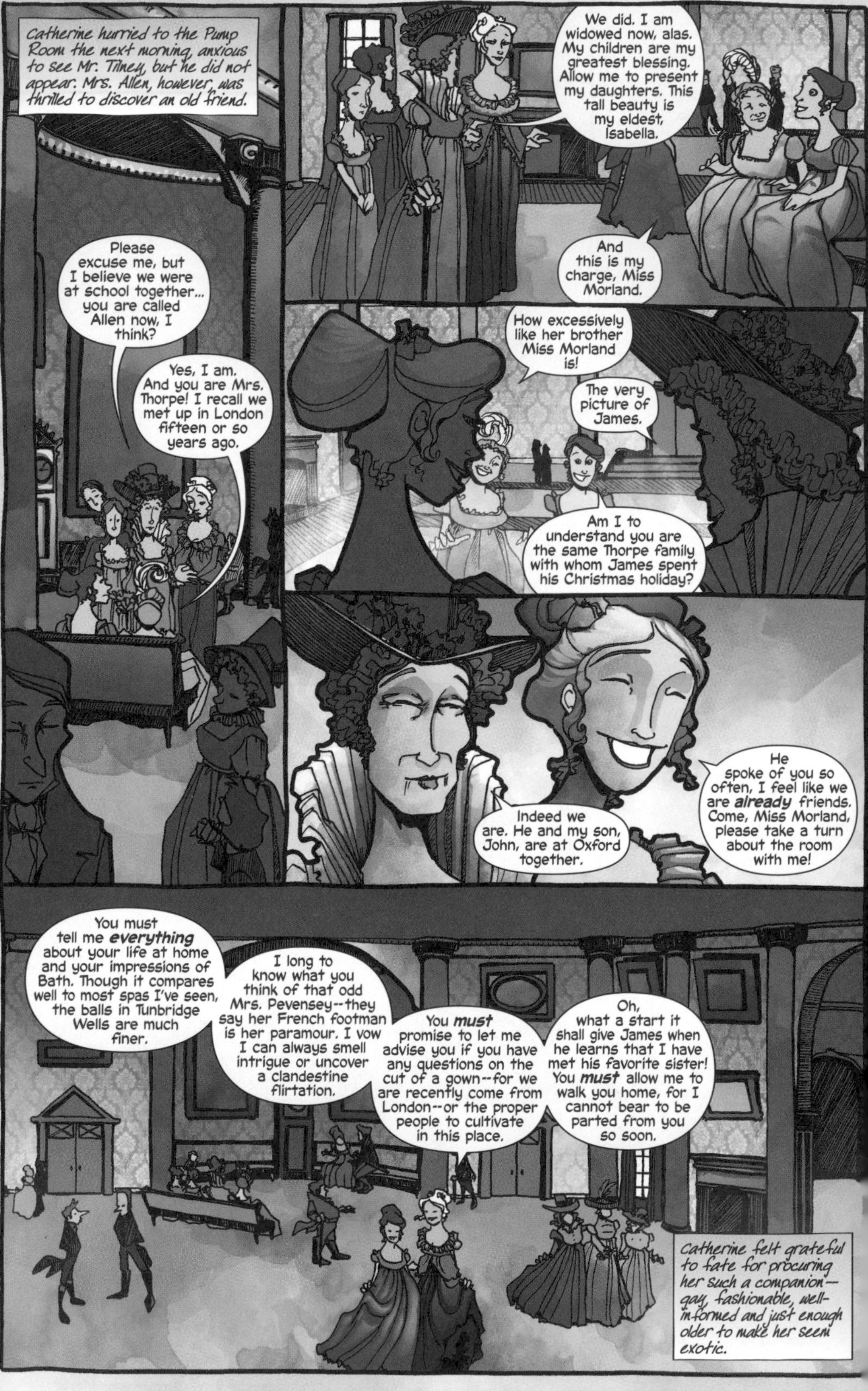
Catherine hurried to the Pump Room the next morning, anxious to see Mr. Tilney, but he did not appear. Mrs. Allen, however, was thrilled to discover an old friend.
Please excuse me, but I believe we were at school together... you are called Allen now, I think?
Yes, I am. And you are Mrs. Thorpe! I recall we met up in London fifteen or so years ago.
We did. I am widowed now, alas. My children are my greatest blessing. Allow me to present my daughters. This tall beauty is my eldest, Isabella.
And this is my charge, Miss Morland.
How excessively like her brother Miss Morland is!
The very picture of James.
Am I to understand you are the same Thorpe family with whom James spent his Christmas holiday?
Indeed we are. He and my son, John, are at Oxford together.
He spoke of you so often, I feel like we are already friends. Come, Miss Morland, please take a turn about the room with me!
You must tell me everything about your life at home and your impressions of Bath. Though it compares well to most spas I've seen, the balls in Tunbridge Wells are much finer.
I long to know what you think of that odd Mrs. Pevensey--they say her French footman is her paramour. I vow I can always smell intrigue or uncover a clandestine flirtation.
You must promise to let me advise you if you have any questions on the cut of a gown--for we are recently come from London--or the proper people to cultivate in this place.
Oh, what a start it shall give James when he learns that I have met his favorite sister! You must allow me to walk you home, for I cannot bear to be parted from you so soon.
Catherine felt grateful to fate for procuring her such a companion--gay, fashionable, well-informed and just enough older to make her seem exotic.

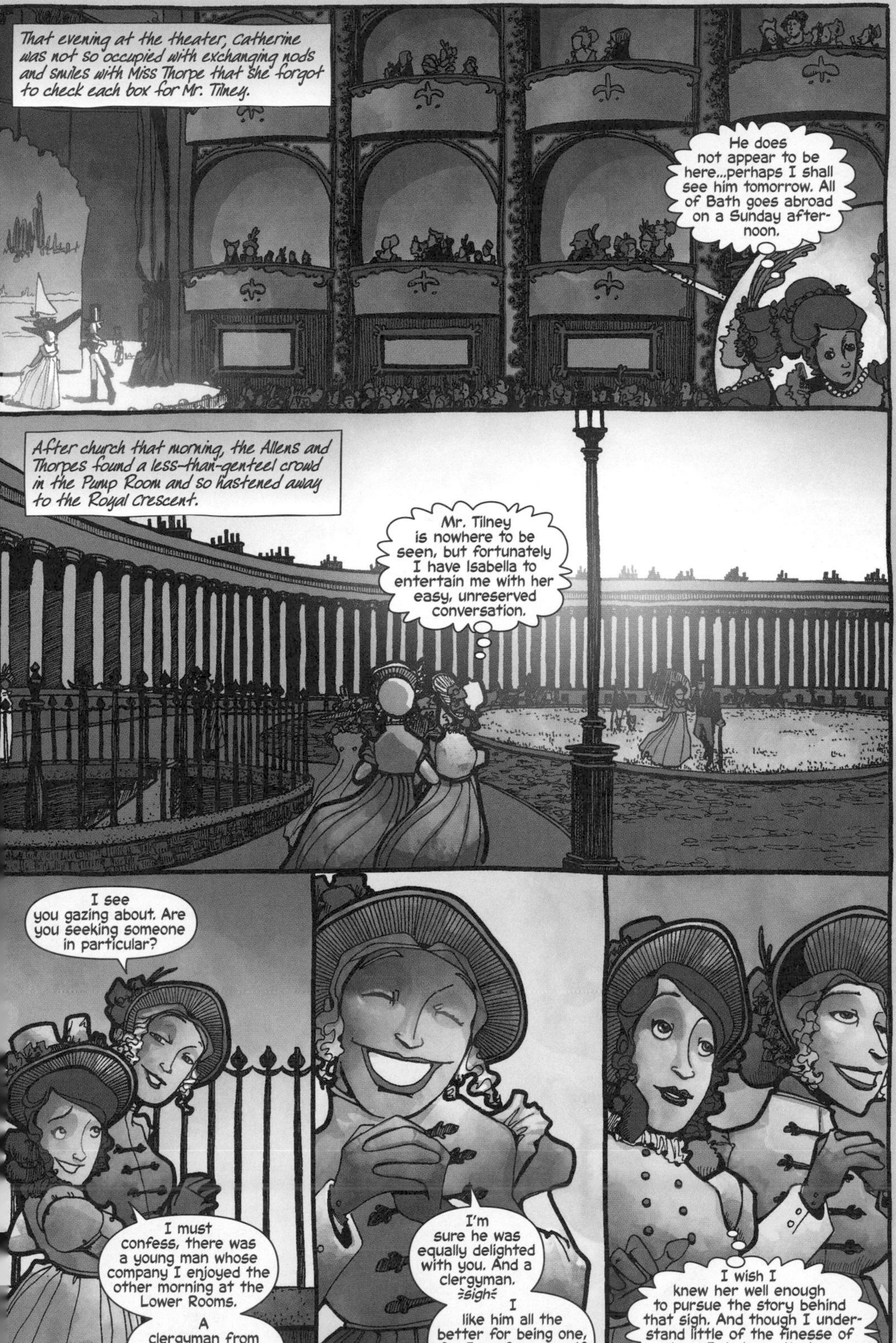
That evening at the theater, Catherine was not so occupied with exchanging nods and smiles with Miss Thorpe that she forgot to check each box for Mr. Tilney.
He does not appear to be here...perhaps I shall see him tomorrow. All of Bath goes abroad on a Sunday after-noon.
After church that morning, the Allens and Thorpes found a less-than-genteel crowd in the Pump Room and so hastened away to the Royal Crescent.
Mr. Tilney is nowhere to be seen, but fortunately I have Isabella to entertain me with her easy, unreserved conversation.
I see you gazing about. Are you seeking someone in particular?
I must confess, there was a young man whose company I enjoyed the other morning at the Lower Rooms.
A clergyman from Gloucestershire. But he has not yet reappeared.
I'm sure he was equally delighted with you. And a clergyman.
sigh
I like him all the better for being one, for I confess myself very partial to the profession.
I wish I knew her well enough to pursue the story behind that sigh. And though I under-stand little of the finesse of love, I do know that a confidence cannot be forced.

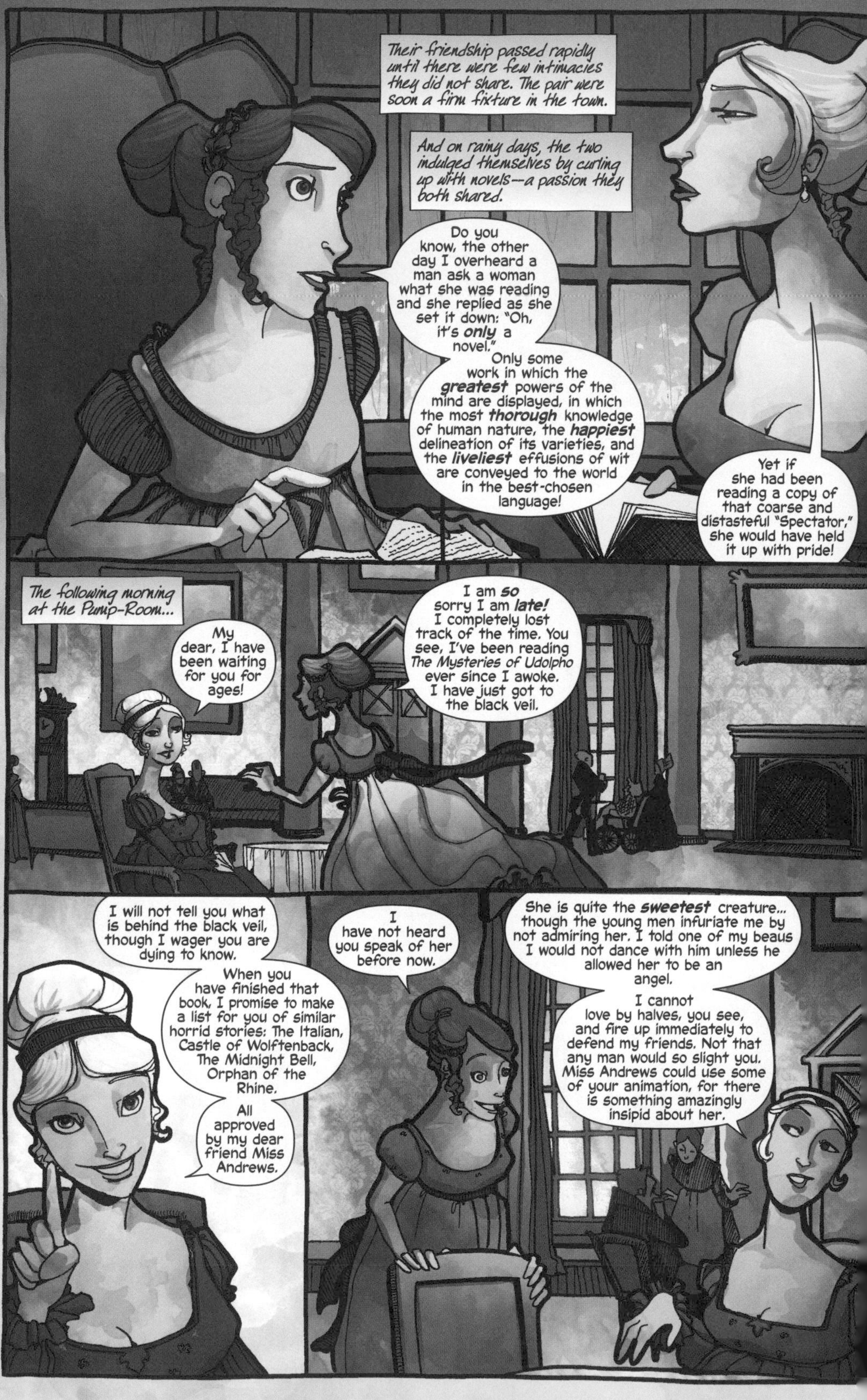
Their friendship passed rapidly until there were few intimacies they did not share. The pair were soon a firm fixture in the town.
And on rainy days, the two indulged themselves by curling up with novels—a passion they both shared.
Do you know, the other day I overheard a man ask a woman what she was reading and she replied as she set it down: "Oh, it's *only* a novel."
Only some work in which the ***greatest*** powers of the mind are displayed, in which the most ***thorough*** knowledge of human nature, the ***happiest*** delineation of its varieties, and the ***liveliest*** effusions of wit are conveyed to the world in the best-chosen language!
Yet if she had been reading a copy of that coarse and distasteful "Spectator," she would have held it up with pride!
The following morning at the Pump-Room...
My dear, I have been waiting for you for ages!
I am ***so*** sorry I am ***late!*** I completely lost track of the time. You see, I've been reading *The Mysteries of Udolpho* ever since I awoke. I have just got to the black veil.
I will not tell you what is behind the black veil, though I wager you are dying to know.
When you have finished that book, I promise to make a list for you of similar horrid stories: The Italian, Castle of Wolftenback, The Midnight Bell, Orphan of the Rhine.
All approved by my dear friend Miss Andrews.
I have not heard you speak of her before now.
She is quite the ***sweetest*** creature... though the young men infuriate me by not admiring her. I told one of my beaus I would not dance with him unless he allowed her to be an angel.
I cannot love by halves, you see, and fire up immediately to defend my friends. Not that any man would so slight you. Miss Andrews could use some of your animation, for there is something amazingly insipid about her.

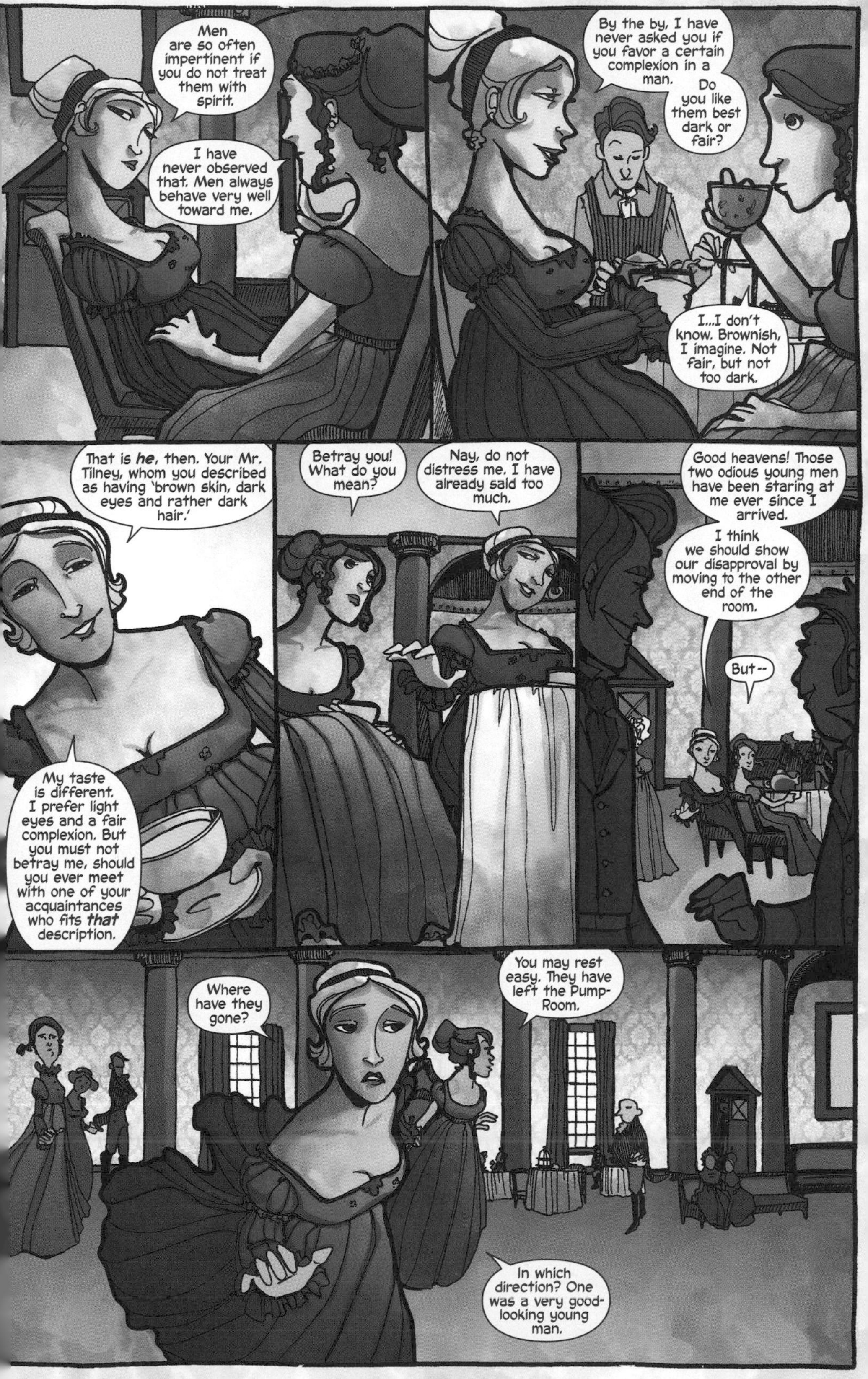
Men are so often impertinent if you do not treat them with spirit.
I have never observed that. Men always behave very well toward me.
By the by, I have never asked you if you favor a certain complexion in a man.
Do you like them best dark or fair?
I...I don't know. Brownish, I imagine. Not fair, but not too dark.
That is **he**, then. Your Mr. Tilney, whom you described as having 'brown skin, dark eyes and rather dark hair.'
My taste is different. I prefer light eyes and a fair complexion. But you must not betray me, should you ever meet with one of your acquaintances who fits **that** description.
Betray you! What do you mean?
Nay, do not distress me. I have already said too much.
Good heavens! Those two odious young men have been staring at me ever since I arrived.
I think we should show our disapproval by moving to the other end of the room.
But--
Where have they gone?
You may rest easy. They have left the Pump-Room.
In which direction? One was a very good-looking young man.

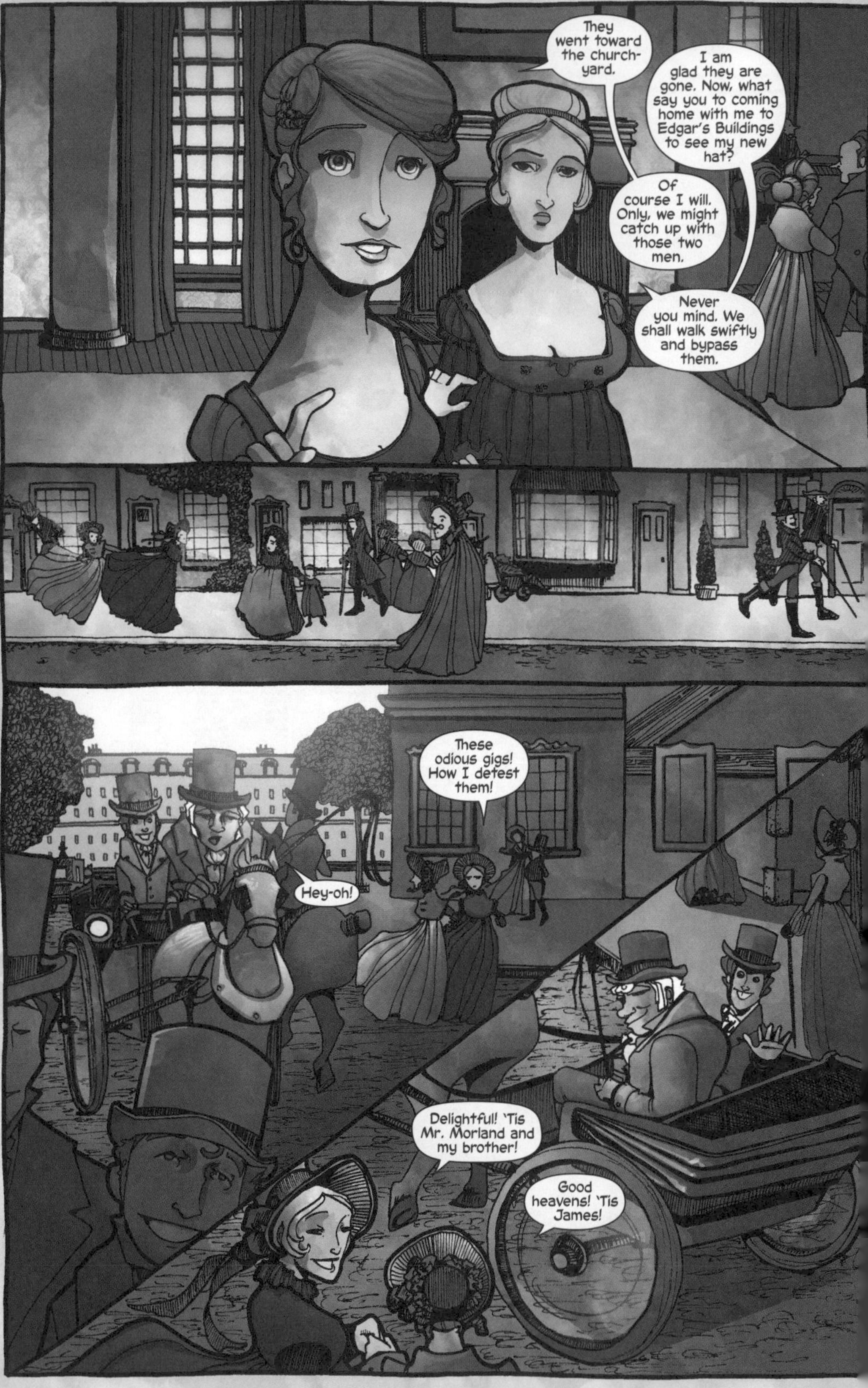
They went toward the church-yard.
I am glad they are gone. Now, what say you to coming home with me to Edgar's Buildings to see my new hat?
Of course I will. Only, we might catch up with those two men.
Never you mind. We shall walk swiftly and bypass them.
These odious gigs! How I detest them!
Hey-oh!
Delightful! 'Tis Mr. Morland and my brother!
Good heavens! 'Tis James!

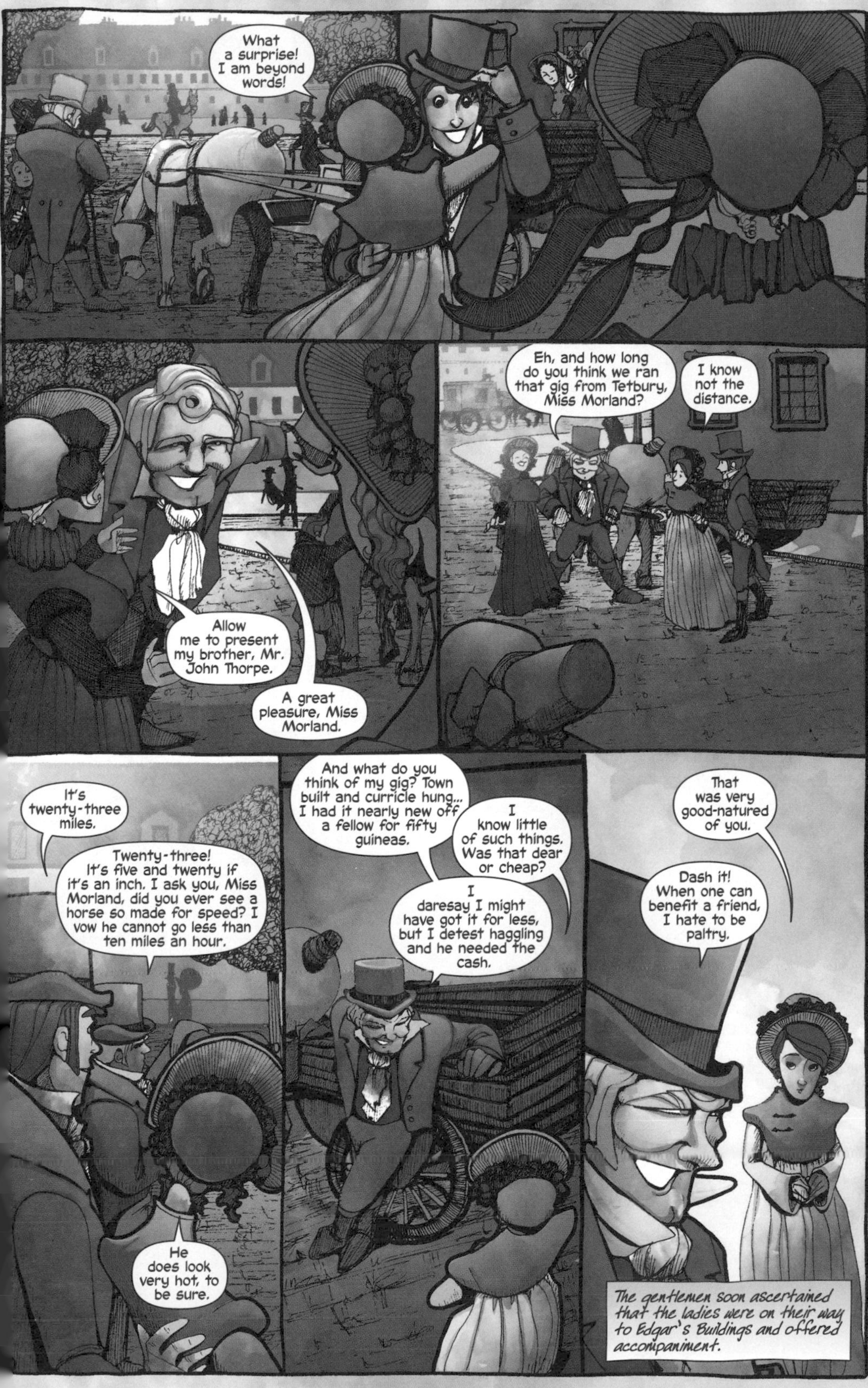
What a surprise! I am beyond words!
Allow me to present my brother, Mr. John Thorpe.
A great pleasure, Miss Morland.
Eh, and how long do you think we ran that gig from Tetbury, Miss Morland?
I know not the distance.
It's twenty-three miles.
Twenty-three! It's five and twenty if it's an inch. I ask you, Miss Morland, did you ever see a horse so made for speed? I vow he cannot go less than ten miles an hour.
He does look very hot, to be sure.
And what do you think of my gig? Town built and curricle hung... I had it nearly new off a fellow for fifty guineas.
I know little of such things. Was that dear or cheap?
I daresay I might have got it for less, but I detest haggling and he needed the cash.
That was very good-natured of you.
Dash it! When one can benefit a friend, I hate to be paltry.
The gentlemen soon ascertained that the ladies were on their way to Edgar's Buildings and offered accompaniment.

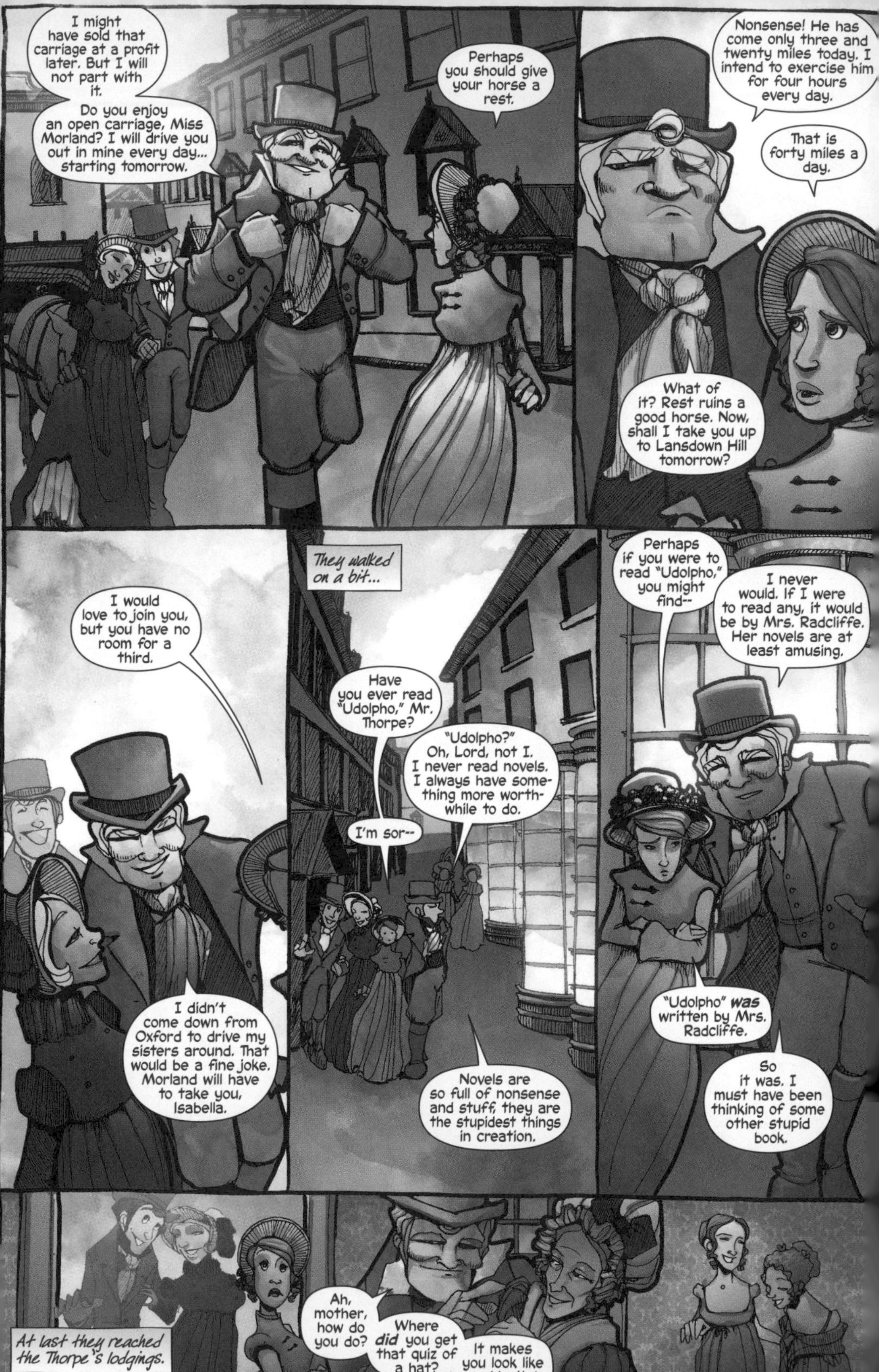
I might have sold that carriage at a profit later. But I will not part with it.
Do you enjoy an open carriage, Miss Morland? I will drive you out in mine every day... starting tomorrow.
Perhaps you should give your horse a rest.
Nonsense! He has come only three and twenty miles today. I intend to exercise him for four hours every day.
That is forty miles a day.
What of it? Rest ruins a good horse. Now, shall I take you up to Lansdown Hill tomorrow?
I would love to join you, but you have no room for a third.
I didn't come down from Oxford to drive my sisters around. That would be a fine joke. Morland will have to take you, Isabella.
They walked on a bit...
Have you ever read "Udolpho," Mr. Thorpe?
"Udolpho?" Oh, Lord, not I. I never read novels. I always have something more worthwhile to do.
I'm sor--
Novels are so full of nonsense and stuff, they are the stupidest things in creation.
Perhaps if you were to read "Udolpho," you might find--
I never would. If I were to read any, it would be by Mrs. Radcliffe. Her novels are at least amusing.
"Udolpho" was written by Mrs. Radcliffe.
So it was. I must have been thinking of some other stupid book.
At last they reached the Thorpe's lodgings.
Ah, mother, how do you do?
Where did you get that quiz of a hat?
It makes you look like an old witch.

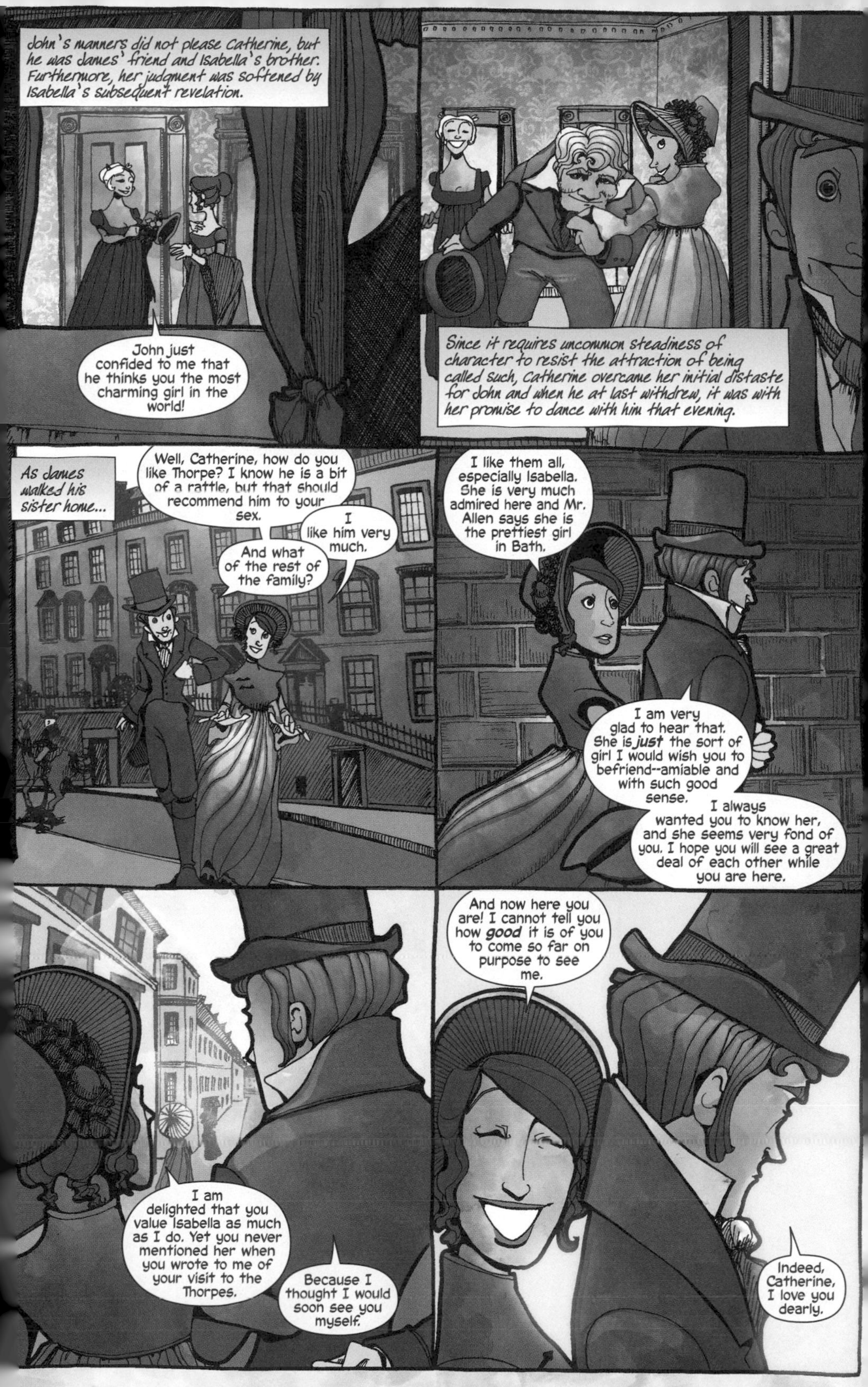
John's manners did not please Catherine, but he was James' friend and Isabella's brother. Furthermore, her judgment was softened by Isabella's subsequent revelation.
John just confided to me that he thinks you the most charming girl in the world!
Since it requires uncommon steadiness of character to resist the attraction of being called such, Catherine overcame her initial distaste for John and when he at last withdrew, it was with her promise to dance with him that evening.
As James walked his sister home...
Well, Catherine, how do you like Thorpe? I know he is a bit of a rattle, but that should recommend him to your sex.
I like him very much.
And what of the rest of the family?
I like them all, especially Isabella. She is very much admired here and Mr. Allen says she is the prettiest girl in Bath.
I am very glad to hear that. She is *just* the sort of girl I would wish you to befriend--amiable and with such good sense.
I always wanted you to know her, and she seems very fond of you. I hope you will see a great deal of each other while you are here.
I am delighted that you value Isabella as much as I do. Yet you never mentioned her when you wrote to me of your visit to the Thorpes.
Because I thought I would soon see you myself.
And now here you are! I cannot tell you how **good** it is of you to come so far on purpose to see me.
Indeed, Catherine, I love you dearly.

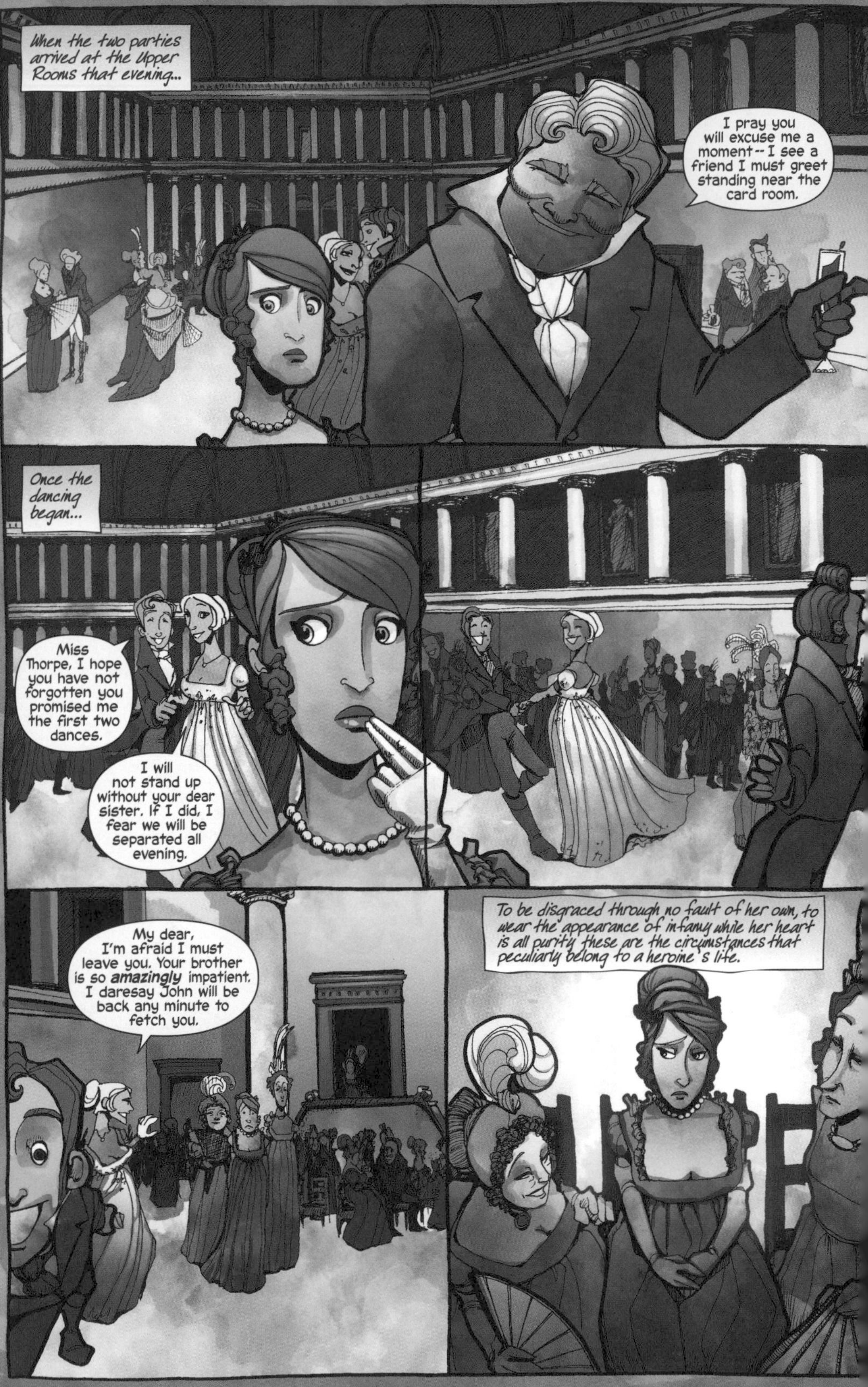
When the two parties arrived at the Upper Rooms that evening...
I pray you will excuse me a moment -- I see a friend I must greet standing near the card room.
Once the dancing began...
Miss Thorpe, I hope you have not forgotten you promised me the first two dances.
I will not stand up without your dear sister. If I did, I fear we will be separated all evening.
My dear, I'm afraid I must leave you. Your brother is so **amazingly** impatient. I daresay John will be back any minute to fetch you.
To be disgraced through no fault of her own, to wear the appearance of infamy while her heart is all purity these are the circumstances that peculiarly belong to a heroine's life.

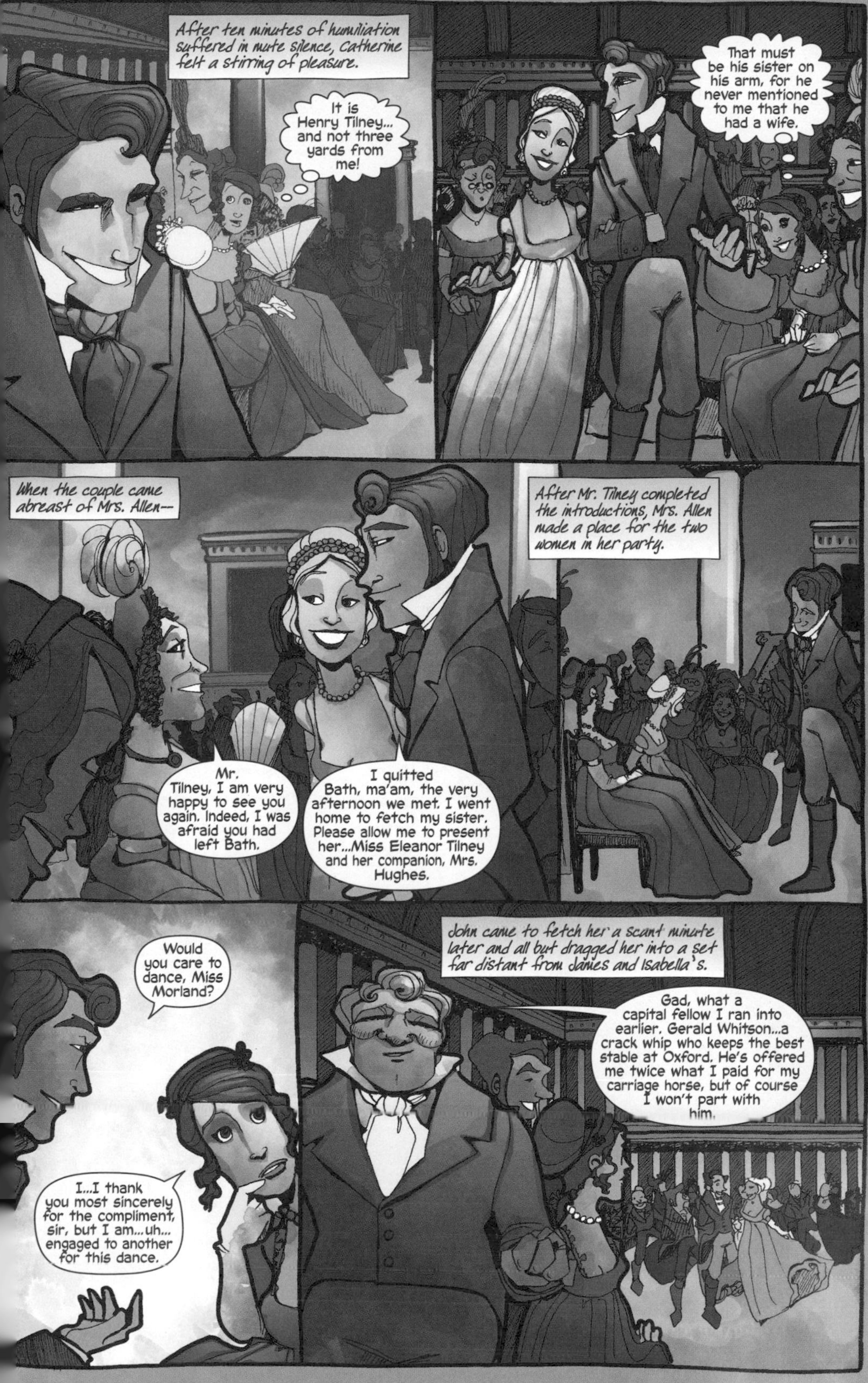
After ten minutes of humiliation suffered in mute silence, Catherine felt a stirring of pleasure.
It is Henry Tilney... and not three yards from me!
That must be his sister on his arm, for he never mentioned to me that he had a wife.
When the couple came abreast of Mrs. Allen--
Mr. Tilney, I am very happy to see you again. Indeed, I was afraid you had left Bath.
I quitted Bath, ma'am, the very afternoon we met. I went home to fetch my sister. Please allow me to present her...Miss Eleanor Tilney and her companion, Mrs. Hughes.
After Mr. Tilney completed the introductions, Mrs. Allen made a place for the two women in her party.
Would you care to dance, Miss Morland?
I...I thank you most sincerely for the compliment, sir, but I am...uh... engaged to another for this dance.
John came to fetch her a scant minute later and all but dragged her into a set far distant from James and Isabella's.
Gad, what a capital fellow I ran into earlier. Gerald Whitson...a crack whip who keeps the best stable at Oxford. He's offered me twice what I paid for my carriage horse, but of course I won't part with him.

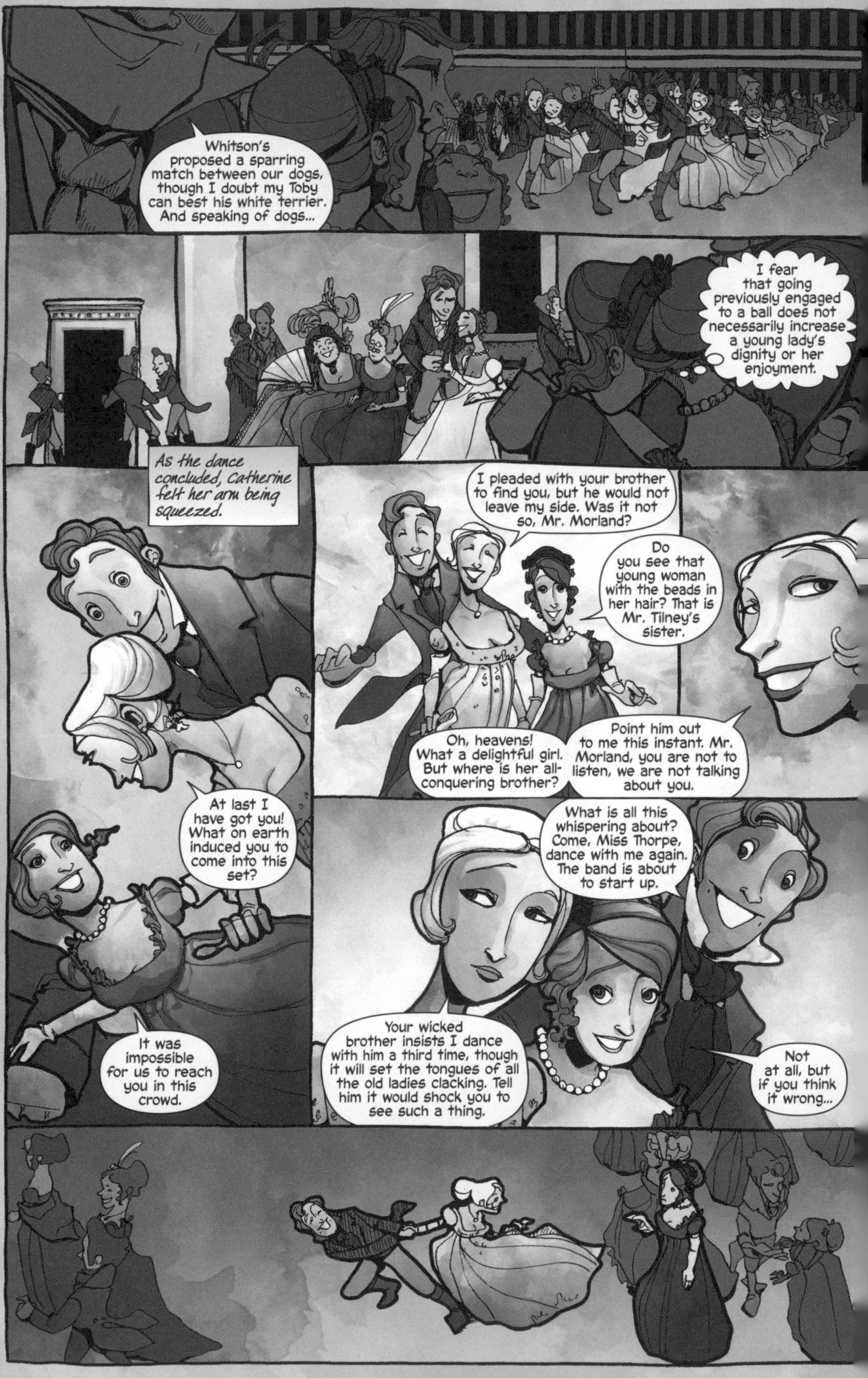
Whitson's proposed a sparring match between our dogs, though I doubt my Toby can best his white terrier. And speaking of dogs...
I fear that going previously engaged to a ball does not necessarily increase a young lady's dignity or her enjoyment.
As the dance concluded, Catherine felt her arm being squeezed.
At last I have got you! What on earth induced you to come into this set?
It was impossible for us to reach you in this crowd.
I pleaded with your brother to find you, but he would not leave my side. Was it not so, Mr. Morland?
Do you see that young woman with the beads in her hair? That is Mr. Tilney's sister.
Oh, heavens! What a delightful girl. But where is her all-conquering brother?
Point him out to me this instant. Mr. Morland, you are not to listen, we are not talking about you.
What is all this whispering about? Come, Miss Thorpe, dance with me again. The band is about to start up.
Your wicked brother insists I dance with him a third time, though it will set the tongues of all the old ladies clacking. Tell him it would shock you to see such a thing.
Not at all, but if you think it wrong...

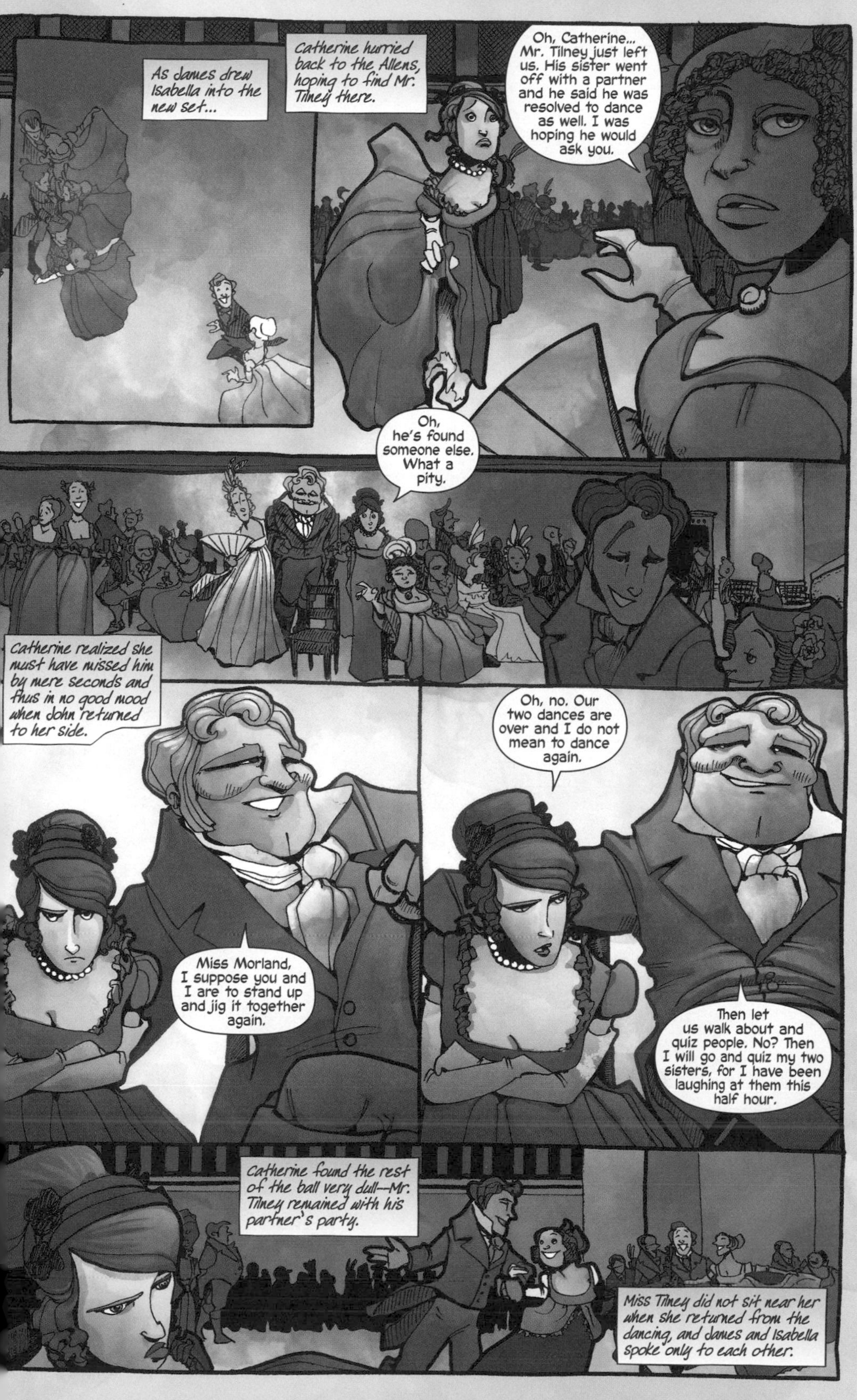

As James drew Isabella into the new set...
Catherine hurried back to the Allens, hoping to find Mr. Tilney there.
Oh, Catherine... Mr. Tilney just left us. His sister went off with a partner and he said he was resolved to dance as well. I was hoping he would ask you.
Oh, he's found someone else. What a pity.
Catherine realized she must have missed him by mere seconds and thus in no good mood when John returned to her side.
Miss Morland, I suppose you and I are to stand up and jig it together again.
Oh, no. Our two dances are over and I do not mean to dance again.
Then let us walk about and quiz people. No? Then I will go and quiz my two sisters, for I have been laughing at them this half hour.
Catherine found the rest of the ball very dull--Mr. Tilney remained with his partner's party.
Miss Tilney did not sit near her when she returned from the dancing, and James and Isabella spoke only to each other.

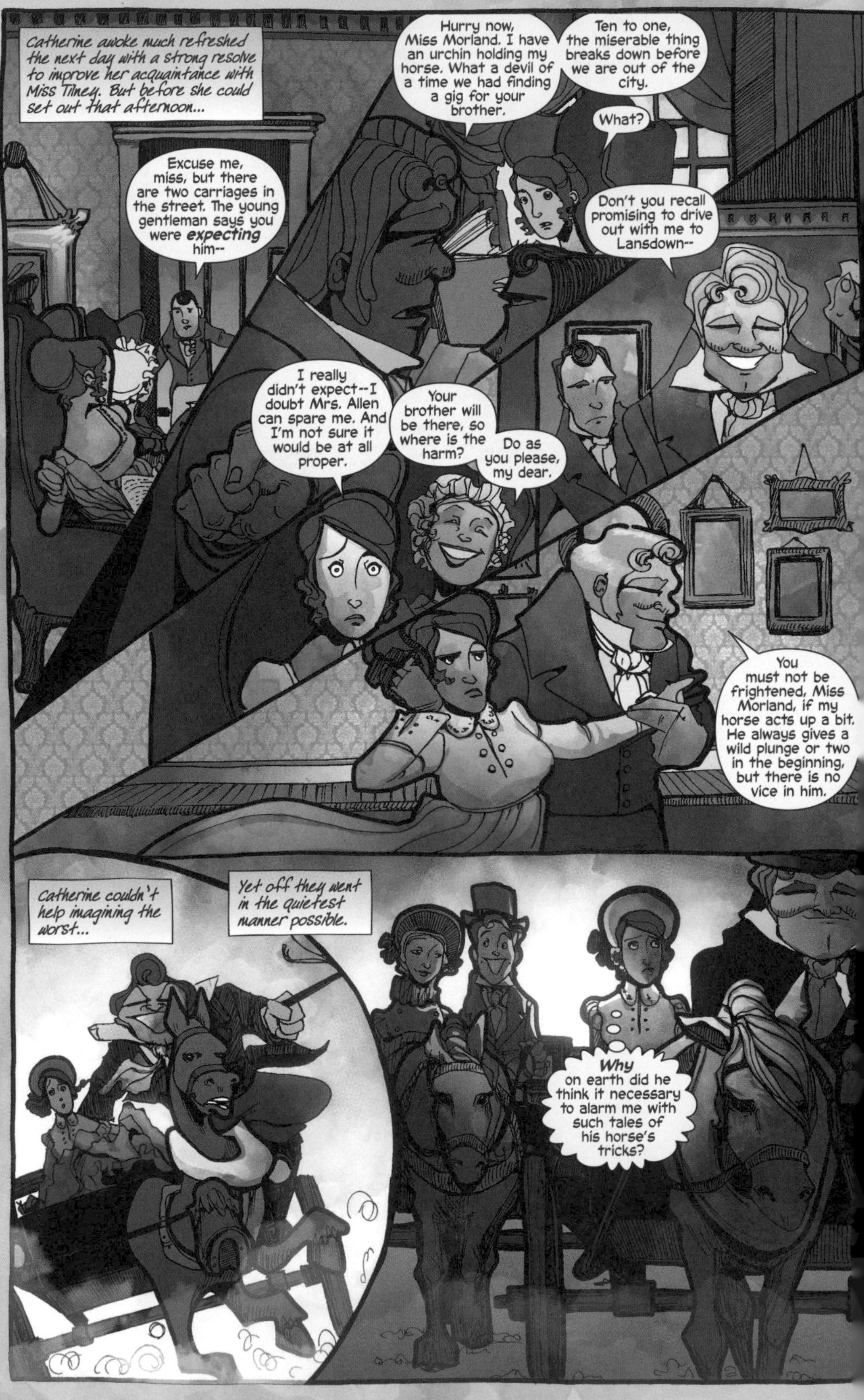
Catherine awoke much refreshed the next day with a strong resolve to improve her acquaintance with Miss Tilney. But before she could set out that afternoon...
Excuse me, miss, but there are two carriages in the street. The young gentleman says you were *expecting* him--
Hurry now, Miss Morland. I have an urchin holding my horse. What a devil of a time we had finding a gig for your brother.
Ten to one, the miserable thing breaks down before we are out of the city.
What?
Don't you recall promising to drive out with me to Lansdown--
I really didn't expect--I doubt Mrs. Allen can spare me. And I'm not sure it would be at all proper.
Your brother will be there, so where is the harm?
Do as you please, my dear.
You must not be frightened, Miss Morland, if my horse acts up a bit. He always gives a wild plunge or two in the beginning, but there is no vice in him.
Catherine couldn't help imagining the worst...
Yet off they went in the quietest manner possible.
Why on earth did he think it necessary to alarm me with such tales of his horse's tricks?

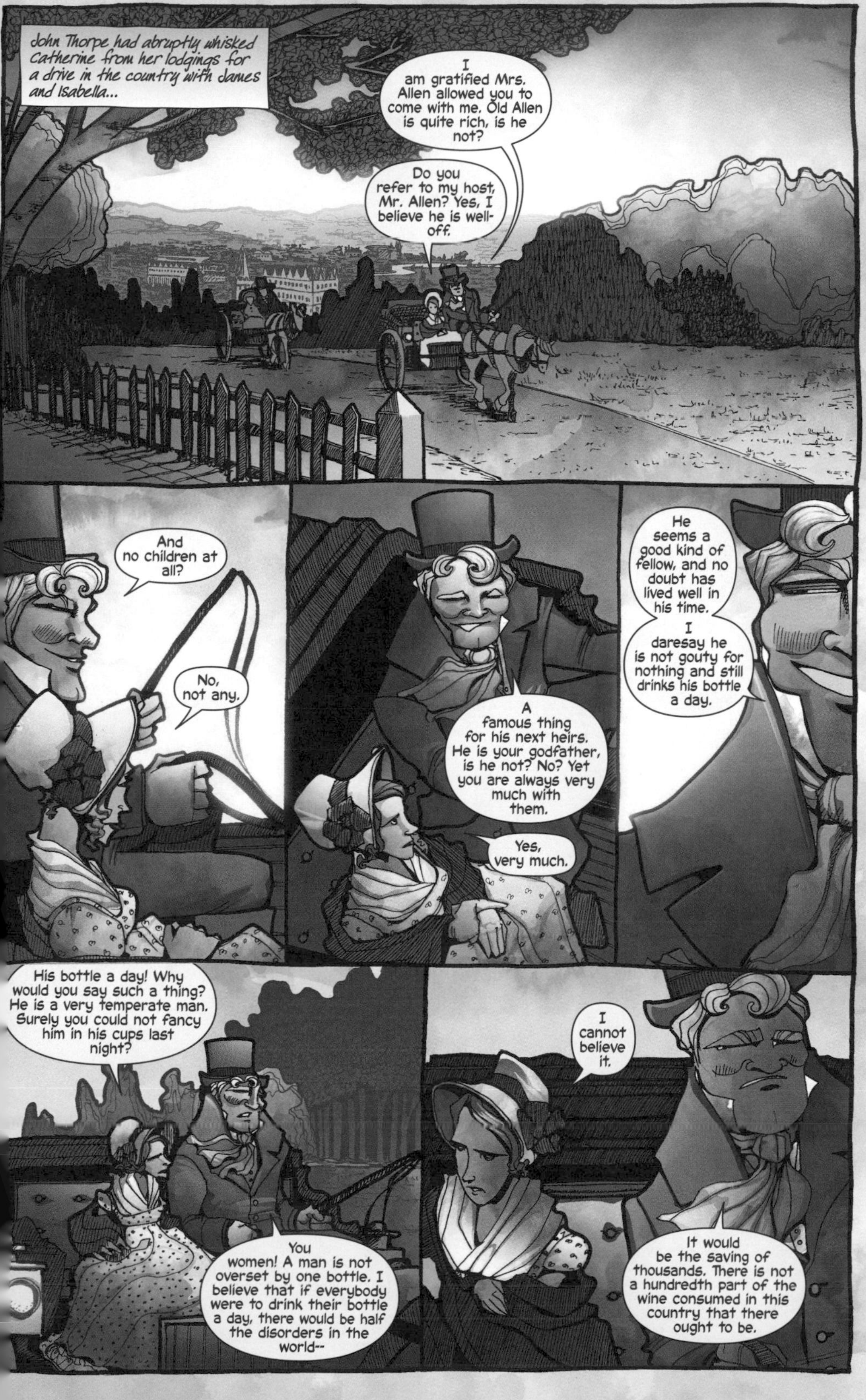
John Thorpe had abruptly whisked Catherine from her lodgings for a drive in the country with James and Isabella...
I am gratified Mrs. Allen allowed you to come with me. Old Allen is quite rich, is he not?
Do you refer to my host, Mr. Allen? Yes, I believe he is well-off.
And no children at all?
No, not any.
A famous thing for his next heirs. He is your godfather, is he not? No? Yet you are always very much with them.
Yes, very much.
He seems a good kind of fellow, and no doubt has lived well in his time.
I daresay he is not gouty for nothing and still drinks his bottle a day.
His bottle a day! Why would you say such a thing? He is a very temperate man. Surely you could not fancy him in his cups last night?
You women! A man is not overset by one bottle. I believe that if everybody were to drink their bottle a day, there would be half the disorders in the world--
I cannot believe it.
It would be the saving of thousands. There is not a hundredth part of the wine consumed in this country that there ought to be.

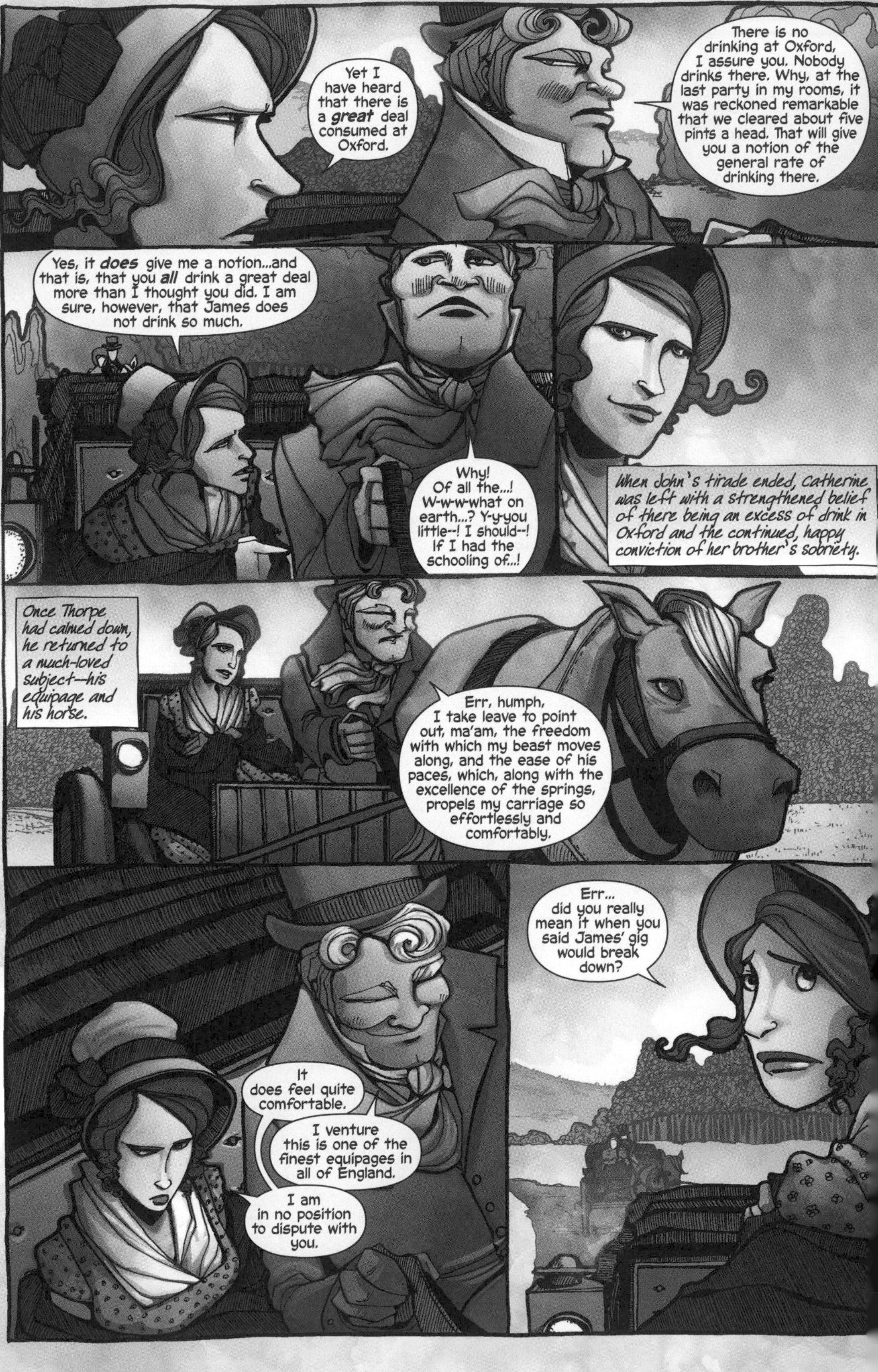
Yet I have heard that there is a great deal consumed at Oxford.
There is no drinking at Oxford, I assure you. Nobody drinks there. Why, at the last party in my rooms, it was reckoned remarkable that we cleared about five pints a head. That will give you a notion of the general rate of drinking there.
Yes, it does give me a notion...and that is, that you all drink a great deal more than I thought you did. I am sure, however, that James does not drink so much.
Why! Of all the...! W-w-w-what on earth...? Y-y-you little--! I should--! If I had the schooling of...!
When John's tirade ended, Catherine was left with a strengthened belief of there being an excess of drink in Oxford and the continued, happy conviction of her brother's sobriety.
Once Thorpe had calmed down, he returned to a much-loved subject--his equipage and his horse.
Err, humph, I take leave to point out, ma'am, the freedom with which my beast moves along, and the ease of his paces, which, along with the excellence of the springs, propels my carriage so effortlessly and comfortably.
It does feel quite comfortable.
I venture this is one of the finest equipages in all of England.
I am in no position to dispute with you.
Err... did you really mean it when you said James' gig would break down?

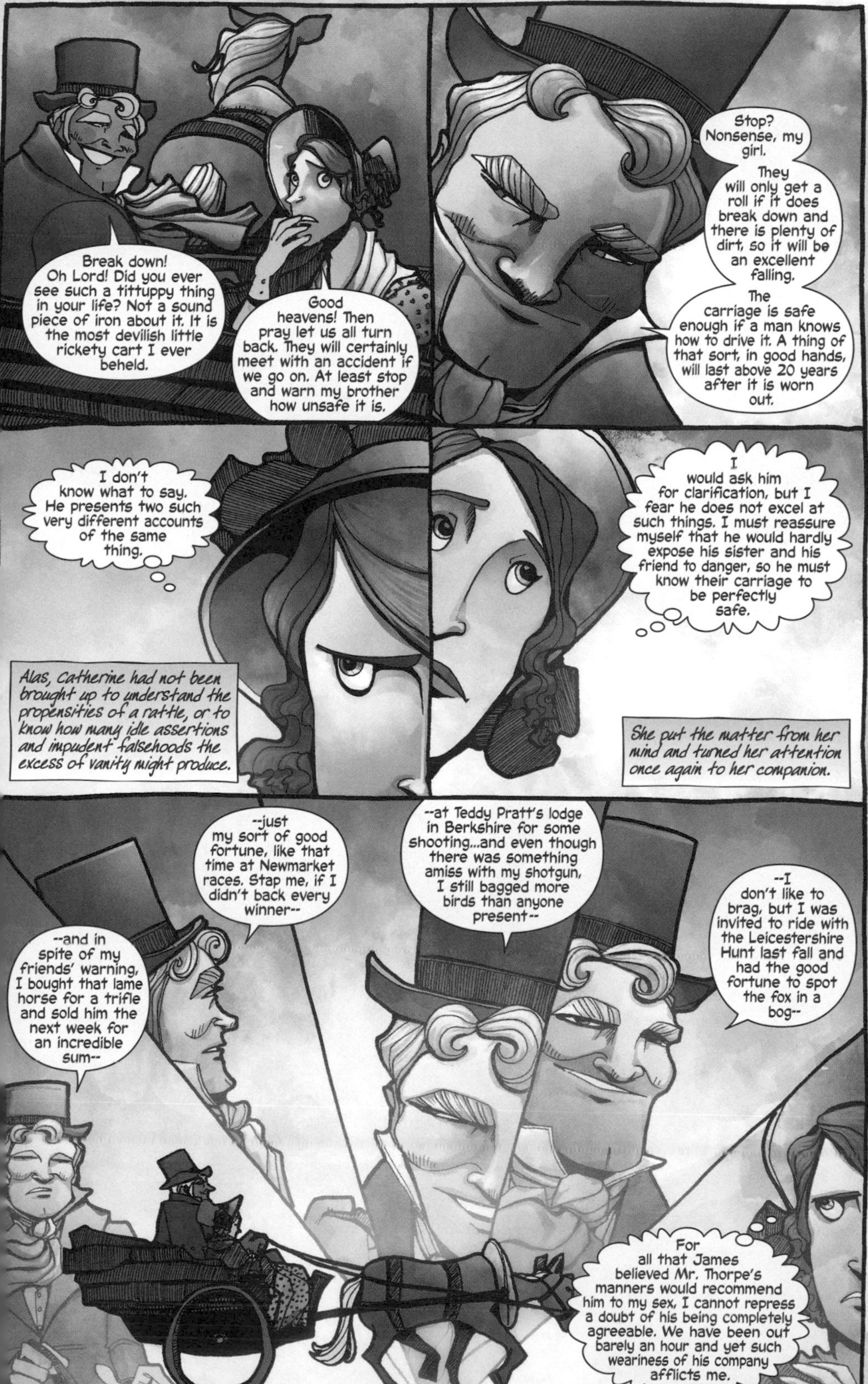
Break down! Oh Lord! Did you ever see such a tittuppy thing in your life? Not a sound piece of iron about it. It is the most devilish little rickety cart I ever beheld.
Good heavens! Then pray let us all turn back. They will certainly meet with an accident if we go on. At least stop and warn my brother how unsafe it is.
Stop? Nonsense, my girl.
They will only get a roll if it does break down and there is plenty of dirt, so it will be an excellent falling.
The carriage is safe enough if a man knows how to drive it. A thing of that sort, in good hands, will last above 20 years after it is worn out.
I don't know what to say. He presents two such very different accounts of the same thing.
I would ask him for clarification, but I fear he does not excel at such things. I must reassure myself that he would hardly expose his sister and his friend to danger, so he must know their carriage to be perfectly safe.
Alas, Catherine had not been brought up to understand the propensities of a rattle, or to know how many idle assertions and impudent falsehoods the excess of vanity might produce.
She put the matter from her mind and turned her attention once again to her companion.
--and in spite of my friends' warning, I bought that lame horse for a trifle and sold him the next week for an incredible sum--
--just my sort of good fortune, like that time at Newmarket races. Stap me, if I didn't back every winner--
--at Teddy Pratt's lodge in Berkshire for some shooting...and even though there was something amiss with my shotgun, I still bagged more birds than anyone present--
--I don't like to brag, but I was invited to ride with the Leicestershire Hunt last fall and had the good fortune to spot the fox in a bog--
For all that James believed Mr. Thorpe's manners would recommend him to my sex, I cannot repress a doubt of his being completely agreeable. We have been out barely an hour and yet such weariness of his company afflicts me.

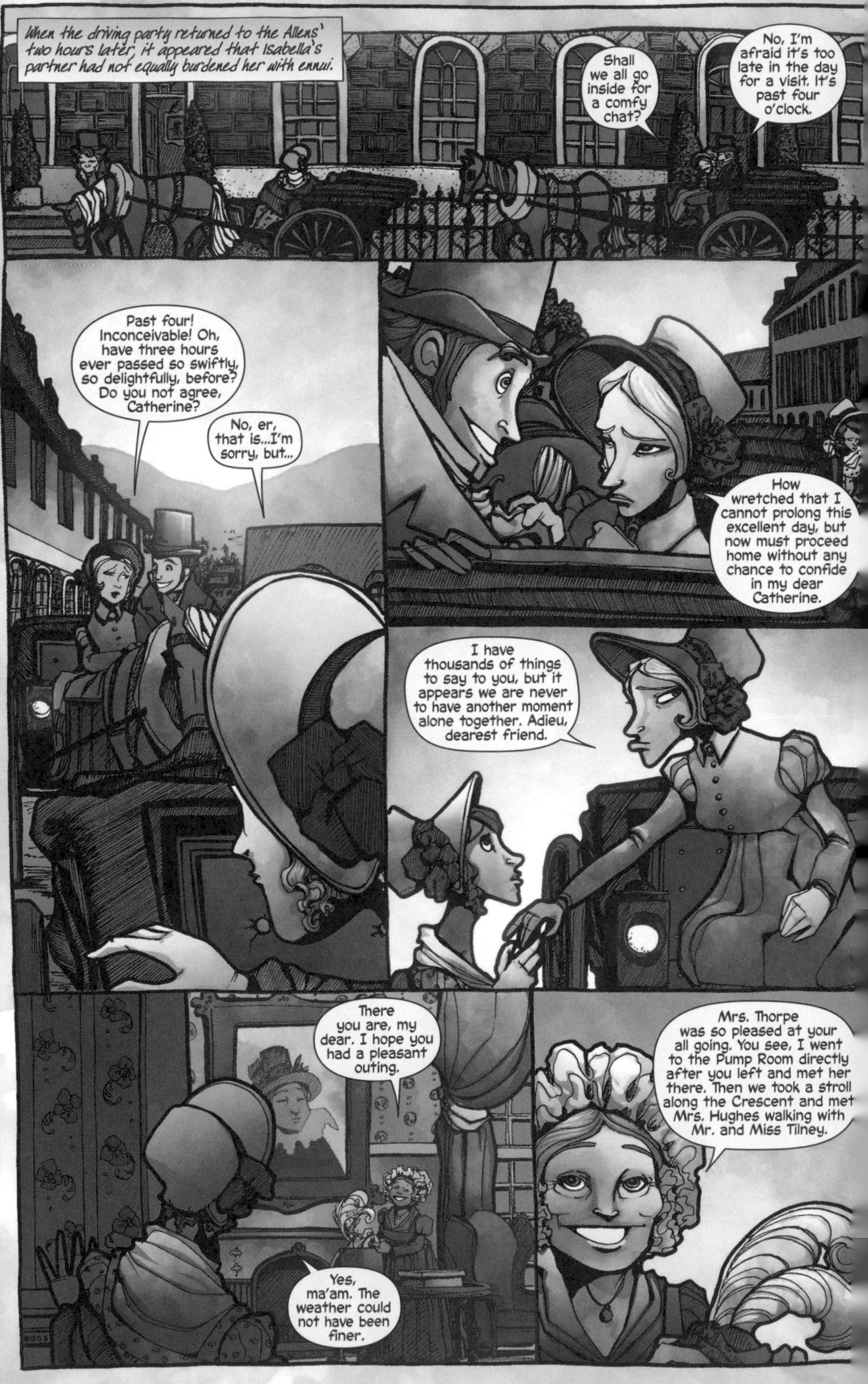
When the driving party returned to the Allens' two hours later, it appeared that Isabella's partner had not equally burdened her with ennui.
Shall we all go inside for a comfy chat?
No, I'm afraid it's too late in the day for a visit. It's past four o'clock.
Past four! Inconceivable! Oh, have three hours ever passed so swiftly, so delightfully, before? Do you not agree, Catherine?
No, er, that is...I'm sorry, but...
How wretched that I cannot prolong this excellent day, but now must proceed home without any chance to confide in my dear Catherine.
I have thousands of things to say to you, but it appears we are never to have another moment alone together. Adieu, dearest friend.
There you are, my dear. I hope you had a pleasant outing.
Yes, ma'am. The weather could not have been finer.
Mrs. Thorpe was so pleased at your all going. You see, I went to the Pump Room directly after you left and met her there. Then we took a stroll along the Crescent and met Mrs. Hughes walking with Mr. and Miss Tilney.

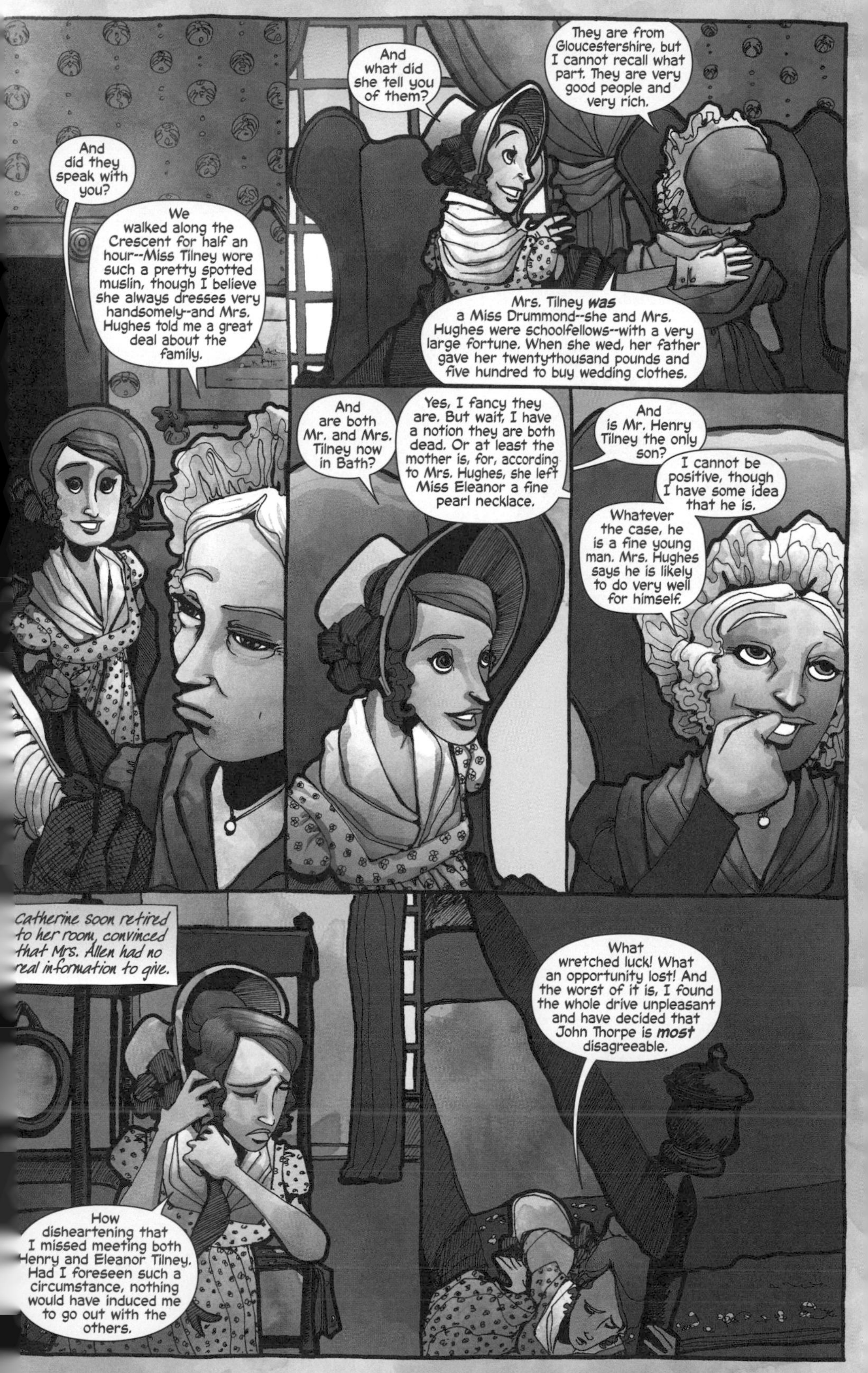
And did they speak with you?
We walked along the Crescent for half an hour--Miss Tilney wore such a pretty spotted muslin, though I believe she always dresses very handsomely--and Mrs. Hughes told me a great deal about the family.
And what did she tell you of them?
They are from Gloucestershire, but I cannot recall what part. They are very good people and very rich.
Mrs. Tilney *was* a Miss Drummond--she and Mrs. Hughes were schoolfellows--with a very large fortune. When she wed, her father gave her twenty-thousand pounds and five hundred to buy wedding clothes.
And are both Mr. and Mrs. Tilney now in Bath?
Yes, I fancy they are. But wait, I have a notion they are both dead. Or at least the mother is, for, according to Mrs. Hughes, she left Miss Eleanor a fine pearl necklace.
And is Mr. Henry Tilney the only son?
I cannot be positive, though I have some idea that he is.
Whatever the case, he is a fine young man. Mrs. Hughes says he is likely to do very well for himself.
Catherine soon retired to her room, convinced that Mrs. Allen had no real information to give.
How disheartening that I missed meeting both Henry and Eleanor Tilney. Had I foreseen such a circumstance, nothing would have induced me to go out with the others.
What wretched luck! What an opportunity lost! And the worst of it is, I found the whole drive unpleasant and have decided that John Thorpe is *most* disagreeable.

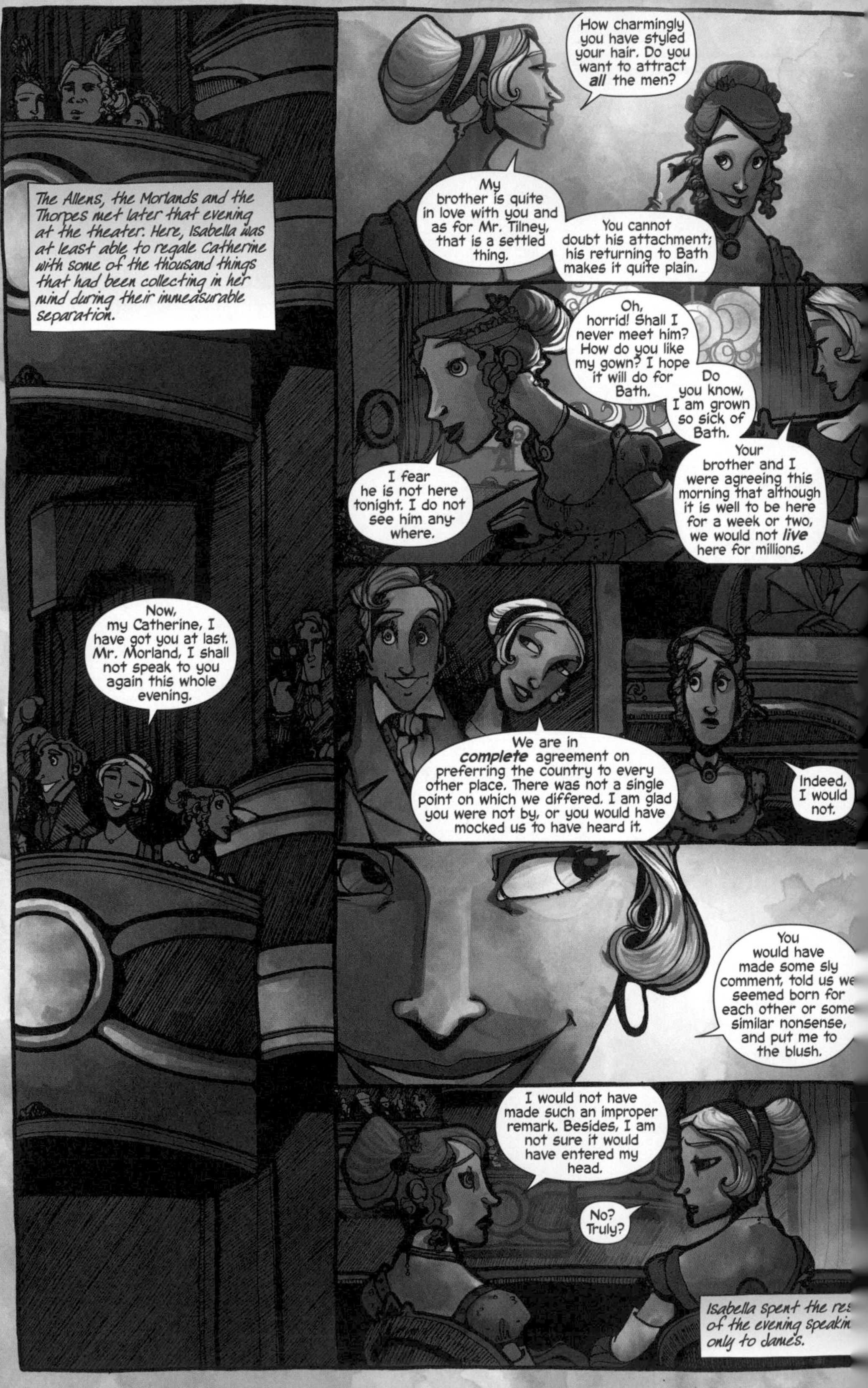
The Allens, the Morlands and the Thorpes met later that evening at the theater. Here, Isabella was at least able to regale Catherine with some of the thousand things that had been collecting in her mind during their immeasurable separation.
How charmingly you have styled your hair. Do you want to attract all the men?
My brother is quite in love with you and as for Mr. Tilney, that is a settled thing.
You cannot doubt his attachment; his returning to Bath makes it quite plain.
I fear he is not here tonight. I do not see him anywhere.
Oh, horrid! Shall I never meet him? How do you like my gown? I hope it will do for Bath.
Do you know, I am grown so sick of Bath.
Your brother and I were agreeing this morning that although it is well to be here for a week or two, we would not live here for millions.
Now, my Catherine, I have got you at last. Mr. Morland, I shall not speak to you again this whole evening.
We are in complete agreement on preferring the country to every other place. There was not a single point on which we differed. I am glad you were not by, or you would have mocked us to have heard it.
Indeed, I would not.
You would have made some sly comment, told us we seemed born for each other or some similar nonsense, and put me to the blush.
I would not have made such an improper remark. Besides, I am not sure it would have entered my head.
No? Truly?
Isabella spent the res of the evening speakin only to James.

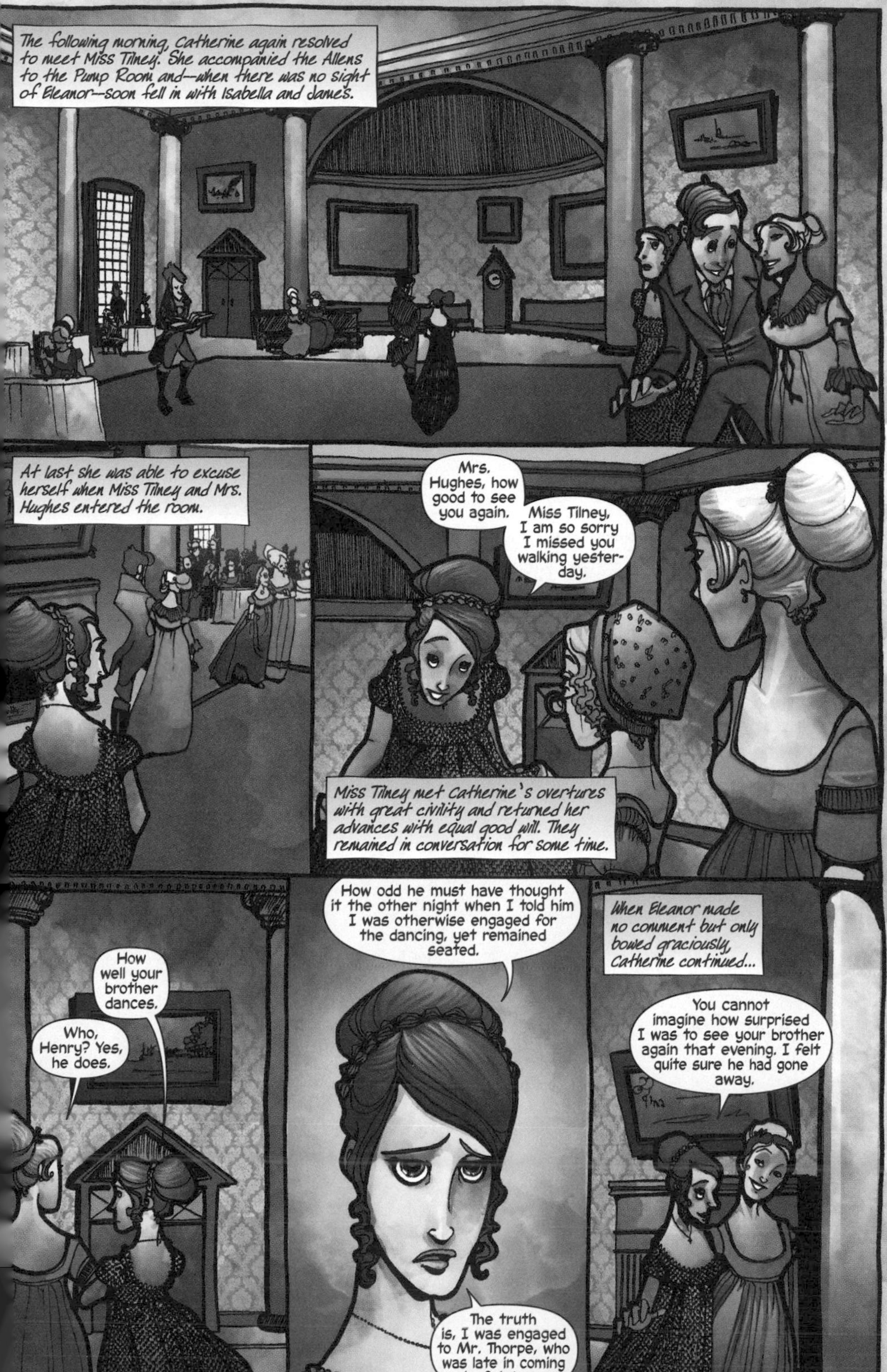
The following morning, Catherine again resolved to meet Miss Tilney. She accompanied the Allens to the Pump Room and--when there was no sight of Eleanor--soon fell in with Isabella and James.
At last she was able to excuse herself when Miss Tilney and Mrs. Hughes entered the room.
Mrs. Hughes, how good to see you again.
Miss Tilney, I am so sorry I missed you walking yester-day.
Miss Tilney met Catherine's overtures with great civility and returned her advances with equal good will. They remained in conversation for some time.
How well your brother dances.
Who, Henry? Yes, he does.
How odd he must have thought it the other night when I told him I was otherwise engaged for the dancing, yet remained seated.
The truth is, I was engaged to Mr. Thorpe, who was late in coming to fetch me.
When Eleanor made no comment but only bowed graciously, Catherine continued...
You cannot imagine how surprised I was to see your brother again that evening. I felt quite sure he had gone away.

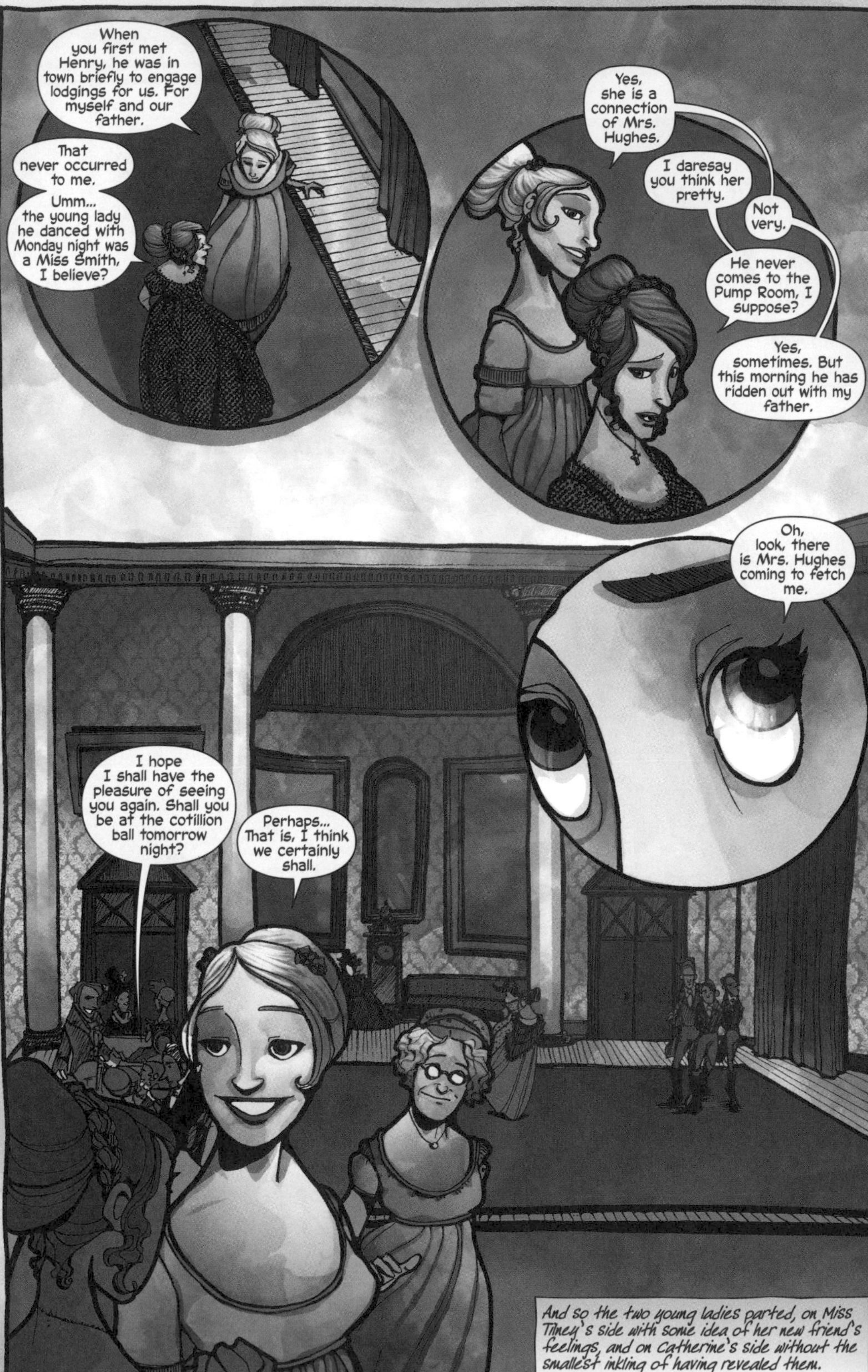
When you first met Henry, he was in town briefly to engage lodgings for us. For myself and our father.
That never occurred to me.
Umm... the young lady he danced with Monday night was a Miss Smith, I believe?
Yes, she is a connection of Mrs. Hughes.
I daresay you think her pretty.
Not very.
He never comes to the Pump Room, I suppose?
Yes, sometimes. But this morning he has ridden out with my father.
Oh, look, there is Mrs. Hughes coming to fetch me.
I hope I shall have the pleasure of seeing you again. Shall you be at the cotillion ball tomorrow night?
Perhaps... That is, I think we certainly shall.
And so the two young ladies parted, on Miss Tilney's side with some idea of her new friend's feelings, and on Catherine's side without the smallest inkling of having revealed them.

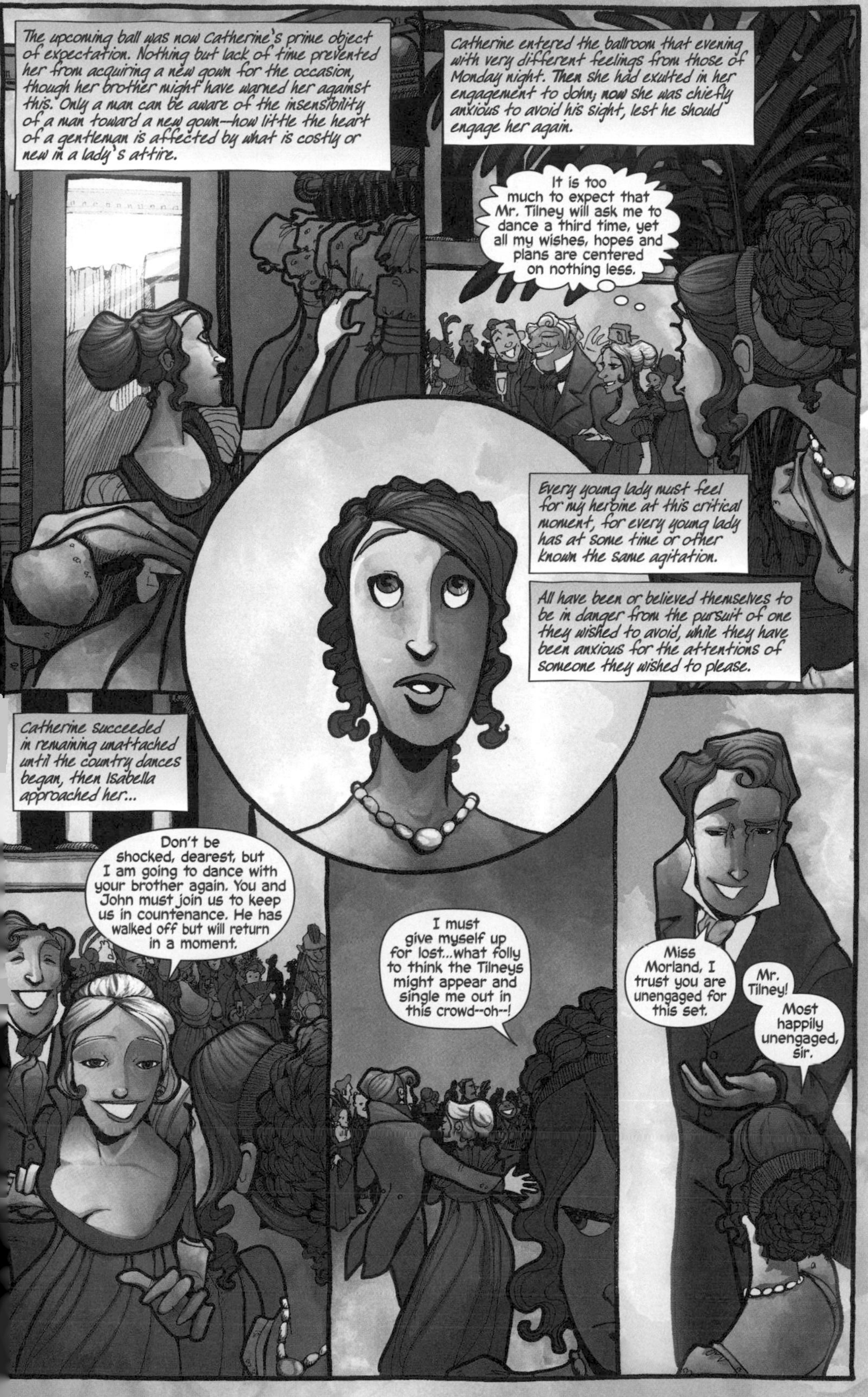

The upcoming ball was now Catherine's prime object of expectation. Nothing but lack of time prevented her from acquiring a new gown for the occasion, though her brother might have warned her against this. Only a man can be aware of the insensibility of a man toward a new gown--how little the heart of a gentleman is affected by what is costly or new in a lady's attire.
Catherine entered the ballroom that evening with very different feelings from those of Monday night. Then she had exulted in her engagement to John; now she was chiefly anxious to avoid his sight, lest he should engage her again.
It is too much to expect that Mr. Tilney will ask me to dance a third time, yet all my wishes, hopes and plans are centered on nothing less.
Every young lady must feel for my heroine at this critical moment, for every young lady has at some time or other known the same agitation.
All have been or believed themselves to be in danger from the pursuit of one they wished to avoid, while they have been anxious for the attentions of someone they wished to please.
Catherine succeeded in remaining unattached until the country dances began, then Isabella approached her...
Don't be shocked, dearest, but I am going to dance with your brother again. You and John must join us to keep us in countenance. He has walked off but will return in a moment.
I must give myself up for lost...what folly to think the Tilneys might appear and single me out in this crowd--oh--!
Miss Morland, I trust you are unengaged for this set.
Mr. Tilney! Most happily unengaged, sir.

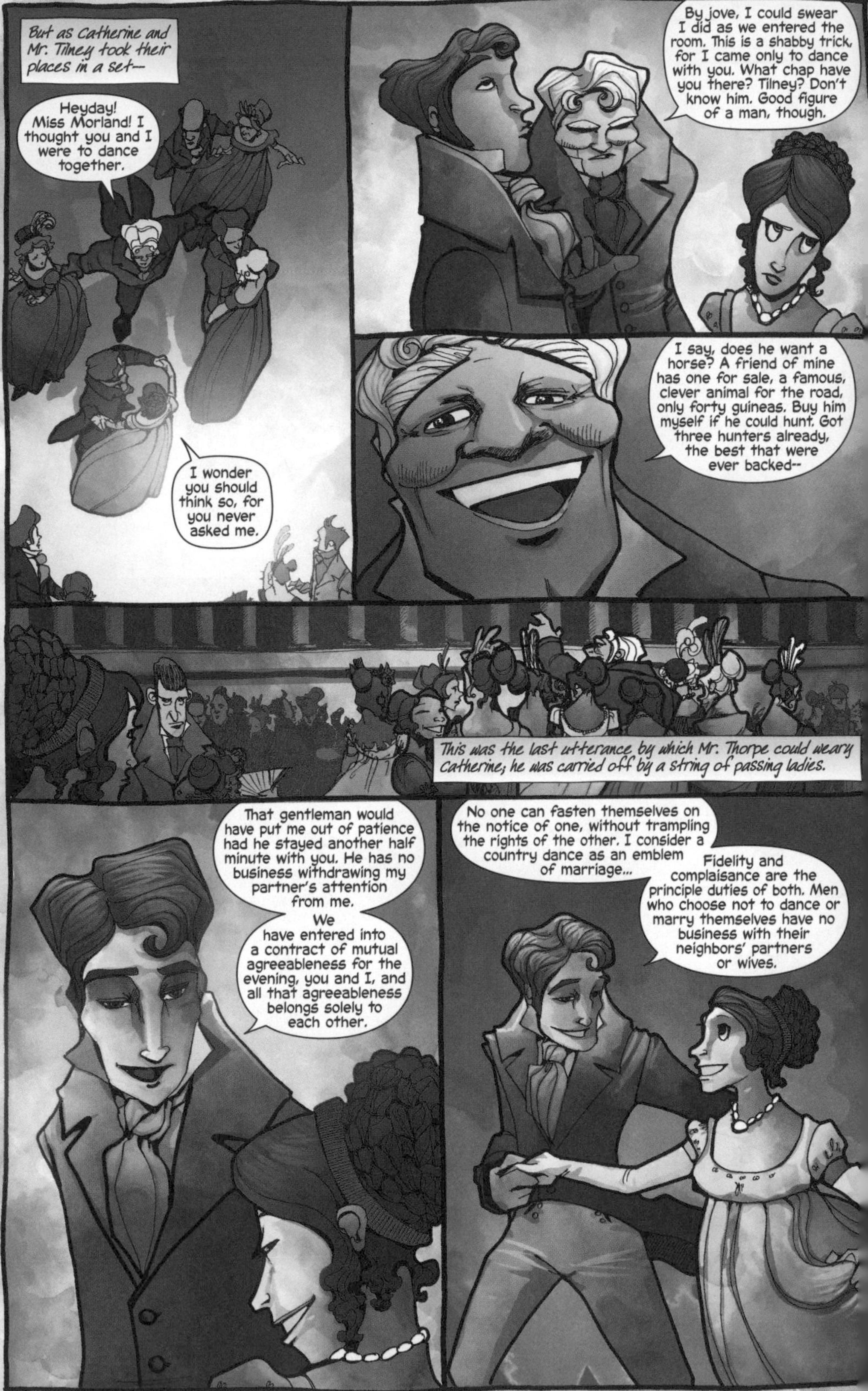
But as Catherine and Mr. Tilney took their places in a set--
Heyday! Miss Morland! I thought you and I were to dance together.
I wonder you should think so, for you never asked me.
By jove, I could swear I did as we entered the room. This is a shabby trick, for I came only to dance with you. What chap have you there? Tilney? Don't know him. Good figure of a man, though.
I say, does he want a horse? A friend of mine has one for sale, a famous, clever animal for the road, only forty guineas. Buy him myself if he could hunt. Got three hunters already, the best that were ever backed--
This was the last utterance by which Mr. Thorpe could weary Catherine; he was carried off by a string of passing ladies.
That gentleman would have put me out of patience had he stayed another half minute with you. He has no business withdrawing my partner's attention from me.
We have entered into a contract of mutual agreeableness for the evening, you and I, and all that agreeableness belongs solely to each other.
No one can fasten themselves on the notice of one, without trampling the rights of the other. I consider a country dance as an emblem of marriage...
Fidelity and complaisance are the principle duties of both. Men who choose not to dance or marry themselves have no business with their neighbors' partners or wives.

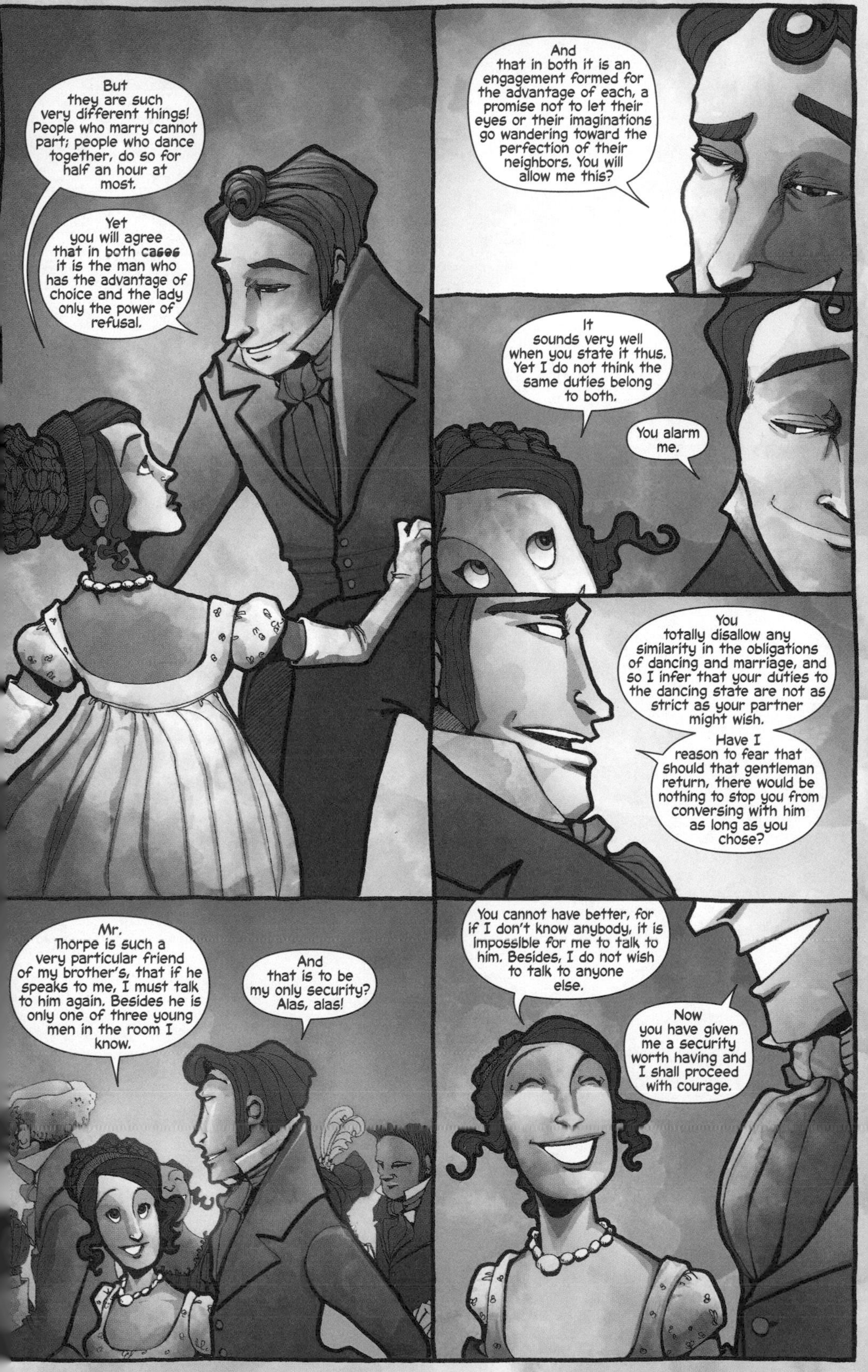

But they are such very different things! People who marry cannot part; people who dance together, do so for half an hour at most.
Yet you will agree that in both cases it is the man who has the advantage of choice and the lady only the power of refusal.
And that in both it is an engagement formed for the advantage of each, a promise not to let their eyes or their imaginations go wandering toward the perfection of their neighbors. You will allow me this?
It sounds very well when you state it thus. Yet I do not think the same duties belong to both.
You alarm me.
You totally disallow any similarity in the obligations of dancing and marriage, and so I infer that your duties to the dancing state are not as strict as your partner might wish.
Have I reason to fear that should that gentleman return, there would be nothing to stop you from conversing with him as long as you chose?
Mr. Thorpe is such a very particular friend of my brother's, that if he speaks to me, I must talk to him again. Besides he is only one of three young men in the room I know.
And that is to be my only security? Alas, alas!
You cannot have better, for if I don't know anybody, it is impossible for me to talk to him. Besides, I do not wish to talk to anyone else.
Now you have given me a security worth having and I shall proceed with courage.

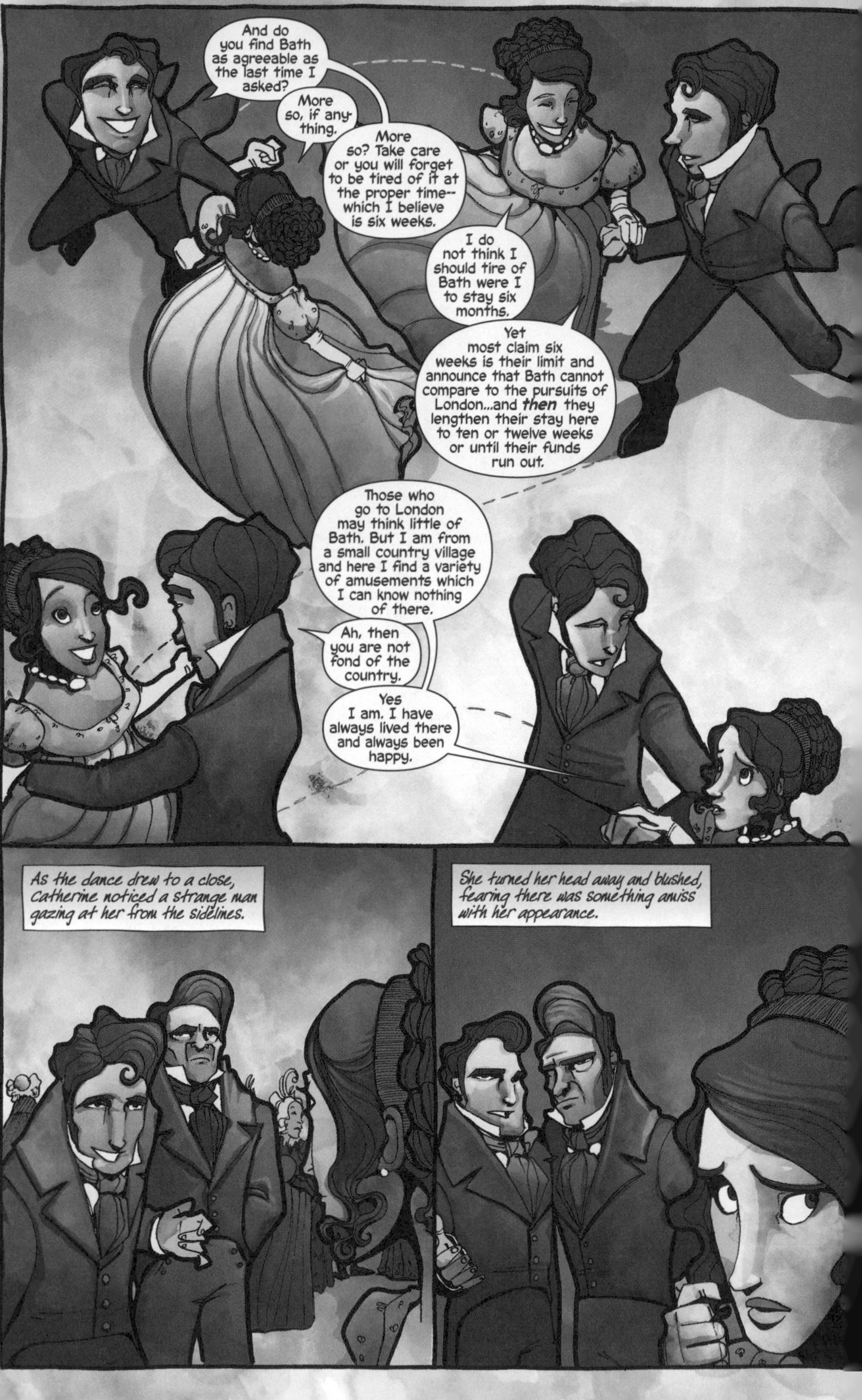

And do you find Bath as agreeable as the last time I asked?
More so, if anything.
More so? Take care or you will forget to be tired of it at the proper time--which I believe is six weeks.
I do not think I should tire of Bath were I to stay six months.
Yet most claim six weeks is their limit and announce that Bath cannot compare to the pursuits of London...and *then* they lengthen their stay here to ten or twelve weeks or until their funds run out.
Those who go to London may think little of Bath. But I am from a small country village and here I find a variety of amusements which I can know nothing of there.
Ah, then you are not fond of the country.
Yes I am. I have always lived there and always been happy.
As the dance drew to a close, Catherine noticed a strange man gazing at her from the sidelines.
She turned her head away and blushed, fearing there was something amiss with her appearance.

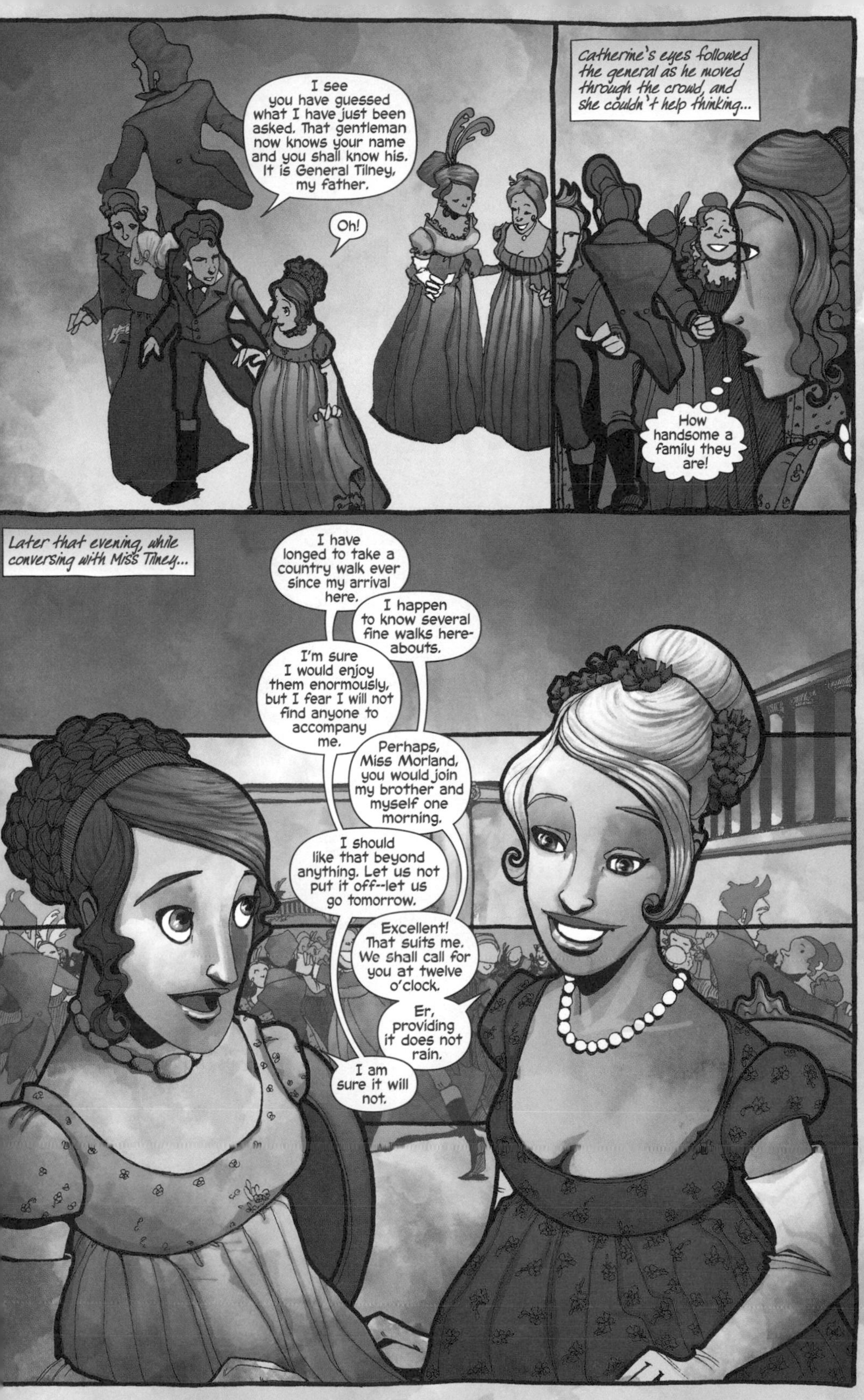
I see you have guessed what I have just been asked. That gentleman now knows your name and you shall know his. It is General Tilney, my father.
Oh!
Catherine's eyes followed the general as he moved through the crowd, and she couldn't help thinking...
How handsome a family they are!
Later that evening, while conversing with Miss Tilney...
I have longed to take a country walk ever since my arrival here.
I happen to know several fine walks hereabouts.
I'm sure I would enjoy them enormously, but I fear I will not find anyone to accompany me.
Perhaps, Miss Morland, you would join my brother and myself one morning.
I should like that beyond anything. Let us not put it off--let us go tomorrow.
Excellent! That suits me. We shall call for you at twelve o'clock.
Er, providing it does not rain.
I am sure it will not.

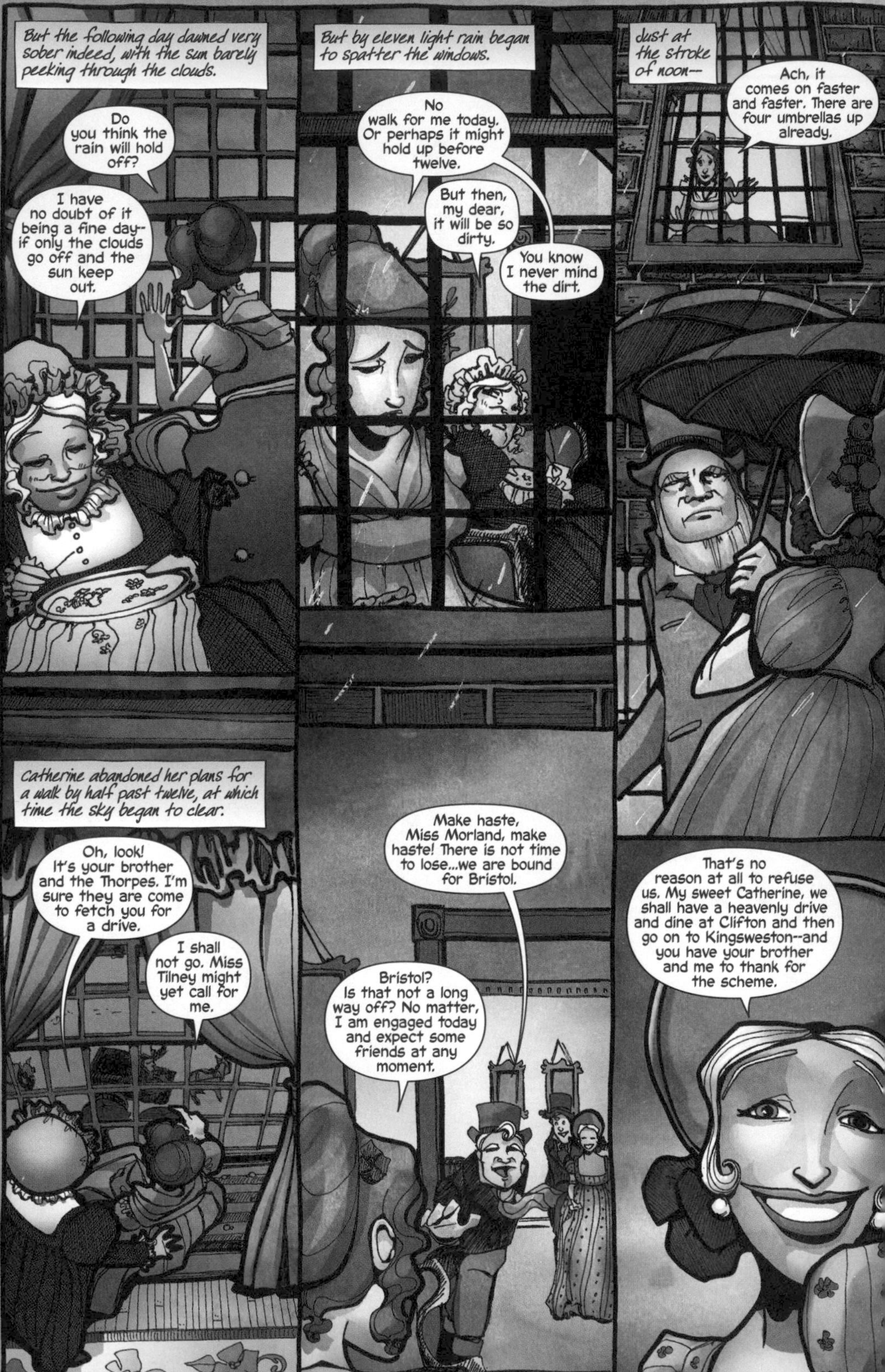
But the following day dawned very sober indeed, with the sun barely peeking through the clouds.
Do you think the rain will hold off?
I have no doubt of it being a fine day--if only the clouds go off and the sun keep out.
But by eleven light rain began to spatter the windows.
No walk for me today. Or perhaps it might hold up before twelve.
But then, my dear, it will be so dirty.
You know I never mind the dirt.
Just at the stroke of noon--
Ach, it comes on faster and faster. There are four umbrellas up already.
Catherine abandoned her plans for a walk by half past twelve, at which time the sky began to clear.
Oh, look! It's your brother and the Thorpes. I'm sure they are come to fetch you for a drive.
I shall not go. Miss Tilney might yet call for me.
Make haste, Miss Morland, make haste! There is not time to lose...we are bound for Bristol.
Bristol? Is that not a long way off? No matter, I am engaged today and expect some friends at any moment.
That's no reason at all to refuse us. My sweet Catherine, we shall have a heavenly drive and dine at Clifton and then go on to Kingsweston--and you have your brother and me to thank for the scheme.

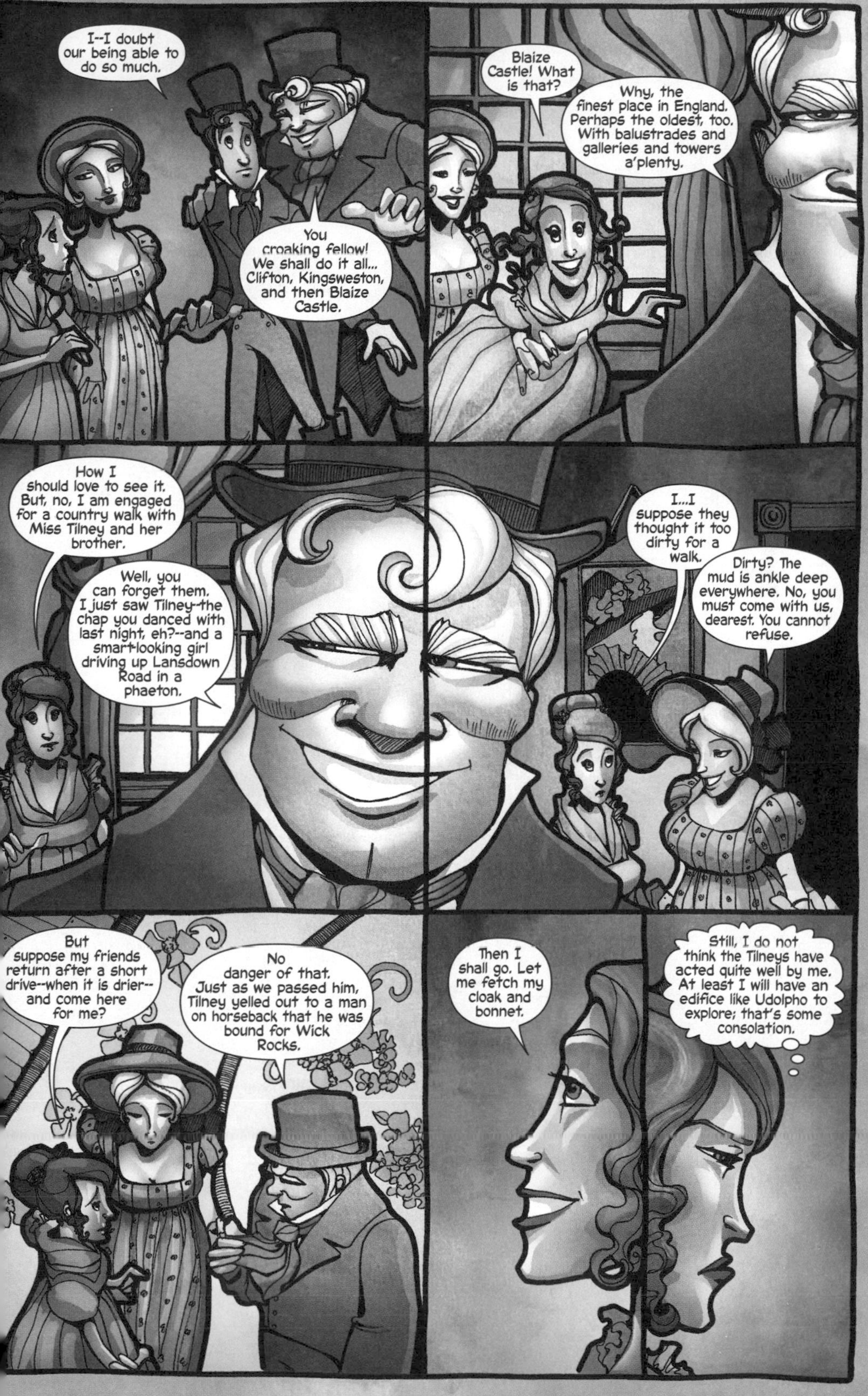
I--I doubt our being able to do so much.
You croaking fellow! We shall do it all... Clifton, Kingsweston, and then Blaize Castle.
Blaize Castle! What is that?
Why, the finest place in England. Perhaps the oldest, too. With balustrades and galleries and towers a'plenty.
How I should love to see it. But, no, I am engaged for a country walk with Miss Tilney and her brother.
Well, you can forget them. I just saw Tilney--the chap you danced with last night, eh?--and a smart-looking girl driving up Lansdown Road in a phaeton.
I...I suppose they thought it too dirty for a walk.
Dirty? The mud is ankle deep everywhere. No, you must come with us, dearest. You cannot refuse.
But suppose my friends return after a short drive--when it is drier--and come here for me?
No danger of that. Just as we passed him, Tilney yelled out to a man on horseback that he was bound for Wick Rocks.
Then I shall go. Let me fetch my cloak and bonnet.
Still, I do not think the Tilneys have acted quite well by me. At least I will have an edifice like Udolpho to explore; that's some consolation.

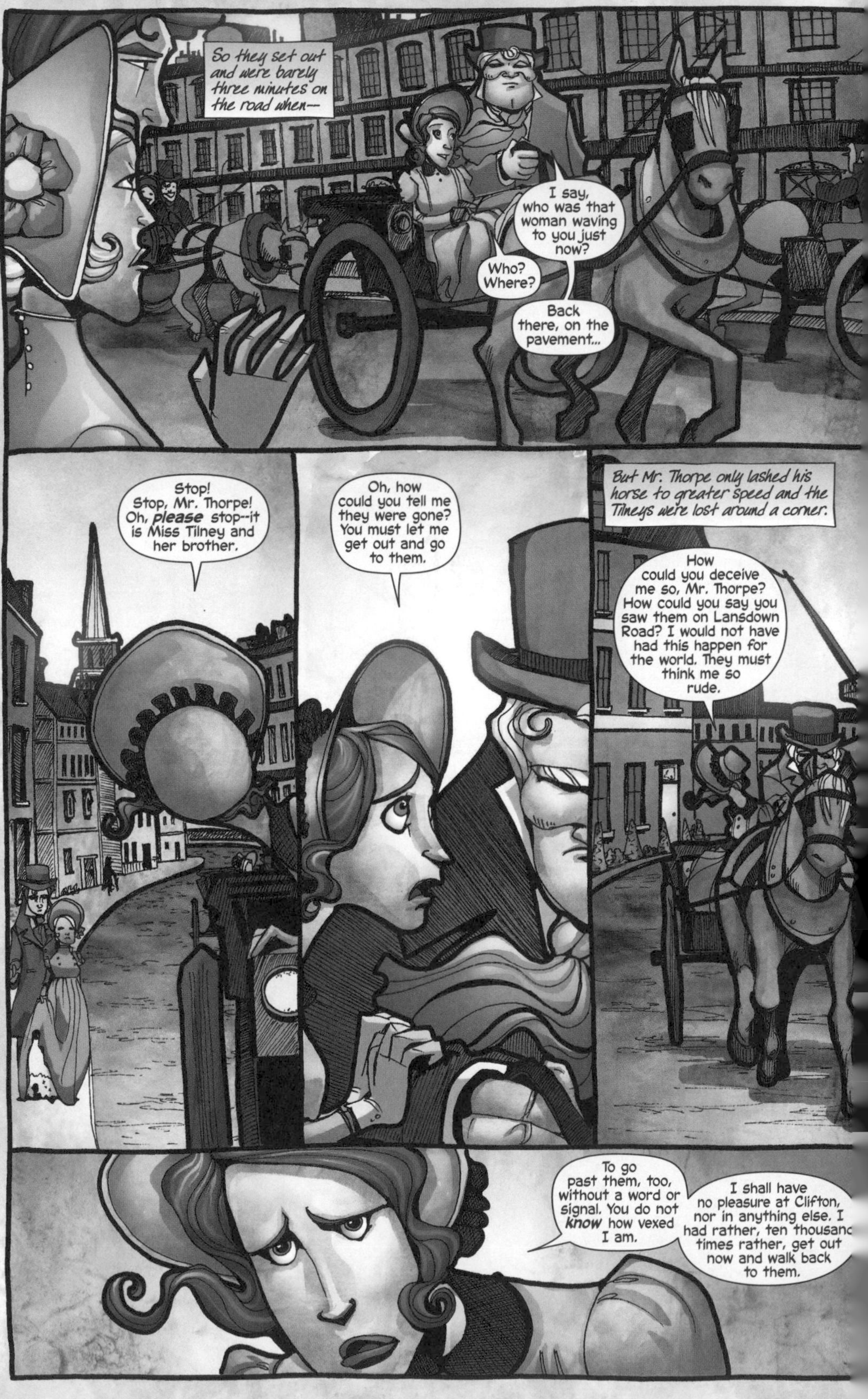
So they set out and were barely three minutes on the road when--
I say, who was that woman waving to you just now?
Who? Where?
Back there, on the pavement...
Stop! Stop, Mr. Thorpe! Oh, please stop--it is Miss Tilney and her brother.
Oh, how could you tell me they were gone? You must let me get out and go to them.
But Mr. Thorpe only lashed his horse to greater speed and the Tilneys were lost around a corner.
How could you deceive me so, Mr. Thorpe? How could you say you saw them on Lansdown Road? I would not have had this happen for the world. They must think me so rude.
To go past them, too, without a word or signal. You do not know how vexed I am.
I shall have no pleasure at Clifton, nor in anything else. I had rather, ten thousanc times rather, get out now and walk back to them.

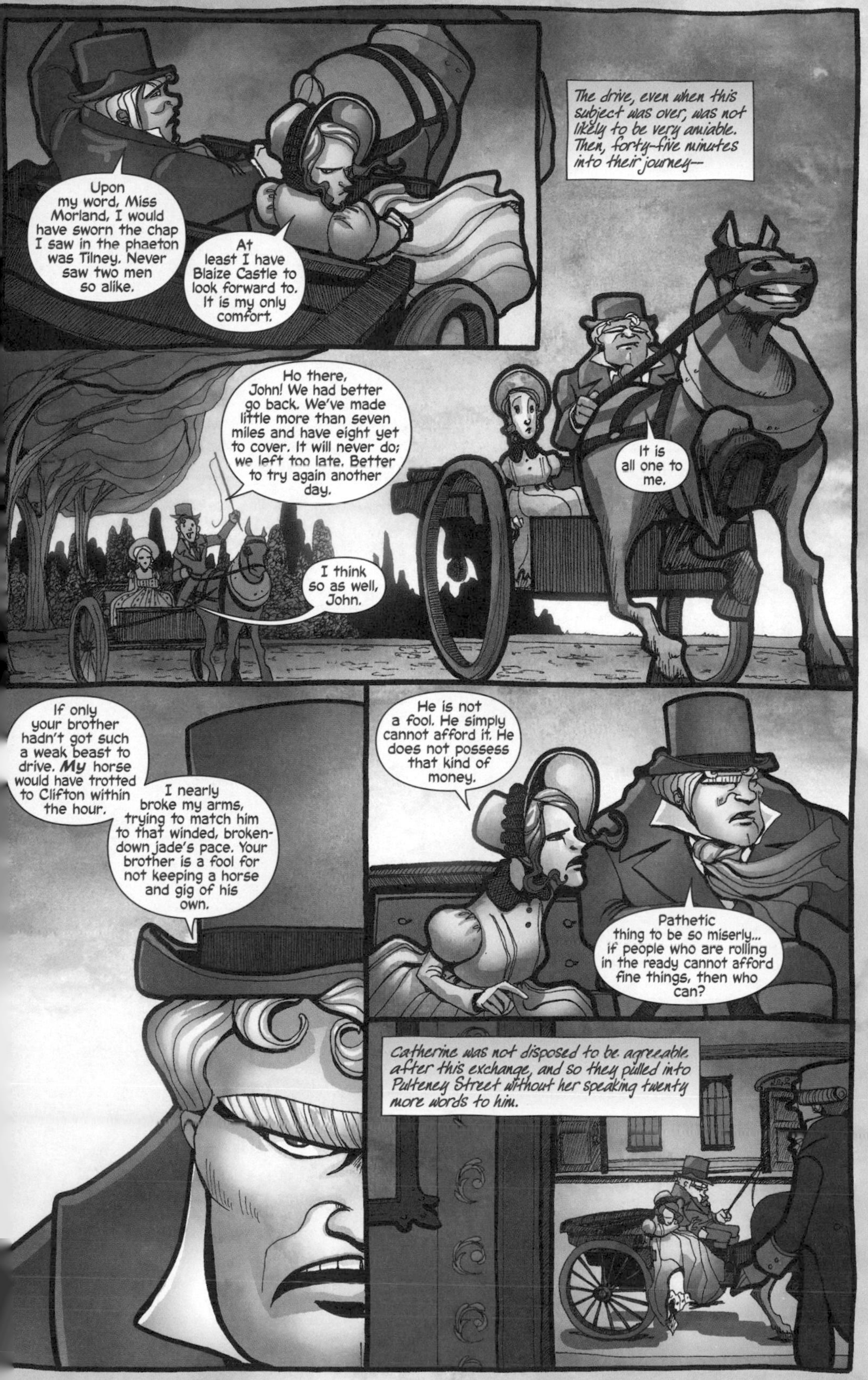
Upon my word, Miss Morland, I would have sworn the chap I saw in the phaeton was Tilney. Never saw two men so alike.
At least I have Blaize Castle to look forward to. It is my only comfort.
The drive, even when this subject was over, was not likely to be very amiable. Then, forty-five minutes into their journey—
Ho there, John! We had better go back. We've made little more than seven miles and have eight yet to cover. It will never do; we left too late. Better to try again another day.
It is all one to me.
I think so as well, John.
If only your brother hadn't got such a weak beast to drive. My horse would have trotted to Clifton within the hour.
I nearly broke my arms, trying to match him to that winded, broken-down jade's pace. Your brother is a fool for not keeping a horse and gig of his own.
He is not a fool. He simply cannot afford it. He does not possess that kind of money.
Pathetic thing to be so miserly... if people who are rolling in the ready cannot afford fine things, then who can?
Catherine was not disposed to be agreeable after this exchange, and so they pulled into Pulteney Street without her speaking twenty more words to him.

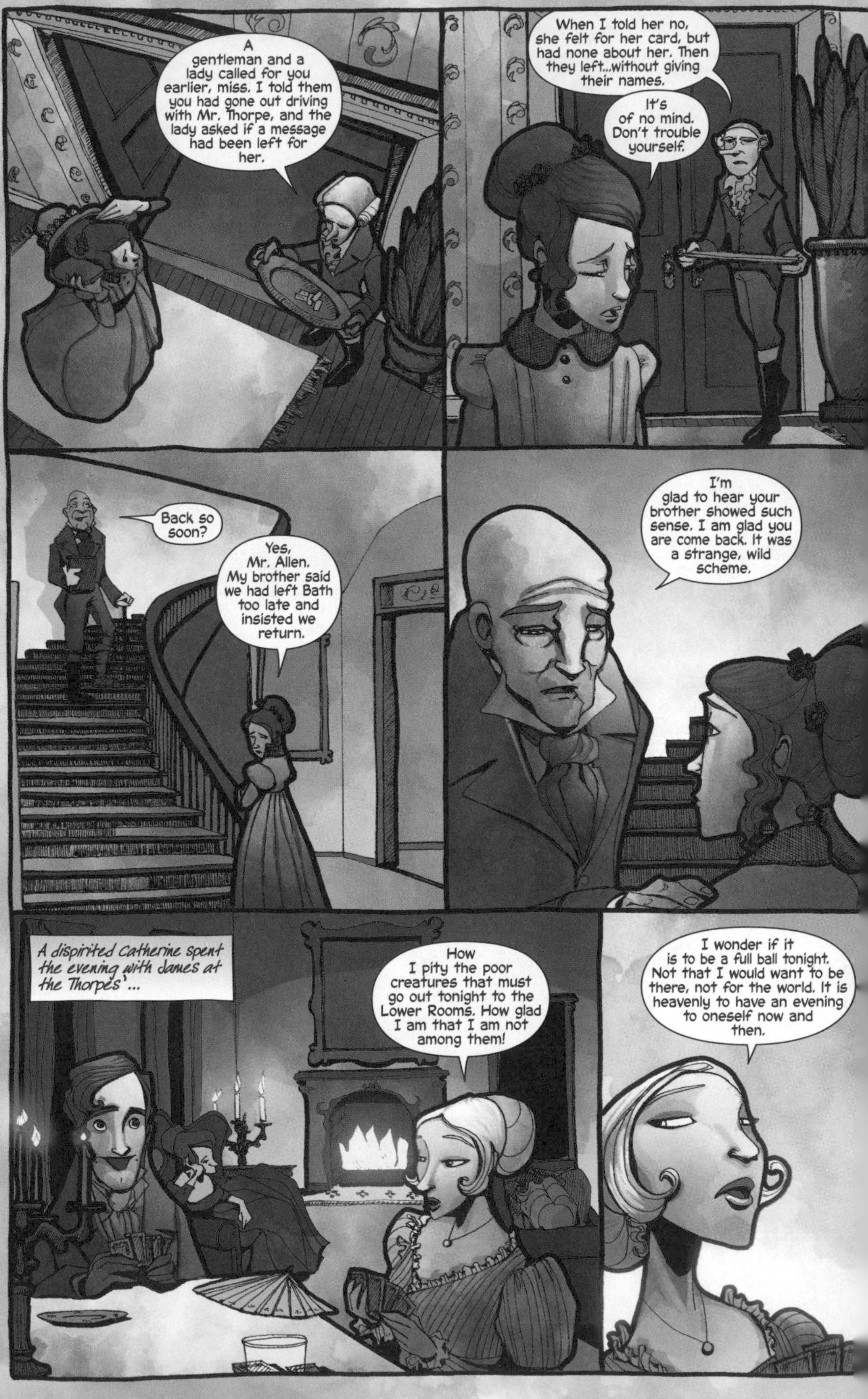
A gentleman and a lady called for you earlier, miss. I told them you had gone out driving with Mr. Thorpe, and the lady asked if a message had been left for her.
When I told her no, she felt for her card, but had none about her. Then they left...without giving their names.
It's of no mind. Don't trouble yourself.
Back so soon?
Yes, Mr. Allen. My brother said we had left Bath too late and insisted we return.
I'm glad to hear your brother showed such sense. I am glad you are come back. It was a strange, wild scheme.
A dispirited Catherine spent the evening with James at the Thorpes'...
How I pity the poor creatures that must go out tonight to the Lower Rooms. How glad I am that I am not among them!
I wonder if it is to be a full ball tonight. Not that I would want to be there, not for the world. It is heavenly to have an evening to oneself now and then.

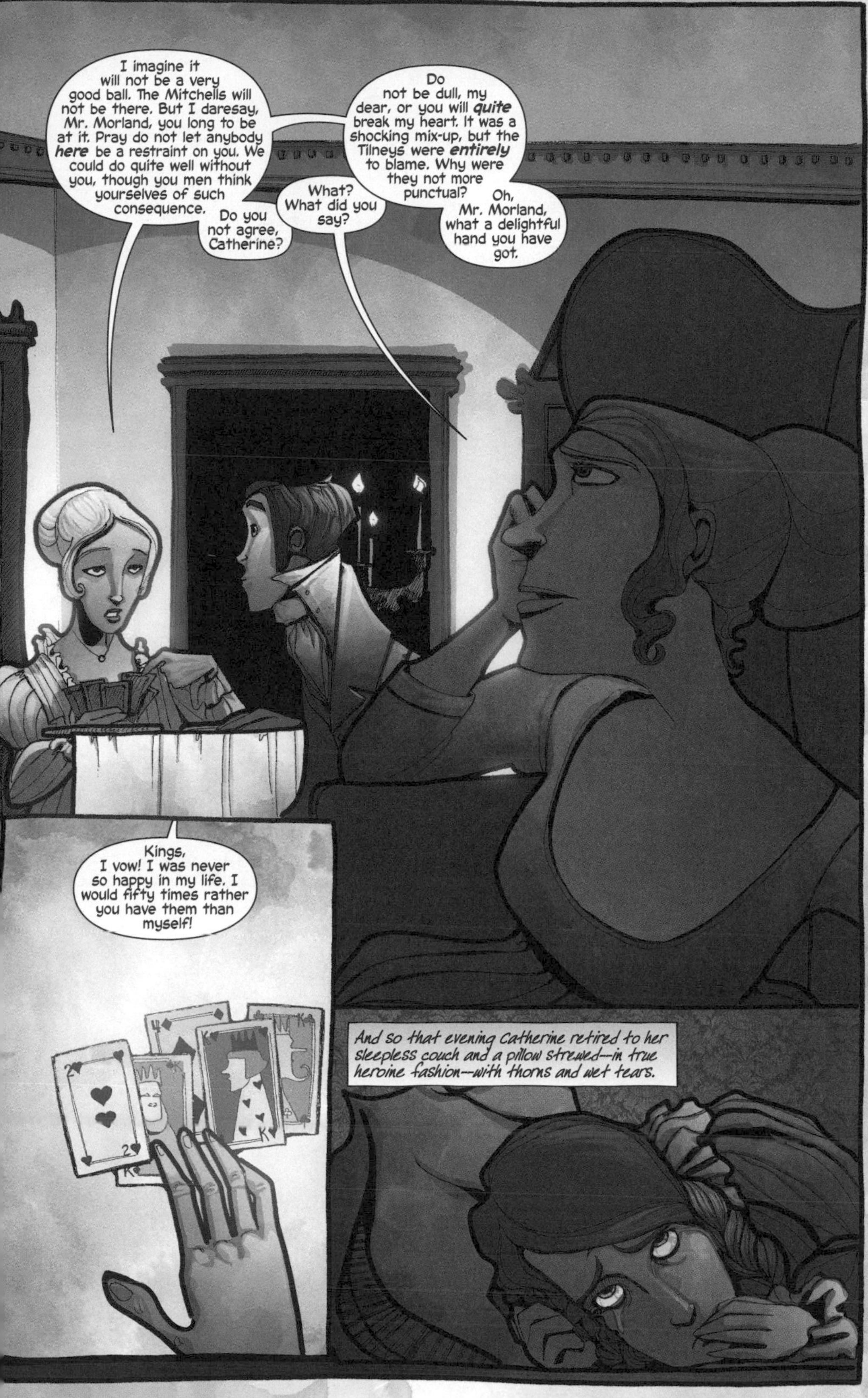
I imagine it will not be a very good ball. The Mitchells will not be there. But I daresay, Mr. Morland, you long to be at it. Pray do not let anybody **here** be a restraint on you. We could do quite well without you, though you men think yourselves of such consequence.
Do you not agree, Catherine?
What? What did you say?
Do not be dull, my dear, or you will ***quite*** break my heart. It was a shocking mix-up, but the Tilneys were ***entirely*** to blame. Why were they not more punctual?
Oh, Mr. Morland, what a delightful hand you have got.
Kings, I vow! I was never so happy in my life. I would fifty times rather you have them than myself!
And so that evening Catherine retired to her sleepless couch and a pillow strewed--in true heroine fashion--with thorns and wet tears.

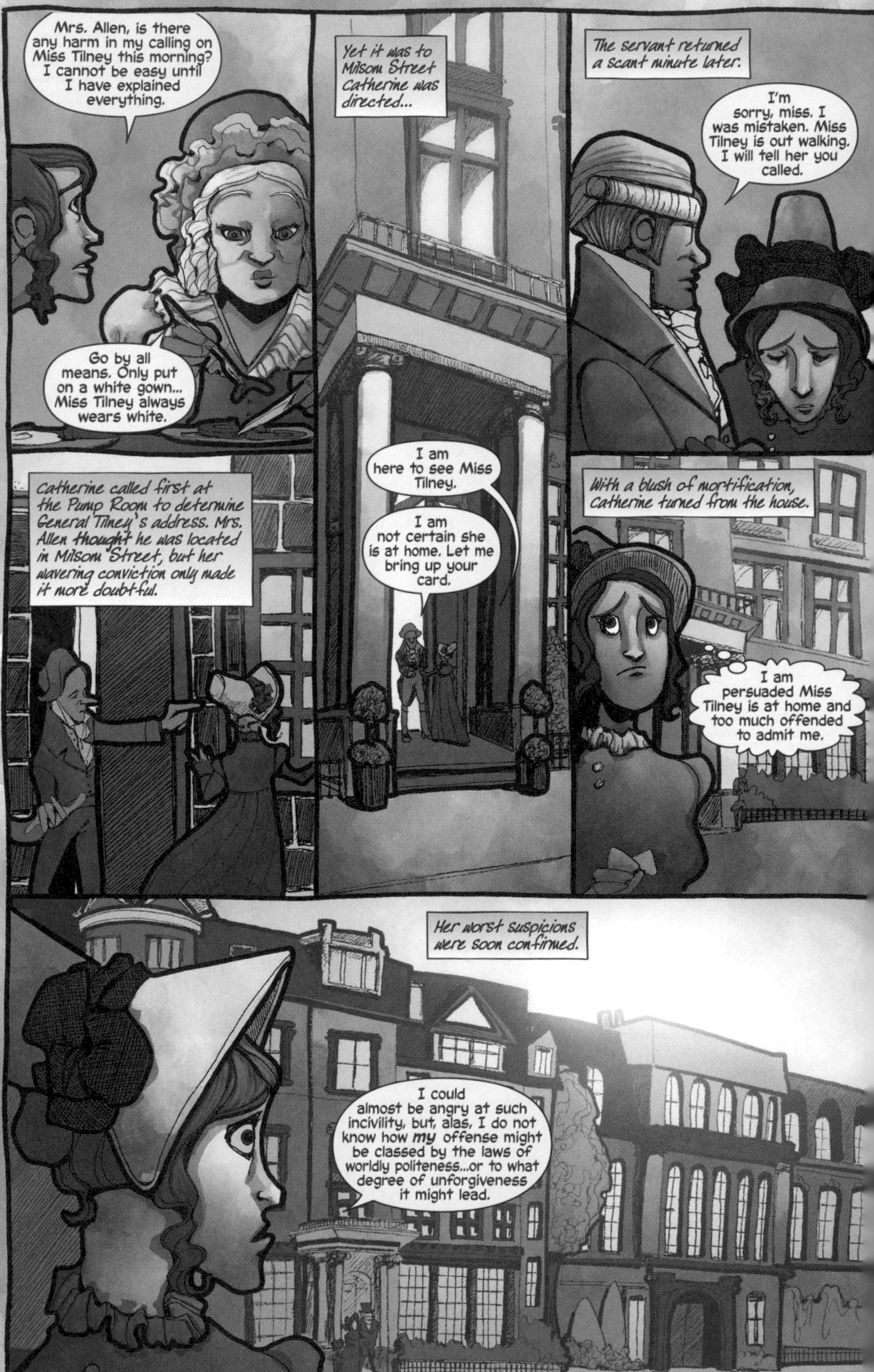
Mrs. Allen, is there any harm in my calling on Miss Tilney this morning? I cannot be easy until I have explained everything.
Go by all means. Only put on a white gown... Miss Tilney always wears white.
Yet it was to Milsom Street Catherine was directed...
The servant returned a scant minute later.
I'm sorry, miss. I was mistaken. Miss Tilney is out walking. I will tell her you called.
Catherine called first at the Pump Room to determine General Tilney's address. Mrs. Allen thought he was located in Milsom Street, but her wavering conviction only made it more doubtful.
I am here to see Miss Tilney.
I am not certain she is at home. Let me bring up your card.
With a blush of mortification, Catherine turned from the house.
I am persuaded Miss Tilney is at home and too much offended to admit me.
Her worst suspicions were soon confirmed.
I could almost be angry at such incivility, but, alas, I do not know how my offense might be classed by the laws of worldly politeness...or to what degree of unforgiveness it might lead.

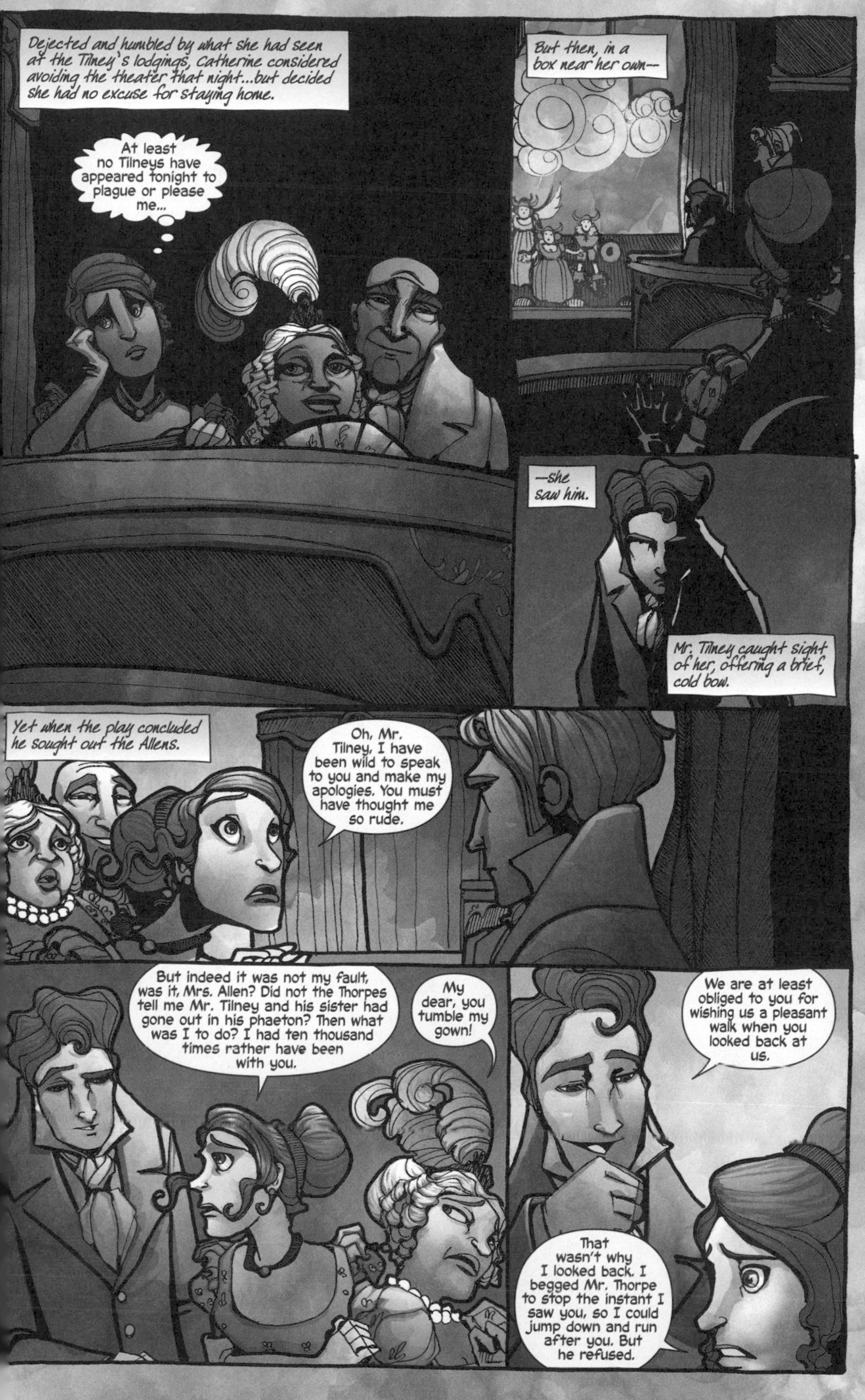
Dejected and humbled by what she had seen at the Tilney's lodgings, Catherine considered avoiding the theater that night...but decided she had no excuse for staying home.
At least no Tilneys have appeared tonight to plague or please me...
But then, in a box near her own--
--she saw him.
Mr. Tilney caught sight of her, offering a brief, cold bow.
Yet when the play concluded he sought out the Allens.
Oh, Mr. Tilney, I have been wild to speak to you and make my apologies. You must have thought me so rude.
But indeed it was not my fault, was it, Mrs. Allen? Did not the Thorpes tell me Mr. Tilney and his sister had gone out in his phaeton? Then what was I to do? I had ten thousand times rather have been with you.
My dear, you tumble my gown!
We are at least obliged to you for wishing us a pleasant walk when you looked back at us.
That wasn't why I looked back. I begged Mr. Thorpe to stop the instant I saw you, so I could jump down and run after you. But he refused.

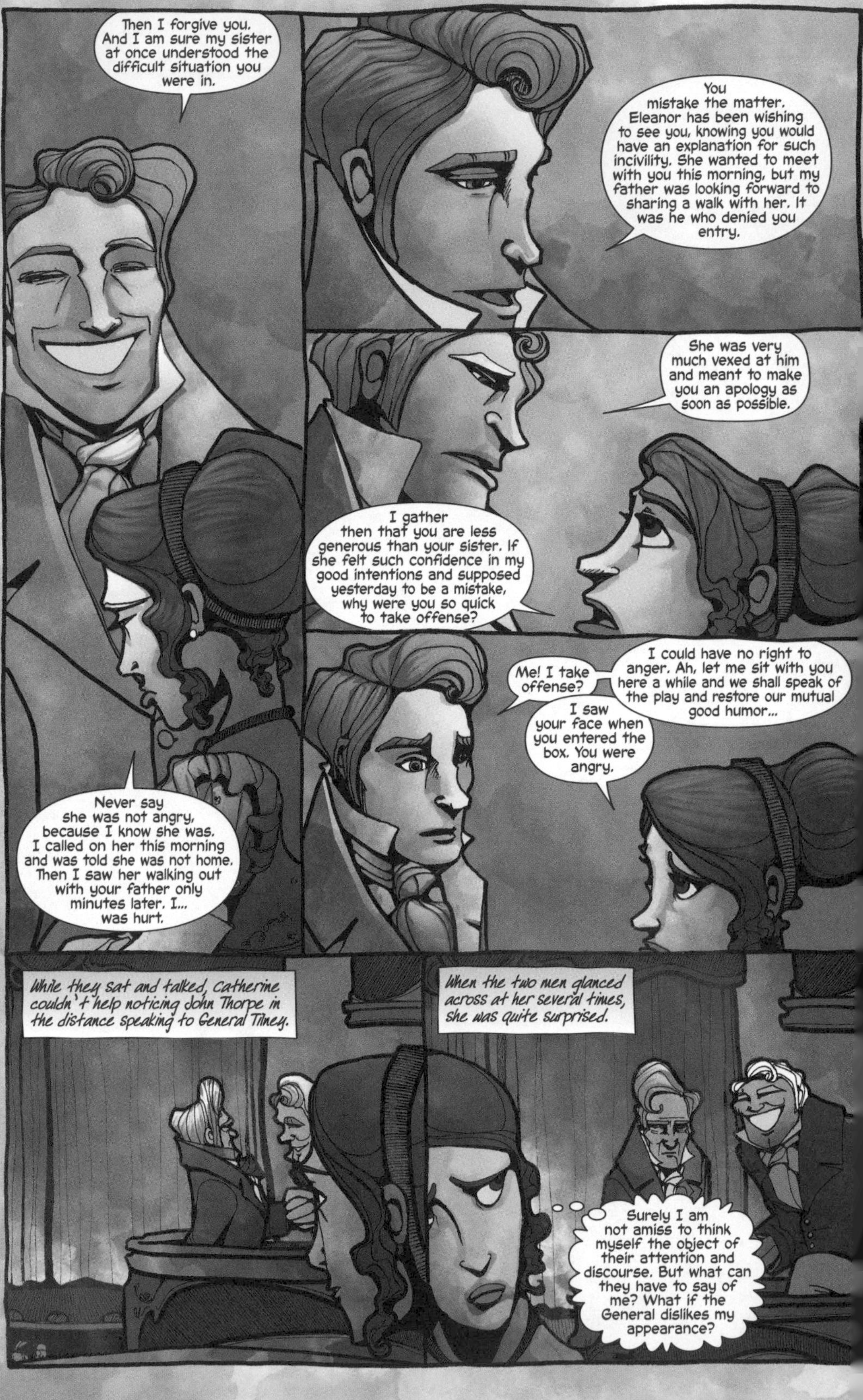
Then I forgive you. And I am sure my sister at once understood the difficult situation you were in.
You mistake the matter. Eleanor has been wishing to see you, knowing you would have an explanation for such incivility. She wanted to meet with you this morning, but my father was looking forward to sharing a walk with her. It was he who denied you entry.
Never say she was not angry, because I know she was. I called on her this morning and was told she was not home. Then I saw her walking out with your father only minutes later. I... was hurt.
She was very much vexed at him and meant to make you an apology as soon as possible.
I gather then that you are less generous than your sister. If she felt such confidence in my good intentions and supposed yesterday to be a mistake, why were you so quick to take offense?
Me! I take offense?
I saw your face when you entered the box. You were angry.
I could have no right to anger. Ah, let me sit with you here a while and we shall speak of the play and restore our mutual good humor...
While they sat and talked, Catherine couldn't help noticing John Thorpe in the distance speaking to General Tilney.
When the two men glanced across at her several times, she was quite surprised.
Surely I am not amiss to think myself the object of their attention and discourse. But what can they have to say of me? What if the General dislikes my appearance?

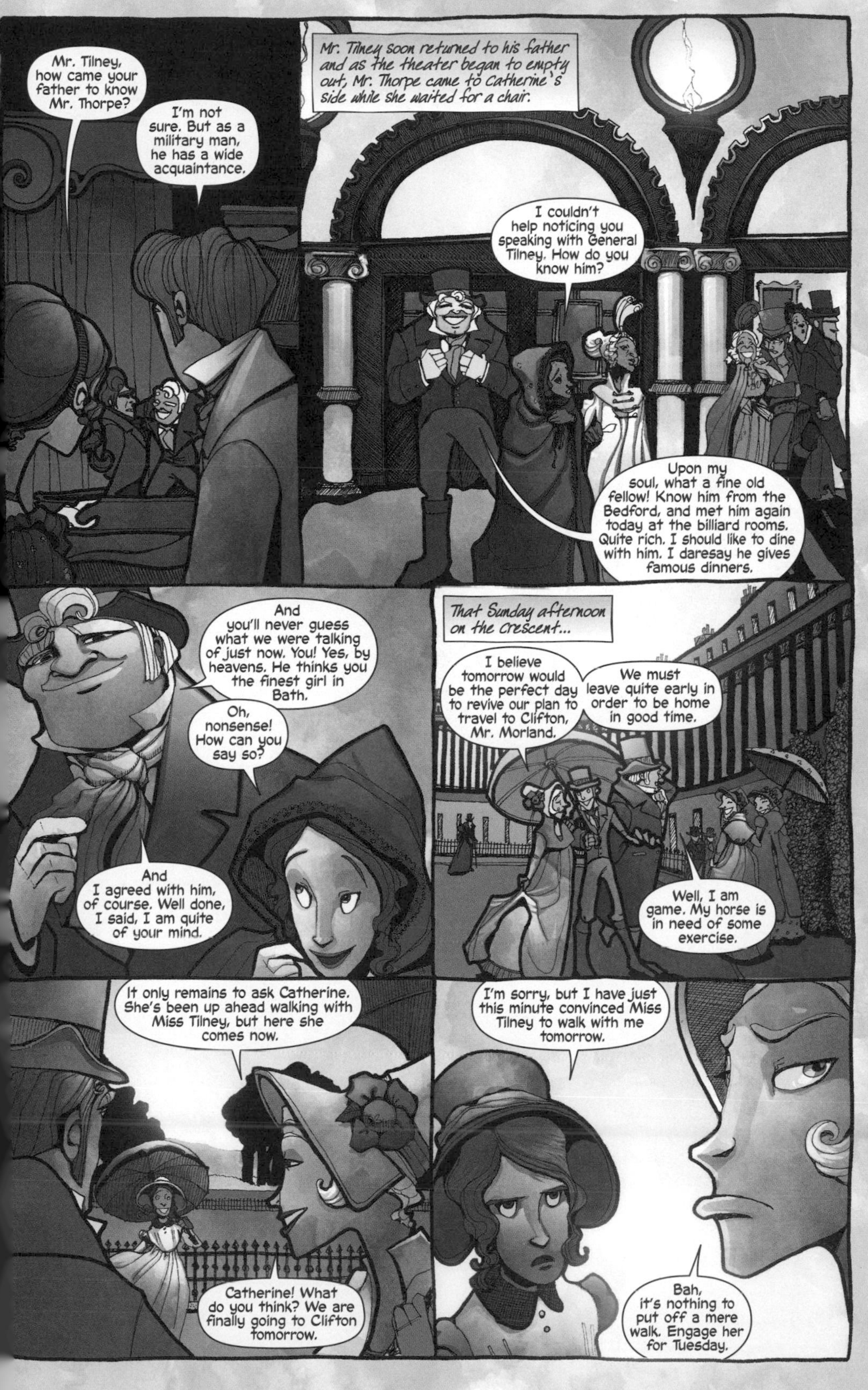
Mr. Tilney, how came your father to know Mr. Thorpe?
I'm not sure. But as a military man, he has a wide acquaintance.
Mr. Tilney soon returned to his father and as the theater began to empty out, Mr. Thorpe came to Catherine's side while she waited for a chair.
I couldn't help noticing you speaking with General Tilney. How do you know him?
Upon my soul, what a fine old fellow! Know him from the Bedford, and met him again today at the billiard rooms. Quite rich. I should like to dine with him. I daresay he gives famous dinners.
And you'll never guess what we were talking of just now. You! Yes, by heavens. He thinks you the finest girl in Bath.
Oh, nonsense! How can you say so?
And I agreed with him, of course. Well done, I said, I am quite of your mind.
That Sunday afternoon on the Crescent...
I believe tomorrow would be the perfect day to revive our plan to travel to Clifton, Mr. Morland.
We must leave quite early in order to be home in good time.
Well, I am game. My horse is in need of some exercise.
It only remains to ask Catherine. She's been up ahead walking with Miss Tilney, but here she comes now.
Catherine! What do you think? We are finally going to Clifton tomorrow.
I'm sorry, but I have just this minute convinced Miss Tilney to walk with me tomorrow.
Bah, it's nothing to put off a mere walk. Engage her for Tuesday.

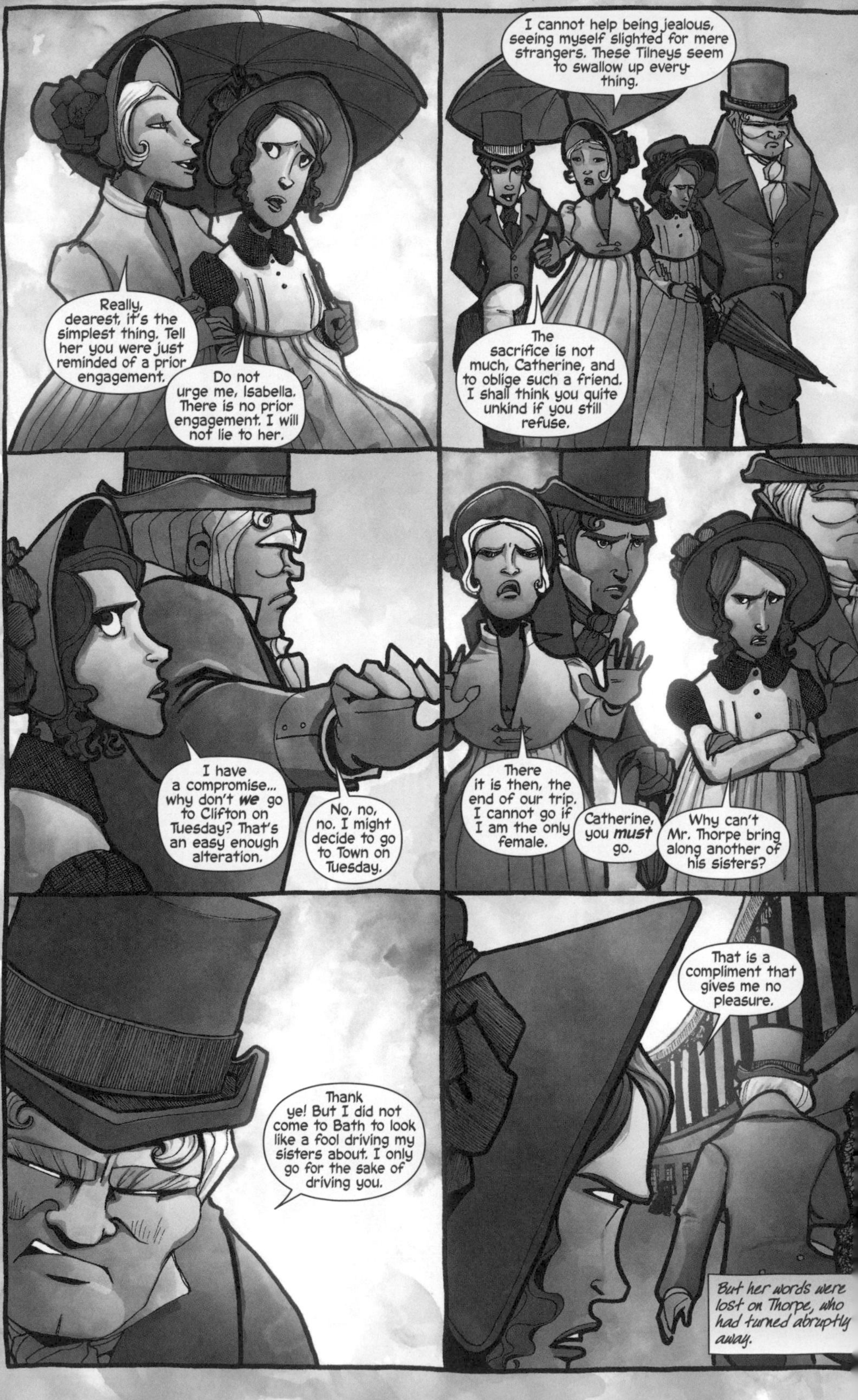
Really, dearest, it's the simplest thing. Tell her you were just reminded of a prior engagement.
Do not urge me, Isabella. There is no prior engagement. I will not lie to her.
I cannot help being jealous, seeing myself slighted for mere strangers. These Tilneys seem to swallow up every-thing.
The sacrifice is not much, Catherine, and to oblige such a friend. I shall think you quite unkind if you still refuse.
I have a compromise... why don't *we* go to Clifton on Tuesday? That's an easy enough alteration.
No, no, no. I might decide to go to Town on Tuesday.
There it is then, the end of our trip. I cannot go if I am the only female.
Catherine, you *must* go.
Why can't Mr. Thorpe bring along another of his sisters?
Thank ye! But I did not come to Bath to look like a fool driving my sisters about. I only go for the sake of driving you.
That is a compliment that gives me no pleasure.
But her words were lost on Thorpe, who had turned abruptly away.

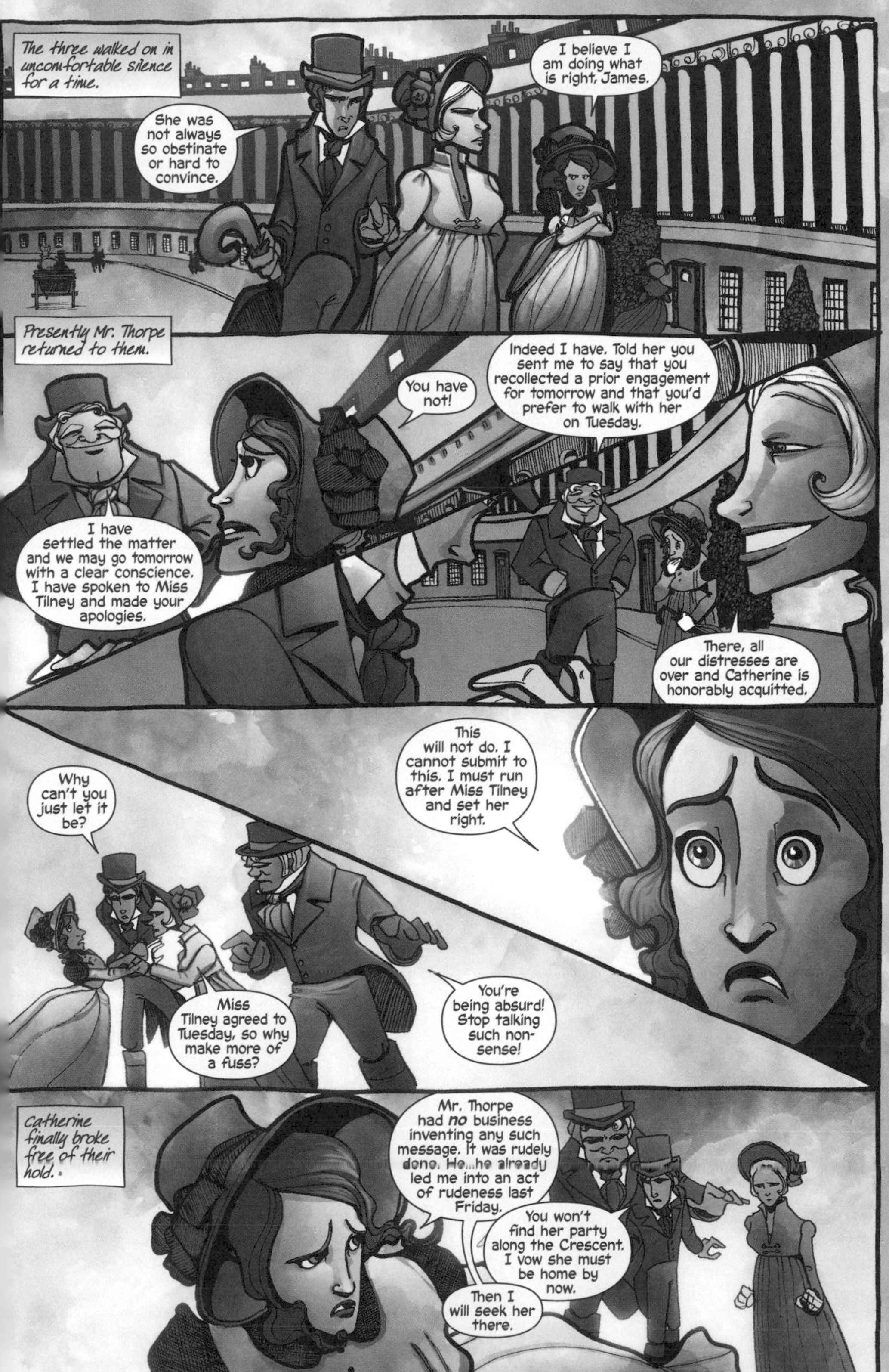
The three walked on in uncomfortable silence for a time.
She was not always so obstinate or hard to convince.
I believe I am doing what is right, James.
Presently Mr. Thorpe returned to them.
I have settled the matter and we may go tomorrow with a clear conscience. I have spoken to Miss Tilney and made your apologies.
You have not!
Indeed I have. Told her you sent me to say that you recollected a prior engagement for tomorrow and that you'd prefer to walk with her on Tuesday.
There, all our distresses are over and Catherine is honorably acquitted.
Why can't you just let it be?
This will not do. I cannot submit to this. I must run after Miss Tilney and set her right.
Miss Tilney agreed to Tuesday, so why make more of a fuss?
You're being absurd! Stop talking such non-sense!
Catherine finally broke free of their hold.
Mr. Thorpe had no business inventing any such message. It was rudely done. He...he already led me into an act of rudeness last Friday.
You won't find her party along the Crescent. I vow she must be home by now.
Then I will seek her there.

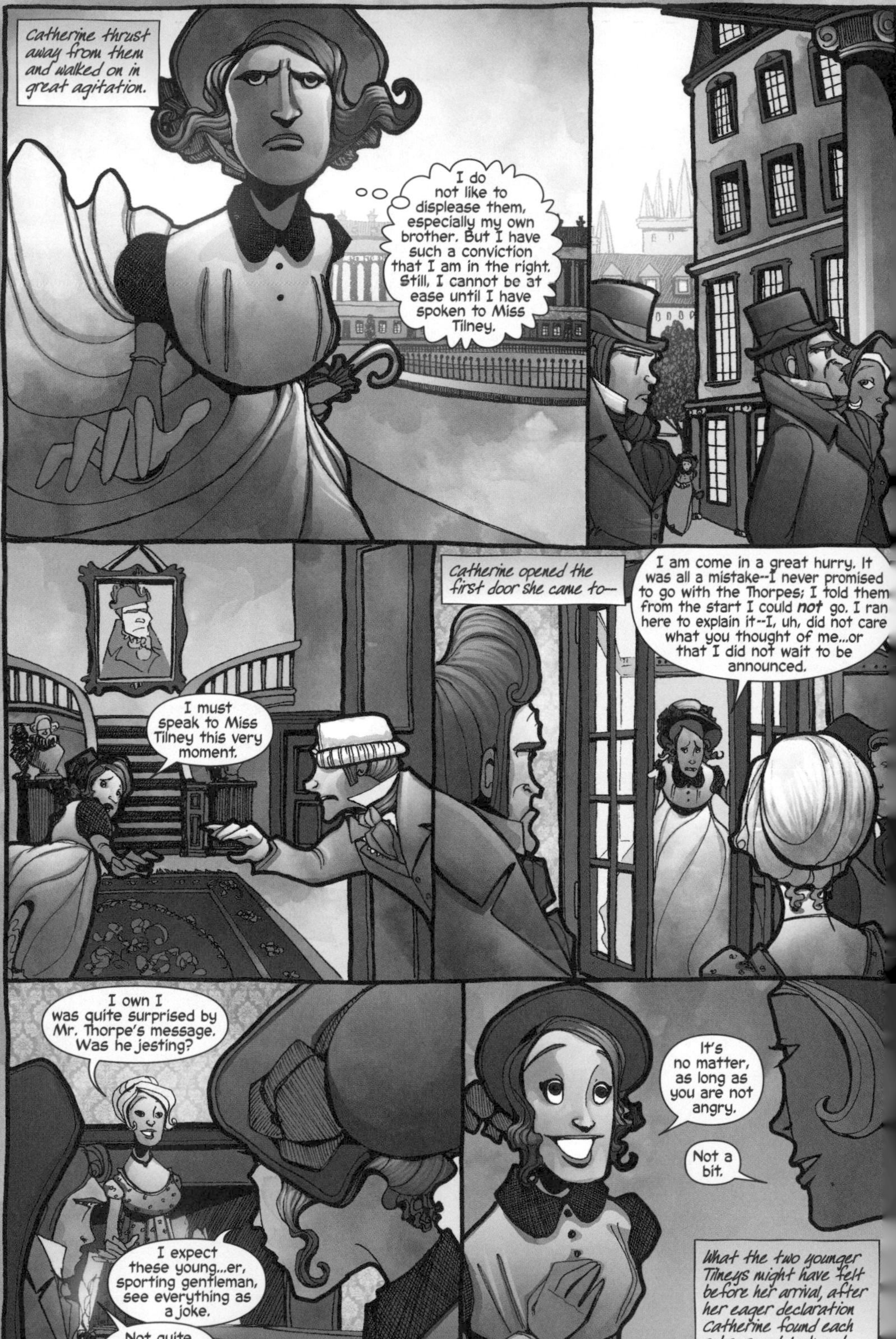
Catherine thrust away from them and walked on in great agitation.
I do not like to displease them, especially my own brother. But I have such a conviction that I am in the right. Still, I cannot be at ease until I have spoken to Miss Tilney.
I must speak to Miss Tilney this very moment.
Catherine opened the first door she came to--
I am come in a great hurry. It was all a mistake--I never promised to go with the Thorpes; I told them from the start I could *not* go. I ran here to explain it--I, uh, did not care what you thought of me...or that I did not wait to be announced.
I own I was quite surprised by Mr. Thorpe's message. Was he jesting?
I expect these young...er, sporting gentleman, see everything as a joke.
Not quite a gentleman if he leaves *you* to straighten things out.
It's no matter, as long as you are not angry.
Not a bit.
What the two younger Tilneys might have felt before her arrival, after her eager declaration Catherine found each subsequent look and sentence as friendly as she could desire.

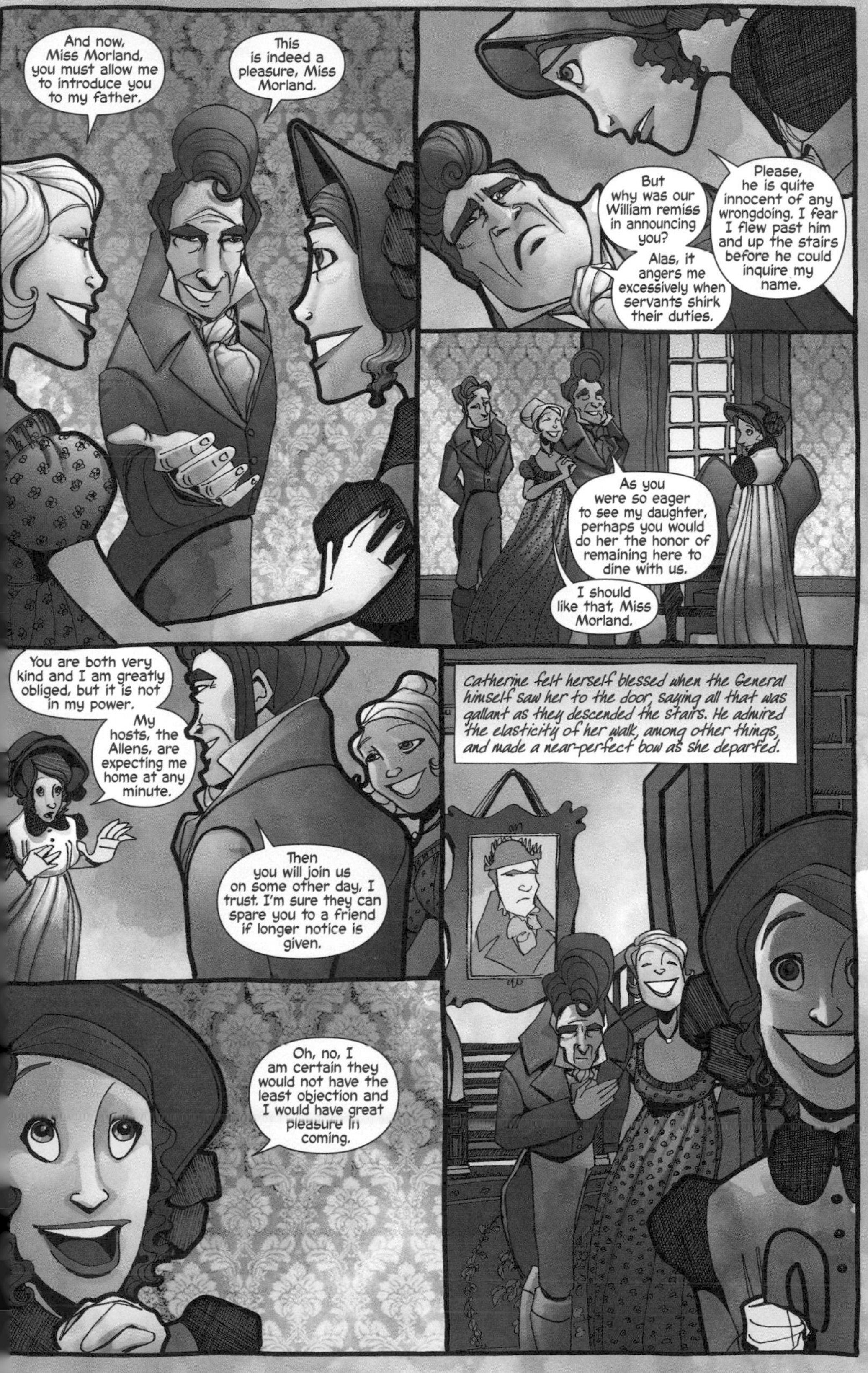
And now, Miss Morland, you must allow me to introduce you to my father.
This is indeed a pleasure, Miss Morland.
But why was our William remiss in announcing you?
Alas, it angers me excessively when servants shirk their duties.
Please, he is quite innocent of any wrongdoing. I fear I flew past him and up the stairs before he could inquire my name.
As you were so eager to see my daughter, perhaps you would do her the honor of remaining here to dine with us.
I should like that, Miss Morland.
You are both very kind and I am greatly obliged, but it is not in my power.
My hosts, the Allens, are expecting me home at any minute.
Then you will join us on some other day, I trust. I'm sure they can spare you to a friend if longer notice is given.
Oh, no, I am certain they would not have the least objection and I would have great pleasure in coming.
Catherine felt herself blessed when the General himself saw her to the door, saying all that was gallant as they descended the stairs. He admired the elasticity of her walk, among other things, and made a near-perfect bow as she departed.

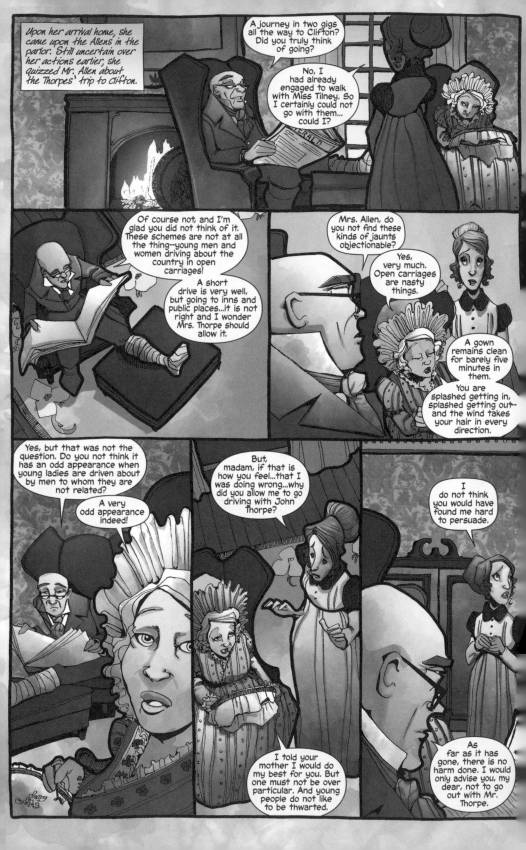

Upon her arrival home, she came upon the Allens in the parlor. Still uncertain over her actions earlier, she quizzed Mr. Allen about the Thorpes' trip to Clifton.

A journey in two gigs all the way to Clifton? Did you truly think of going?

No, I had already engaged to walk with Miss Tilney. So I certainly could not go with them... could I?

Of course not, and I'm glad you did not think of it. These schemes are not at all the thing--young men and women driving about the country in open carriages!

A short drive is very well, but going to inns and public places...it is not right and I wonder Mrs. Thorpe should allow it.

Mrs. Allen, do you not find these kinds of jaunts objectionable?

Yes, very much. Open carriages are nasty things.

A gown remains clean for barely five minutes in them.

You are splashed getting in, splashed getting out-- and the wind takes your hair in every direction.

Yes, but that was not the question. Do you not think it has an odd appearance when young ladies are driven about by men to whom they are not related?

A very odd appearance indeed!

But, madam, if that is how you feel...that I was doing wrong...why did you allow me to go driving with John Thorpe?

I do not think you would have found me hard to persuade.

I told your mother I would do my best for you. But one must not be over particular. And young people do not like to be thwarted.

As far as it has gone, there is no harm done. I would only advise you, my dear, not to go out with Mr. Thorpe.

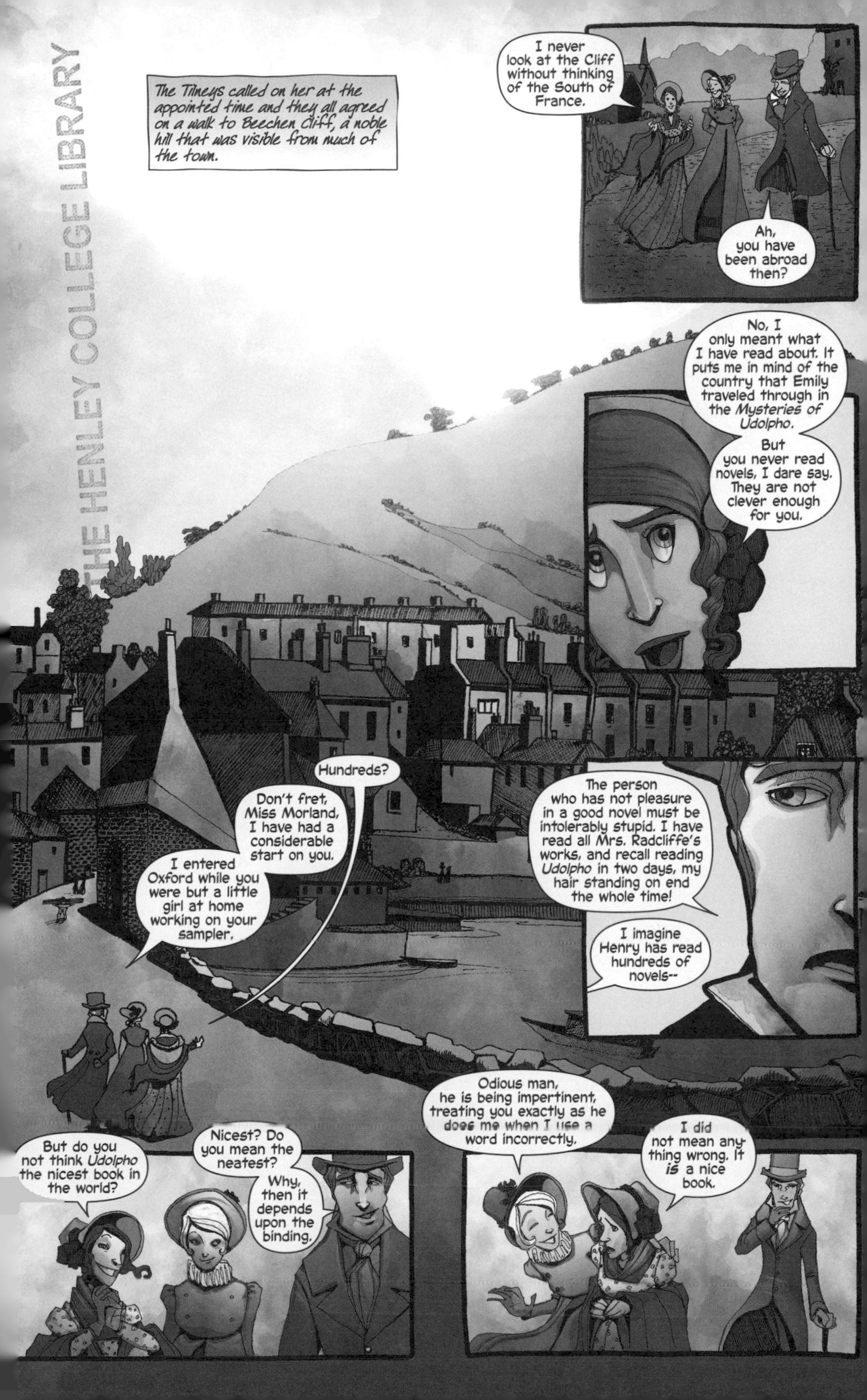
The Tilneys called on her at the appointed time and they all agreed on a walk to Beechen Cliff, a noble hill that was visible from much of the town.
I never look at the Cliff without thinking of the South of France.
Ah, you have been abroad then?
No, I only meant what I have read about. It puts me in mind of the country that Emily traveled through in the *Mysteries of Udolpho*.
But you never read novels, I dare say. They are not clever enough for you.
The person who has not pleasure in a good novel must be intolerably stupid. I have read all Mrs. Radcliffe's works, and recall reading *Udolpho* in two days, my hair standing on end the whole time!
I imagine Henry has read hundreds of novels--
Hundreds?
Don't fret, Miss Morland, I have had a considerable start on you.
I entered Oxford while you were but a little girl at home working on your sampler.
But do you not think *Udolpho* the nicest book in the world?
Nicest? Do you mean the neatest?
Why, then it depends upon the binding.
Odious man, he is being impertinent, treating you exactly as he does me when I use a word incorrectly.
I did not mean anything wrong. It *is* a nice book.

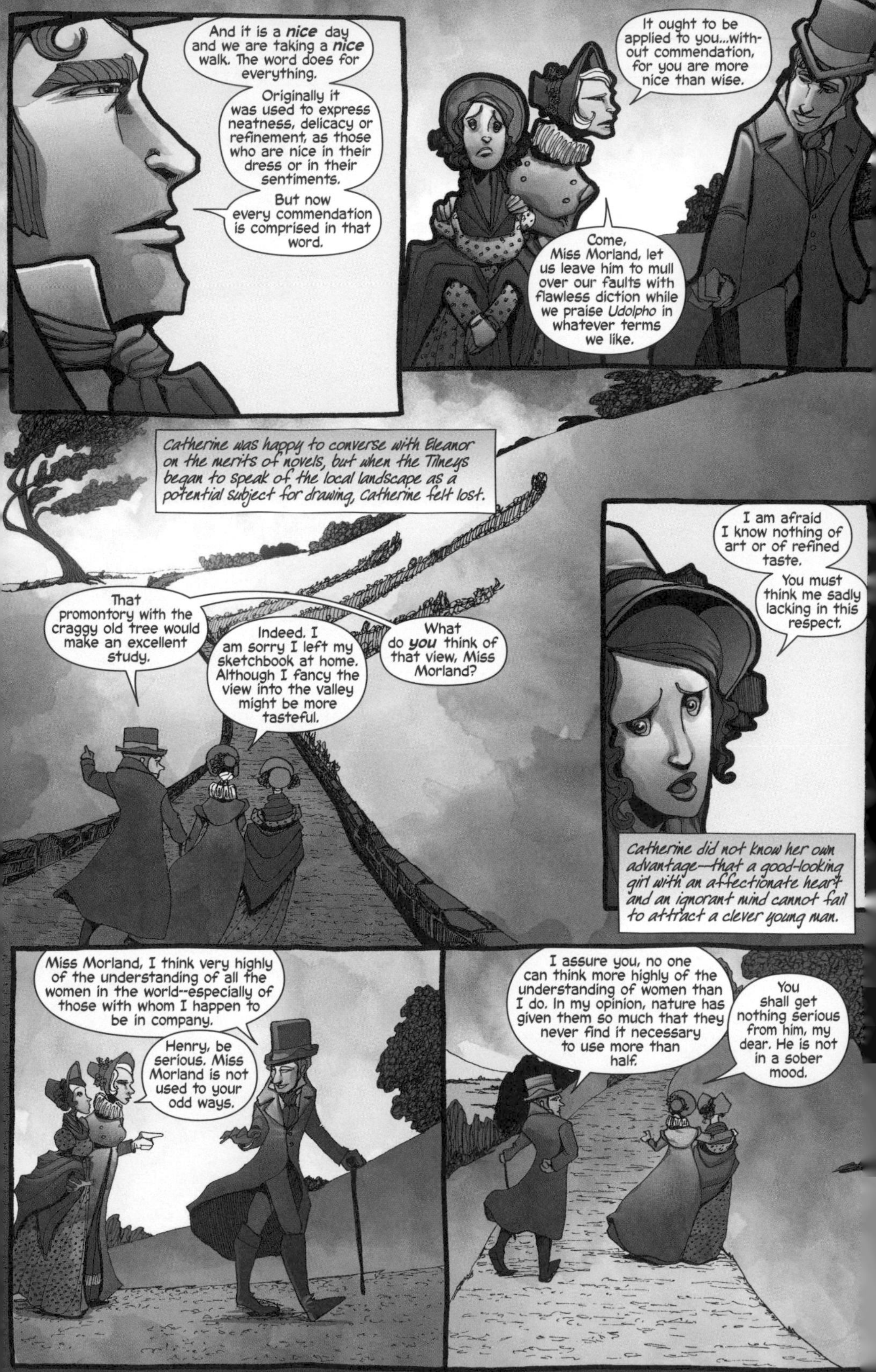
And it is a *nice* day and we are taking a *nice* walk. The word does for everything.
Originally it was used to express neatness, delicacy or refinement, as those who are nice in their dress or in their sentiments.
But now every commendation is comprised in that word.
It ought to be applied to you...without commendation, for you are more nice than wise.
Come, Miss Morland, let us leave him to mull over our faults with flawless diction while we praise *Udolpho* in whatever terms we like.
Catherine was happy to converse with Eleanor on the merits of novels, but when the Tilneys began to speak of the local landscape as a potential subject for drawing, Catherine felt lost.
That promontory with the craggy old tree would make an excellent study.
Indeed. I am sorry I left my sketchbook at home. Although I fancy the view into the valley might be more tasteful.
What do *you* think of that view, Miss Morland?
I am afraid I know nothing of art or of refined taste.
You must think me sadly lacking in this respect.
Catherine did not know her own advantage—that a good-looking girl with an affectionate heart and an ignorant mind cannot fail to attract a clever young man.
Miss Morland, I think very highly of the understanding of all the women in the world--especially of those with whom I happen to be in company.
Henry, be serious. Miss Morland is not used to your odd ways.
I assure you, no one can think more highly of the understanding of women than I do. In my opinion, nature has given them so much that they never find it necessary to use more than half.
You shall get nothing serious from him, my dear. He is not in a sober mood.

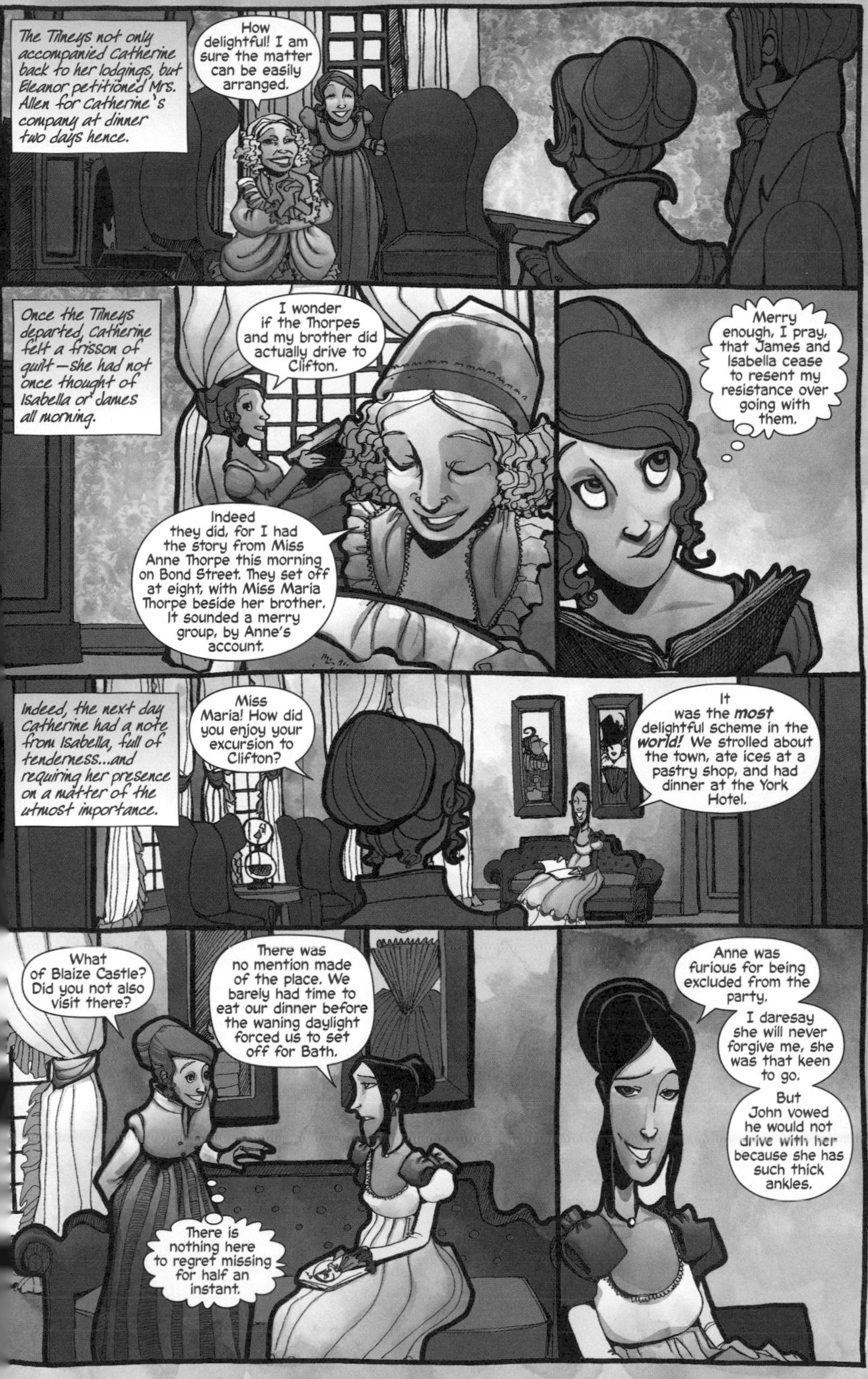
The Tilneys not only accompanied Catherine back to her lodgings, but Eleanor petitioned Mrs. Allen for Catherine's company at dinner two days hence.
How delightful! I am sure the matter can be easily arranged.
Once the Tilneys departed, Catherine felt a frisson of guilt—she had not once thought of Isabella or James all morning.
I wonder if the Thorpes and my brother did actually drive to Clifton.
Indeed they did, for I had the story from Miss Anne Thorpe this morning on Bond Street. They set off at eight, with Miss Maria Thorpe beside her brother. It sounded a merry group, by Anne's account.
Merry enough, I pray, that James and Isabella cease to resent my resistance over going with them.
Indeed, the next day Catherine had a note from Isabella, full of tenderness...and requiring her presence on a matter of the utmost importance.
Miss Maria! How did you enjoy your excursion to Clifton?
It was the **most** delightful scheme in the ***world!*** We strolled about the town, ate ices at a pastry shop, and had dinner at the York Hotel.
What of Blaize Castle? Did you not also visit there?
There was no mention made of the place. We barely had time to eat our dinner before the waning daylight forced us to set off for Bath.
There is nothing here to regret missing for half an instant.
Anne was furious for being excluded from the party.
I daresay she will never forgive me, she was that keen to go.
But John vowed he would not drive with her because she has such thick ankles.

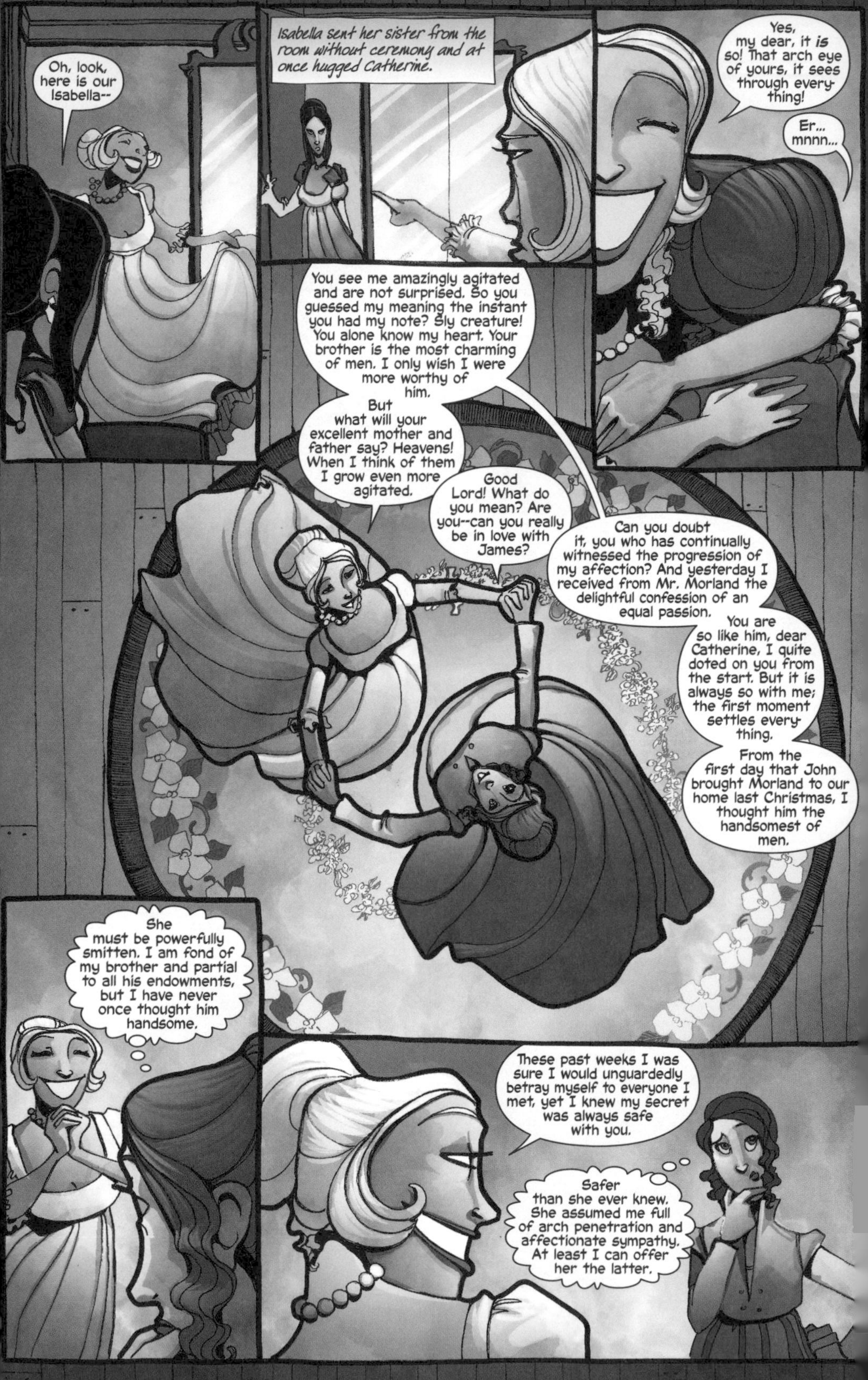
Oh, look, here is our Isabella--
Isabella sent her sister from the room without ceremony and at once hugged Catherine.
Yes, my dear, it is so! That arch eye of yours, it sees through everything!
Er... mnnn...
You see me amazingly agitated and are not surprised. So you guessed my meaning the instant you had my note? Sly creature! You alone know my heart. Your brother is the most charming of men. I only wish I were more worthy of him.
But what will your excellent mother and father say? Heavens! When I think of them I grow even more agitated.
Good Lord! What do you mean? Are you--can you really be in love with James?
Can you doubt it, you who has continually witnessed the progression of my affection? And yesterday I received from Mr. Morland the delightful confession of an equal passion.
You are so like him, dear Catherine, I quite doted on you from the start. But it is always so with me; the first moment settles everything.
From the first day that John brought Morland to our home last Christmas, I thought him the handsomest of men.
She must be powerfully smitten. I am fond of my brother and partial to all his endowments, but I have never once thought him handsome.
These past weeks I was sure I would unguardedly betray myself to everyone I met, yet I knew my secret was always safe with you.
Safer than she ever knew. She assumed me full of arch penetration and affectionate sympathy. At least I can offer her the latter.

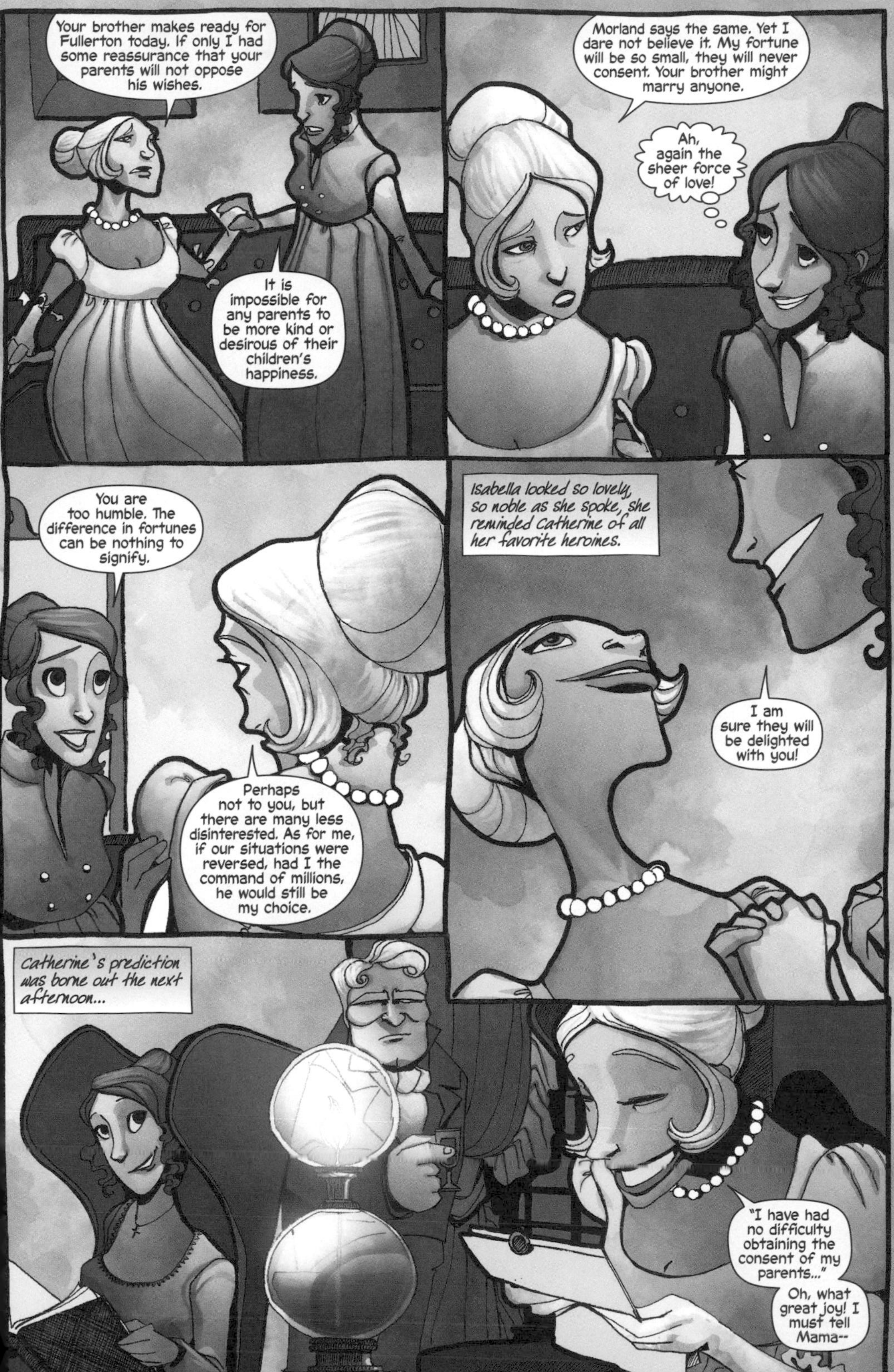
Your brother makes ready for Fullerton today. If only I had some reassurance that your parents will not oppose his wishes.
It is impossible for any parents to be more kind or desirous of their children's happiness.
Morland says the same. Yet I dare not believe it. My fortune will be so small, they will never consent. Your brother might marry anyone.
Ah, again the sheer force of love!
You are too humble. The difference in fortunes can be nothing to signify.
Perhaps not to you, but there are many less disinterested. As for me, if our situations were reversed, had I the command of millions, he would still be my choice.
Isabella looked so lovely, so noble as she spoke, she reminded Catherine of all her favorite heroines.
I am sure they will be delighted with you!
Catherine's prediction was borne out the next afternoon...
"I have had no difficulty obtaining the consent of my parents..."
Oh, what great joy! I must tell Mama--

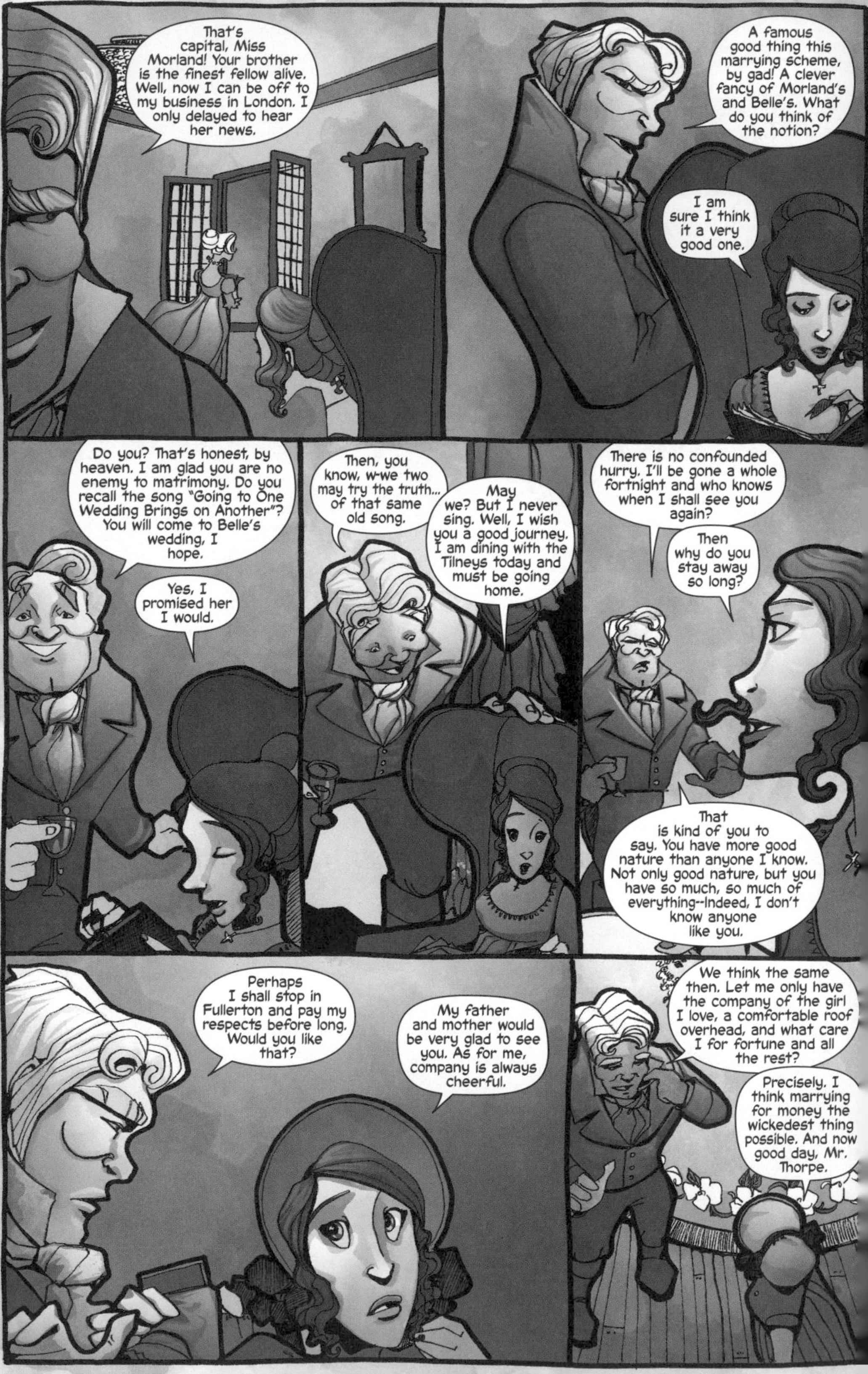
That's capital, Miss Morland! Your brother is the finest fellow alive. Well, now I can be off to my business in London. I only delayed to hear her news.
A famous good thing this marrying scheme, by gad! A clever fancy of Morland's and Belle's. What do you think of the notion?
I am sure I think it a very good one.
Do you? That's honest, by heaven. I am glad you are no enemy to matrimony. Do you recall the song "Going to One Wedding Brings on Another"? You will come to Belle's wedding, I hope.
Yes, I promised her I would.
Then, you know, w-we two may try the truth... of that same old song.
May we? But I never sing. Well, I wish you a good journey. I am dining with the Tilneys today and must be going home.
There is no confounded hurry. I'll be gone a whole fortnight and who knows when I shall see you again?
Then why do you stay away so long?
That is kind of you to say. You have more good nature than anyone I know. Not only good nature, but you have so much, so much of everything--Indeed, I don't know anyone like you.
Perhaps I shall stop in Fullerton and pay my respects before long. Would you like that?
My father and mother would be very glad to see you. As for me, company is always cheerful.
We think the same then. Let me only have the company of the girl I love, a comfortable roof overhead, and what care I for fortune and all the rest?
Precisely. I think marrying for money the wickedest thing possible. And now good day, Mr. Thorpe.

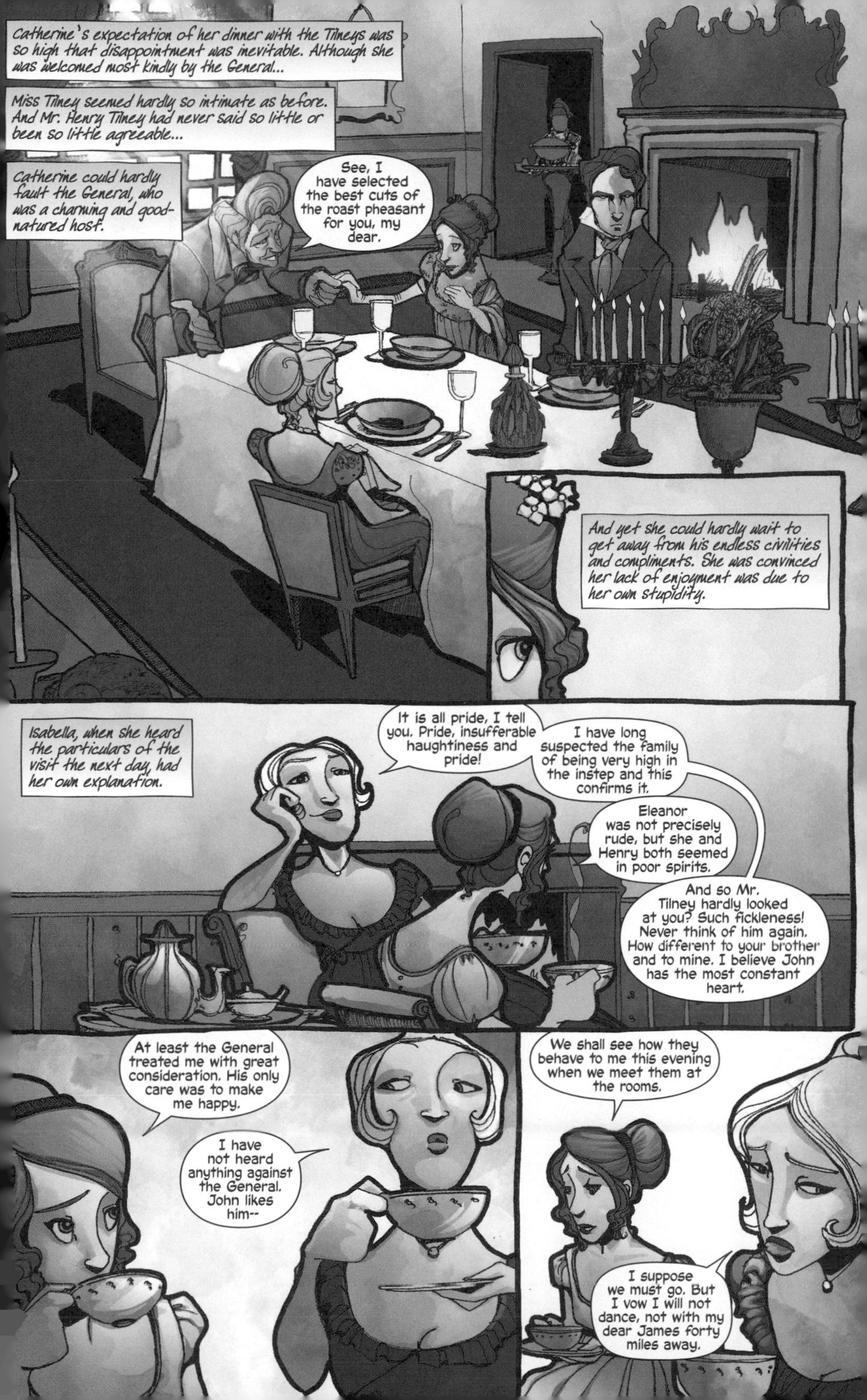
Catherine's expectation of her dinner with the Tilneys was so high that disappointment was inevitable. Although she was welcomed most kindly by the General...
Miss Tilney seemed hardly so intimate as before. And Mr. Henry Tilney had never said so little or been so little agreeable...
Catherine could hardly fault the General, who was a charming and good-natured host.
See, I have selected the best cuts of the roast pheasant for you, my dear.
And yet she could hardly wait to get away from his endless civilities and compliments. She was convinced her lack of enjoyment was due to her own stupidity.
Isabella, when she heard the particulars of the visit the next day, had her own explanation.
It is all pride, I tell you. Pride, insufferable haughtiness and pride!
I have long suspected the family of being very high in the instep and this confirms it.
Eleanor was not precisely rude, but she and Henry both seemed in poor spirits.
And so Mr. Tilney hardly looked at you? Such fickleness! Never think of him again. How different to your brother and to mine. I believe John has the most constant heart.
At least the General treated me with great consideration. His only care was to make me happy.
I have not heard anything against the General. John likes him--
We shall see how they behave to me this evening when we meet them at the rooms.
I suppose we must go. But I vow I will not dance, not with my dear James forty miles away.

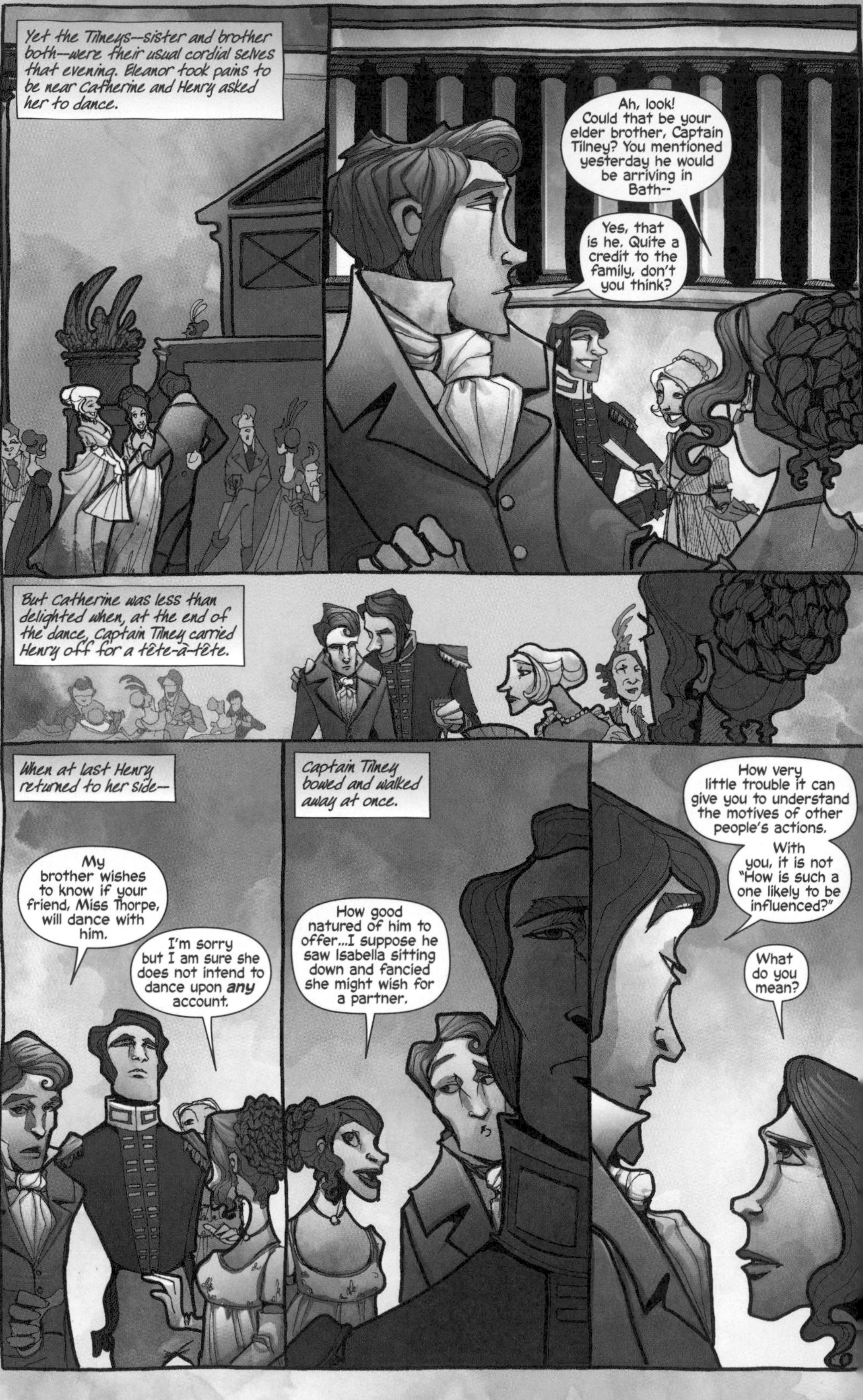

Yet the Tilneys--sister and brother both--were their usual cordial selves that evening. Eleanor took pains to be near Catherine and Henry asked her to dance.
Ah, look! Could that be your elder brother, Captain Tilney? You mentioned yesterday he would be arriving in Bath--
Yes, that is he. Quite a credit to the family, don't you think?
But Catherine was less than delighted when, at the end of the dance, Captain Tilney carried Henry off for a tête-à-tête.
When at last Henry returned to her side--
My brother wishes to know if your friend, Miss Thorpe, will dance with him.
I'm sorry but I am sure she does not intend to dance upon **any** account.
Captain Tilney bowed and walked away at once.
How good natured of him to offer...I suppose he saw Isabella sitting down and fancied she might wish for a partner.
How very little trouble it can give you to understand the motives of other people's actions.
With you, it is not "How is such a one likely to be influenced?"
What do you mean?

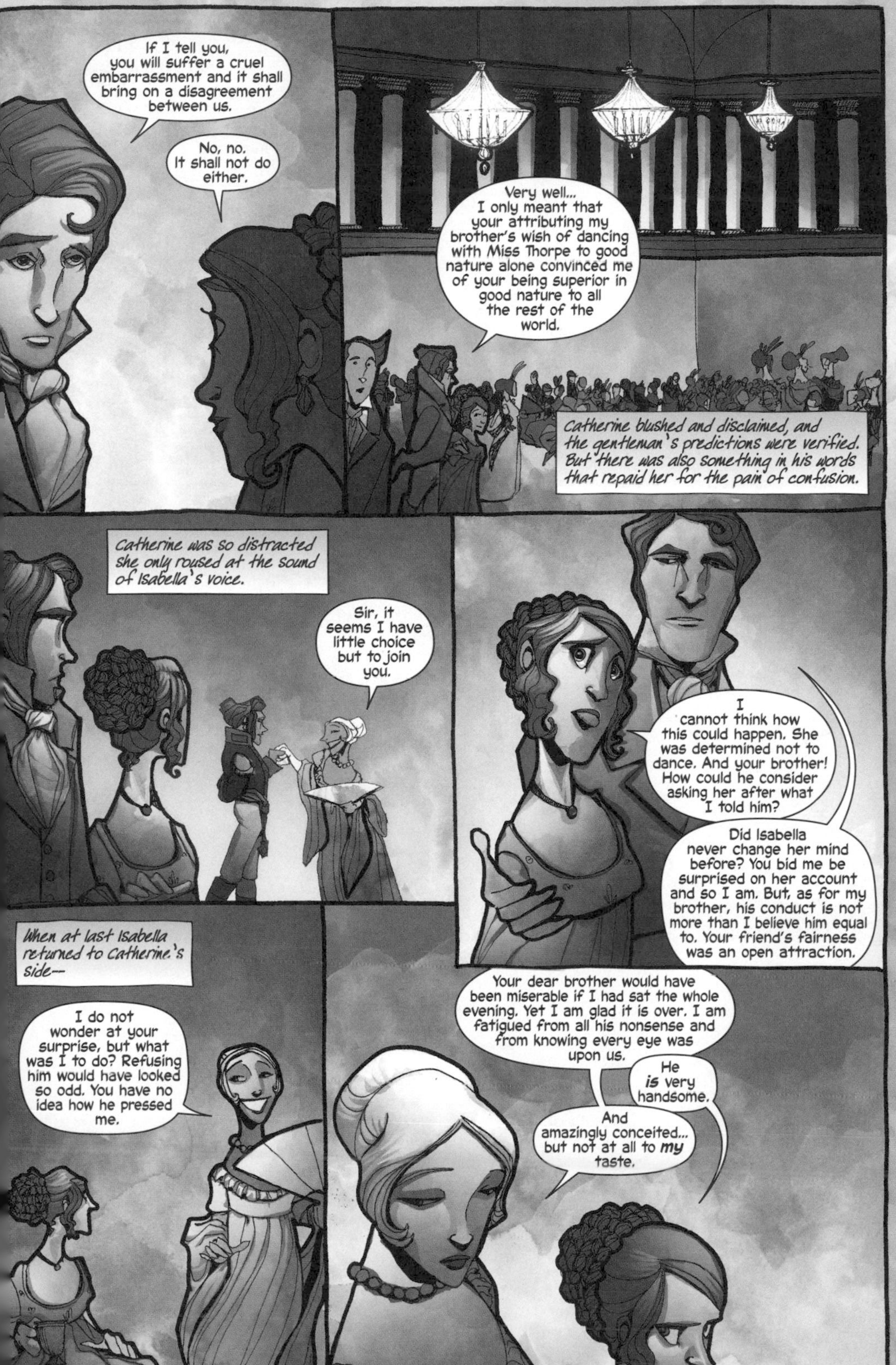
If I tell you, you will suffer a cruel embarrassment and it shall bring on a disagreement between us.
No, no. It shall not do either.
Very well... I only meant that your attributing my brother's wish of dancing with Miss Thorpe to good nature alone convinced me of your being superior in good nature to all the rest of the world.
Catherine blushed and disclaimed, and the gentleman's predictions were verified. But there was also something in his words that repaid her for the pain of confusion.
Catherine was so distracted she only roused at the sound of Isabella's voice.
Sir, it seems I have little choice but to join you.
I cannot think how this could happen. She was determined not to dance. And your brother! How could he consider asking her after what I told him?
Did Isabella never change her mind before? You bid me be surprised on her account and so I am. But, as for my brother, his conduct is not more than I believe him equal to. Your friend's fairness was an open attraction.
When at last Isabella returned to Catherine's side—
I do not wonder at your surprise, but what was I to do? Refusing him would have looked so odd. You have no idea how he pressed me.
Your dear brother would have been miserable if I had sat the whole evening. Yet I am glad it is over. I am fatigued from all his nonsense and from knowing every eye was upon us.
He *is* very handsome.
And amazingly conceited... but not at all to *my* taste.

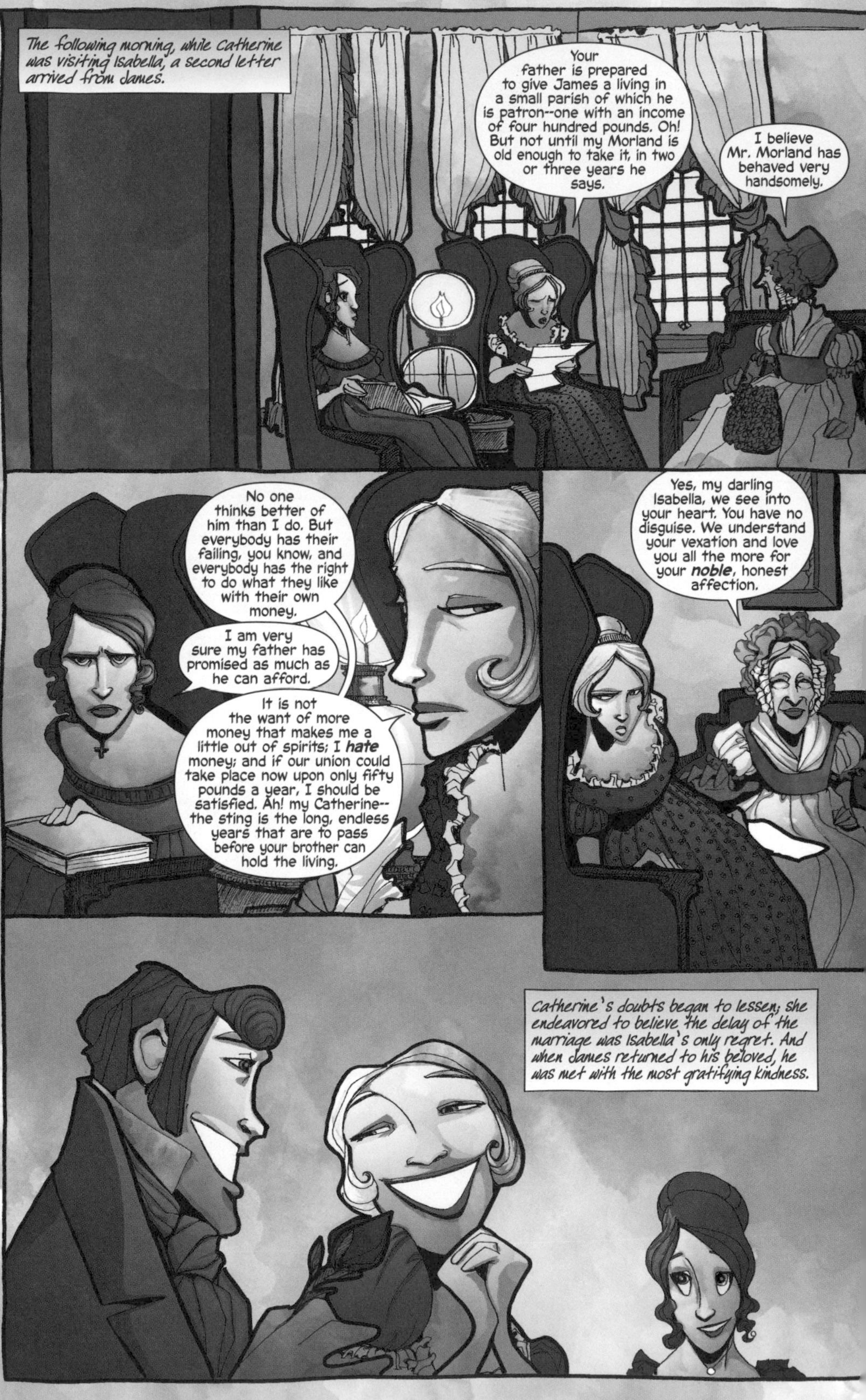
The following morning, while Catherine was visiting Isabella, a second letter arrived from James.
Your father is prepared to give James a living in a small parish of which he is patron--one with an income of four hundred pounds. Oh! But not until my Morland is old enough to take it, in two or three years he says.
I believe Mr. Morland has behaved very handsomely.
No one thinks better of him than I do. But everybody has their failing, you know, and everybody has the right to do what they like with their own money.
I am very sure my father has promised as much as he can afford.
It is not the want of more money that makes me a little out of spirits; I *hate* money; and if our union could take place now upon only fifty pounds a year, I should be satisfied. Ah! my Catherine-- the sting is the long, endless years that are to pass before your brother can hold the living.
Yes, my darling Isabella, we see into your heart. You have no disguise. We understand your vexation and love you all the more for your *noble*, honest affection.
Catherine's doubts began to lessen; she endeavored to believe the delay of the marriage was Isabella's only regret. And when James returned to his beloved, he was met with the most gratifying kindness.

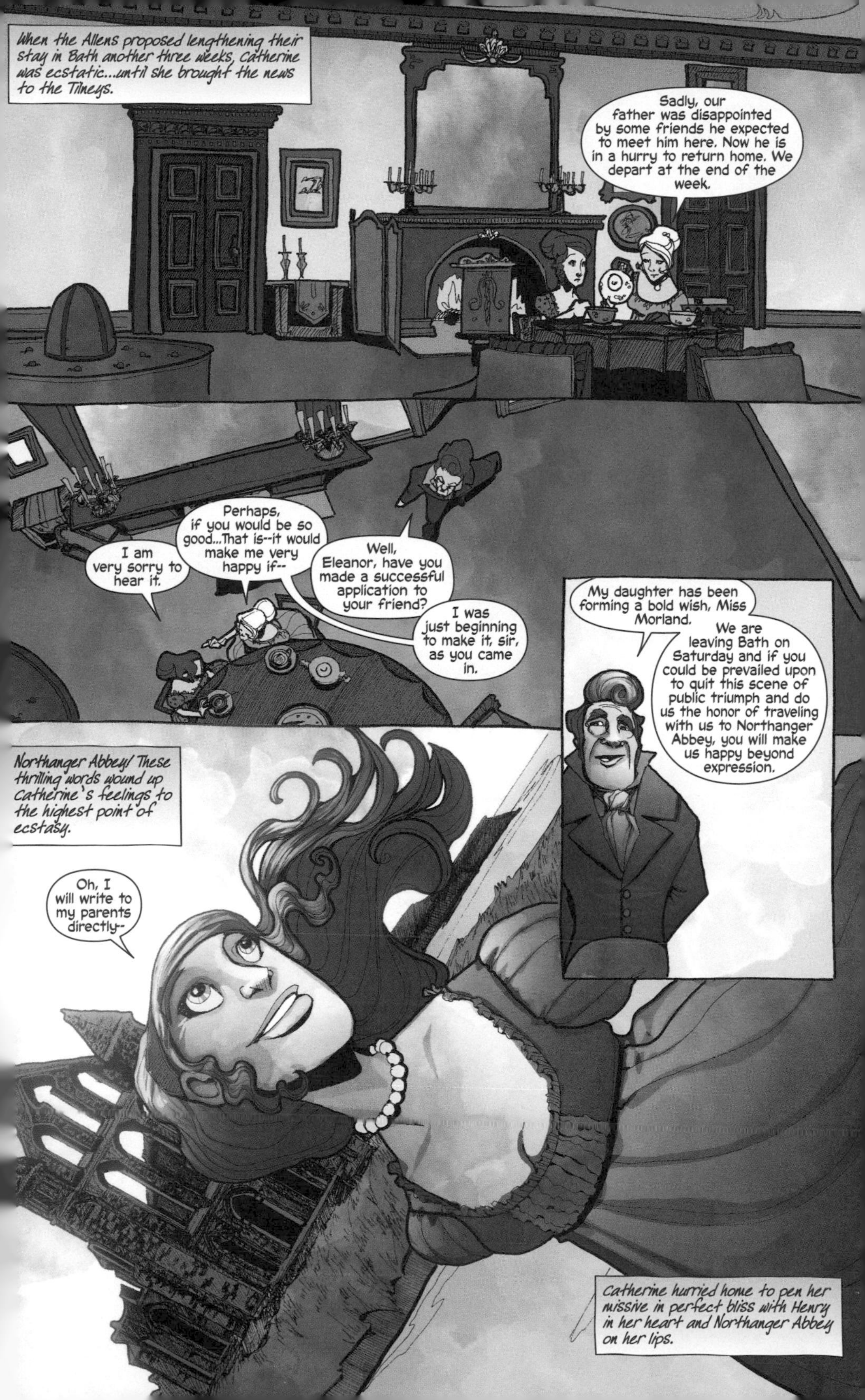
When the Allens proposed lengthening their stay in Bath another three weeks, Catherine was ecstatic...until she brought the news to the Tilneys.
Sadly, our father was disappointed by some friends he expected to meet him here. Now he is in a hurry to return home. We depart at the end of the week.
I am very sorry to hear it.
Perhaps, if you would be so good...That is--it would make me very happy if--
Well, Eleanor, have you made a successful application to your friend?
I was just beginning to make it, sir, as you came in.
My daughter has been forming a bold wish, Miss Morland.
We are leaving Bath on Saturday and if you could be prevailed upon to quit this scene of public triumph and do us the honor of traveling with us to Northanger Abbey, you will make us happy beyond expression.
Northanger Abbey! These thrilling words wound up Catherine's feelings to the highest point of ecstasy.
Oh, I will write to my parents directly--
Catherine hurried home to pen her missive in perfect bliss with Henry in her heart and Northanger Abbey on her lips.

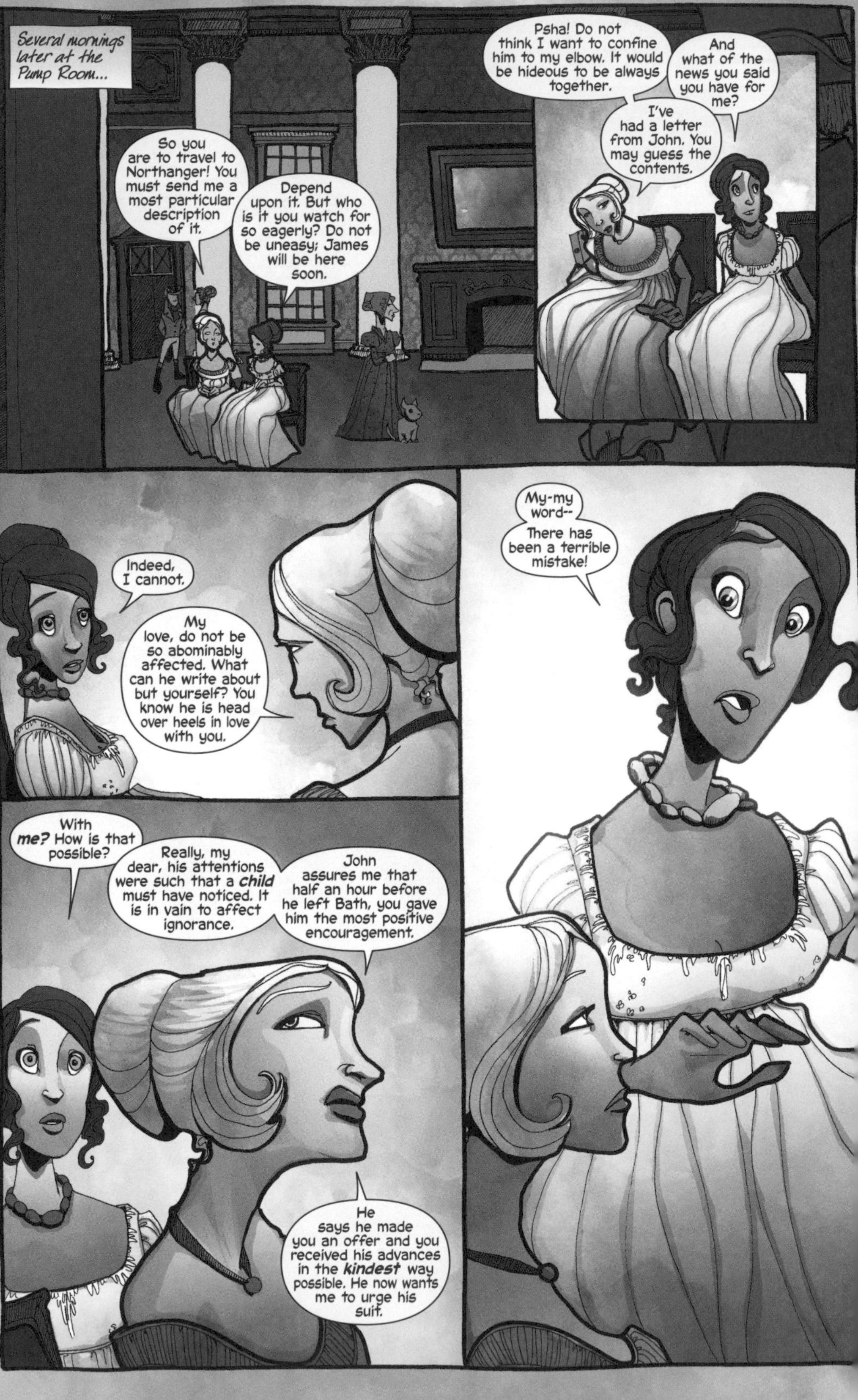

Several mornings later at the Pump Room...
So you are to travel to Northanger! You must send me a most particular description of it.
Depend upon it. But who is it you watch for so eagerly? Do not be uneasy; James will be here soon.
Psha! Do not think I want to confine him to my elbow. It would be hideous to be always together.
And what of the news you said you have for me?
I've had a letter from John. You may guess the contents.
Indeed, I cannot.
My love, do not be so abominably affected. What can he write about but yourself? You know he is head over heels in love with you.
With *me?* How is that possible?
Really, my dear, his attentions were such that a *child* must have noticed. It is in vain to affect ignorance.
John assures me that half an hour before he left Bath, you gave him the most positive encouragement.
He says he made you an offer and you received his advances in the *kindest* way possible. He now wants me to urge his suit.
My-my word--
There has been a terrible mistake!

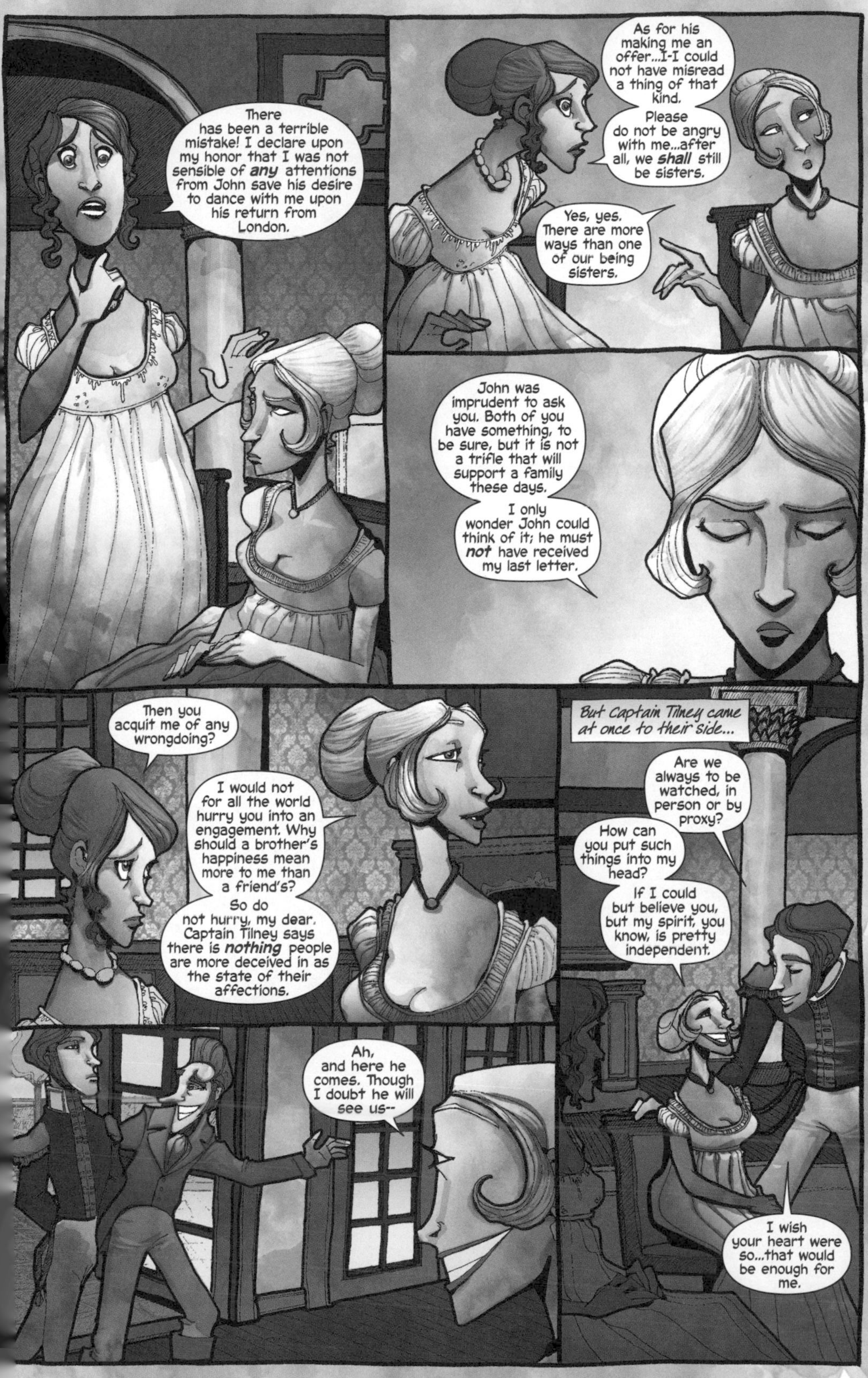
There has been a terrible mistake! I declare upon my honor that I was not sensible of *any* attentions from John save his desire to dance with me upon his return from London.
As for his making me an offer...I-I could not have misread a thing of that kind.
Please do not be angry with me...after all, we *shall* still be sisters.
Yes, yes. There are more ways than one of our being sisters.
John was imprudent to ask you. Both of you have something, to be sure, but it is not a trifle that will support a family these days.
I only wonder John could think of it; he must *not* have received my last letter.
Then you acquit me of any wrongdoing?
I would not for all the world hurry you into an engagement. Why should a brother's happiness mean more to me than a friend's?
So do not hurry, my dear. Captain Tilney says there is *nothing* people are more deceived in as the state of their affections.
Ah, and here he comes. Though I doubt he will see us--
But Captain Tilney came at once to their side...
Are we always to be watched, in person or by proxy?
How can you put such things into my head?
If I could but believe you, but my spirit, you know, is pretty independent.
I wish your heart were so...that would be enough for me.

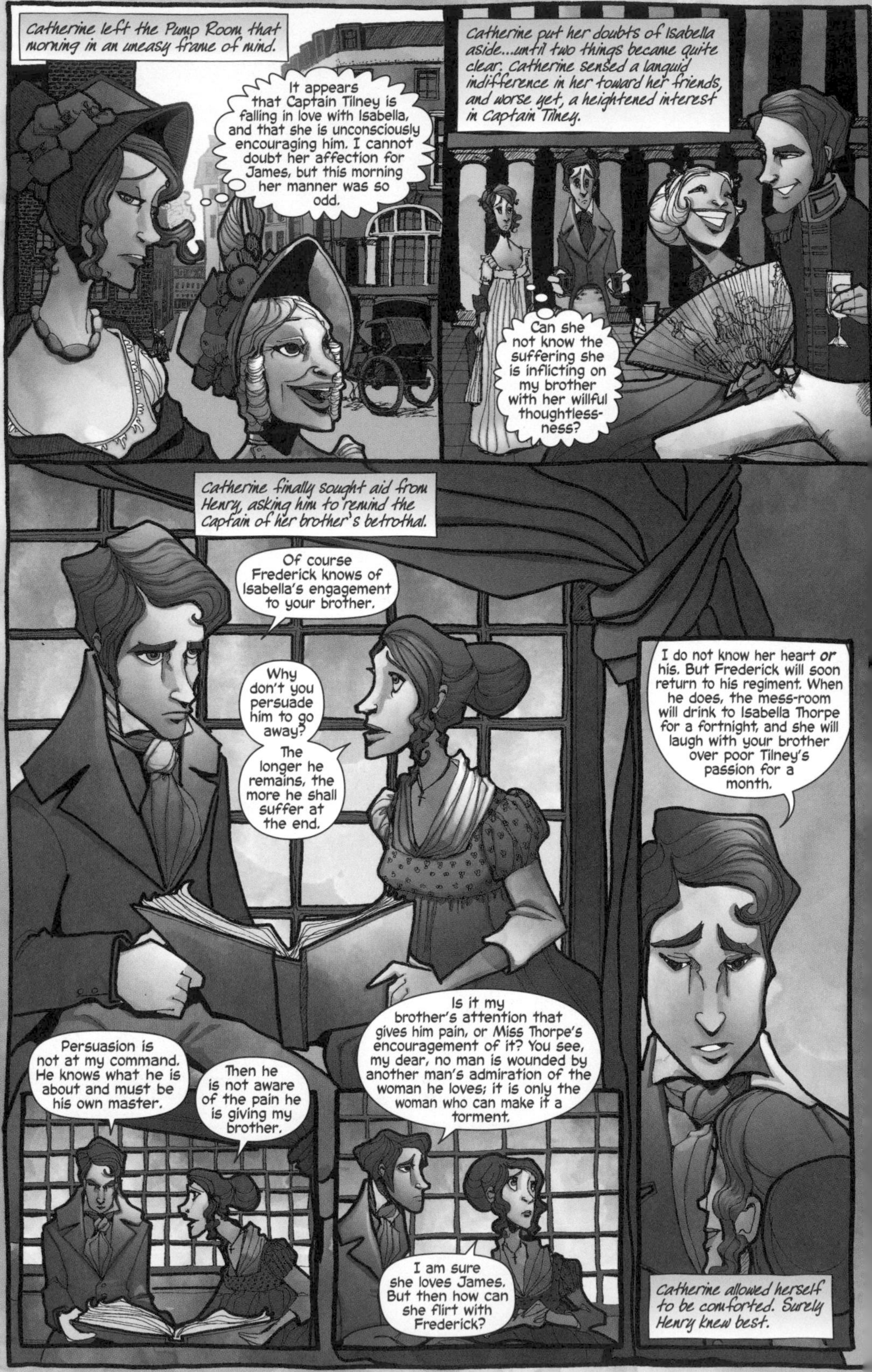

Catherine left the Pump Room that morning in an uneasy frame of mind.
It appears that Captain Tilney is falling in love with Isabella, and that she is unconsciously encouraging him. I cannot doubt her affection for James, but this morning her manner was so odd.
Catherine put her doubts of Isabella aside...until two things became quite clear. Catherine sensed a languid indifference in her toward her friends, and worse yet, a heightened interest in Captain Tilney.
Can she not know the suffering she is inflicting on my brother with her willful thoughtless-ness?
Catherine finally sought aid from Henry, asking him to remind the Captain of her brother's betrothal.
Of course Frederick knows of Isabella's engagement to your brother.
Why don't you persuade him to go away?
The longer he remains, the more he shall suffer at the end.
Persuasion is not at my command. He knows what he is about and must be his own master.
Then he is not aware of the pain he is giving my brother.
Is it my brother's attention that gives him pain, or Miss Thorpe's encouragement of it? You see, my dear, no man is wounded by another man's admiration of the woman he loves; it is only the woman who can make it a torment.
I am sure she loves James. But then how can she flirt with Frederick?
I do not know her heart *or* his. But Frederick will soon return to his regiment. When he does, the mess-room will drink to Isabella Thorpe for a fortnight, and she will laugh with your brother over poor Tilney's passion for a month.
Catherine allowed herself to be comforted. Surely Henry knew best.

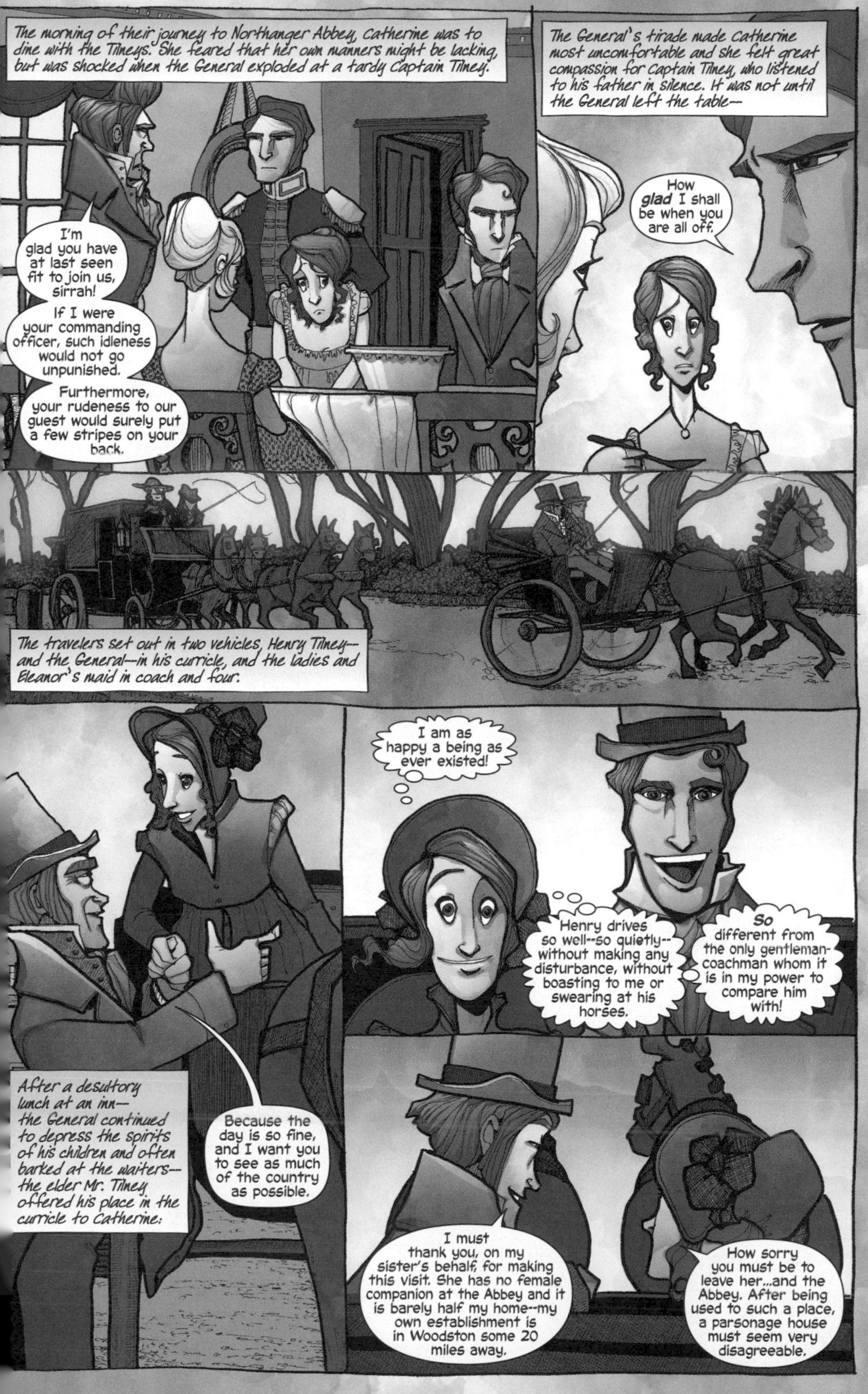
The morning of their journey to Northanger Abbey, Catherine was to dine with the Tilneys. She feared that her own manners might be lacking, but was shocked when the General exploded at a tardy Captain Tilney.
I'm glad you have at last seen fit to join us, sirrah!
If I were your commanding officer, such idleness would not go unpunished.
Furthermore, your rudeness to our guest would surely put a few stripes on your back.
The General's tirade made Catherine most uncomfortable and she felt great compassion for Captain Tilney, who listened to his father in silence. It was not until the General left the table--
How glad I shall be when you are all off.
The travelers set out in two vehicles, Henry Tilney-- and the General--in his curricle, and the ladies and Eleanor's maid in coach and four.
After a desultory lunch at an inn-- the General continued to depress the spirits of his children and often barked at the waiters-- the elder Mr. Tilney offered his place in the curricle to Catherine:
Because the day is so fine, and I want you to see as much of the country as possible.
I am as happy a being as ever existed!
Henry drives so well--so quietly--without making any disturbance, without boasting to me or swearing at his horses.
So different from the only gentleman-coachman whom it is in my power to compare him with!
I must thank you, on my sister's behalf, for making this visit. She has no female companion at the Abbey and it is barely half my home--my own establishment is in Woodston some 20 miles away.
How sorry you must be to leave her...and the Abbey. After being used to such a place, a parsonage house must seem very disagreeable.

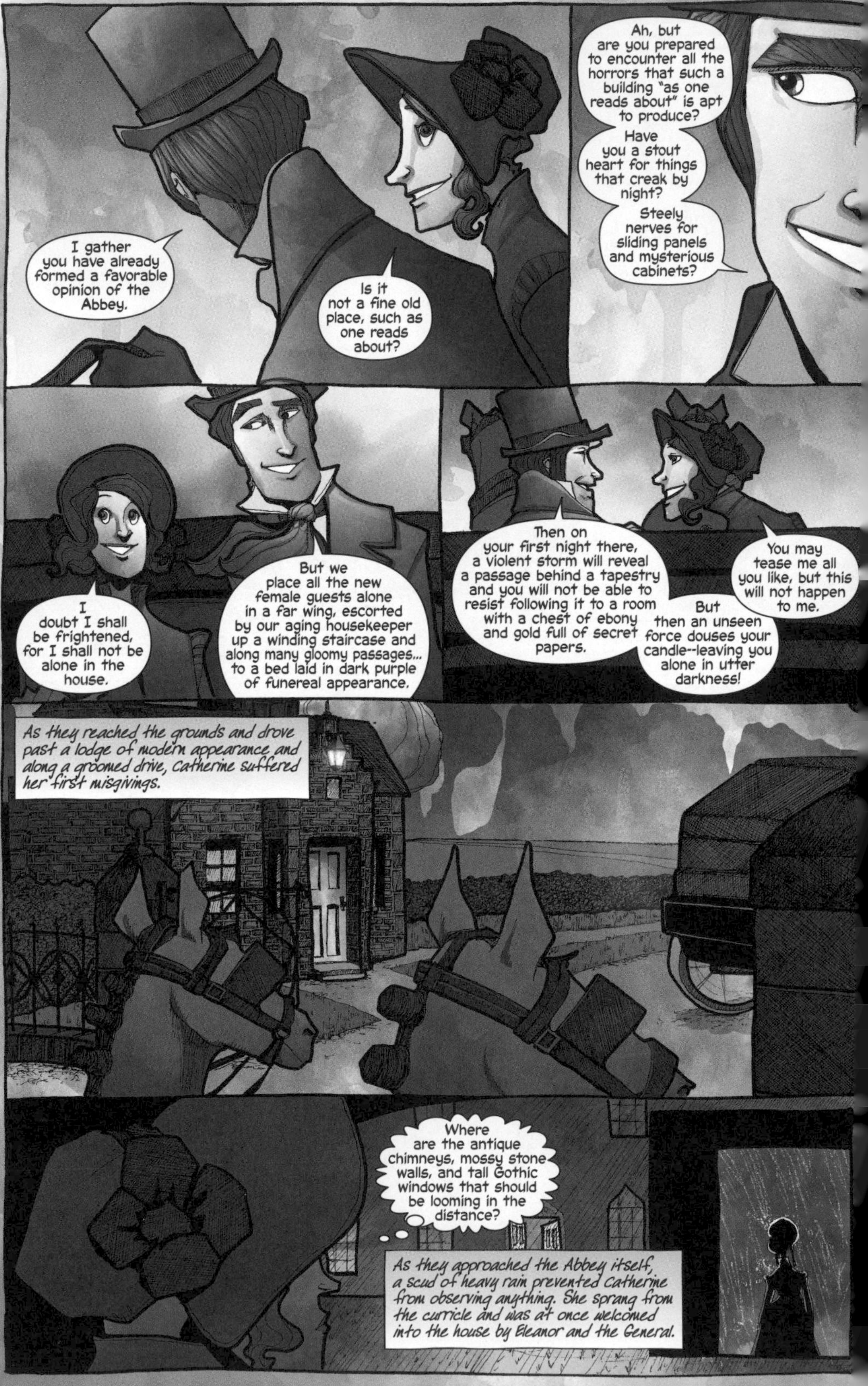
I gather you have already formed a favorable opinion of the Abbey.
Is it not a fine old place, such as one reads about?
Ah, but are you prepared to encounter all the horrors that such a building "as one reads about" is apt to produce?
Have you a stout heart for things that creak by night?
Steely nerves for sliding panels and mysterious cabinets?
I doubt I shall be frightened, for I shall not be alone in the house.
But we place all the new female guests alone in a far wing, escorted by our aging housekeeper up a winding staircase and along many gloomy passages... to a bed laid in dark purple of funereal appearance.
Then on your first night there, a violent storm will reveal a passage behind a tapestry and you will not be able to resist following it to a room with a chest of ebony and gold full of secret papers.
But then an unseen force douses your candle--leaving you alone in utter darkness!
You may tease me all you like, but this will not happen to me.
As they reached the grounds and drove past a lodge of modern appearance and along a groomed drive, Catherine suffered her first misgivings.
Where are the antique chimneys, mossy stone walls, and tall Gothic windows that should be looming in the distance?
As they approached the Abbey itself, a scud of heavy rain prevented Catherine from observing anything. She sprang from the curricle and was at once welcomed into the house by Eleanor and the General.

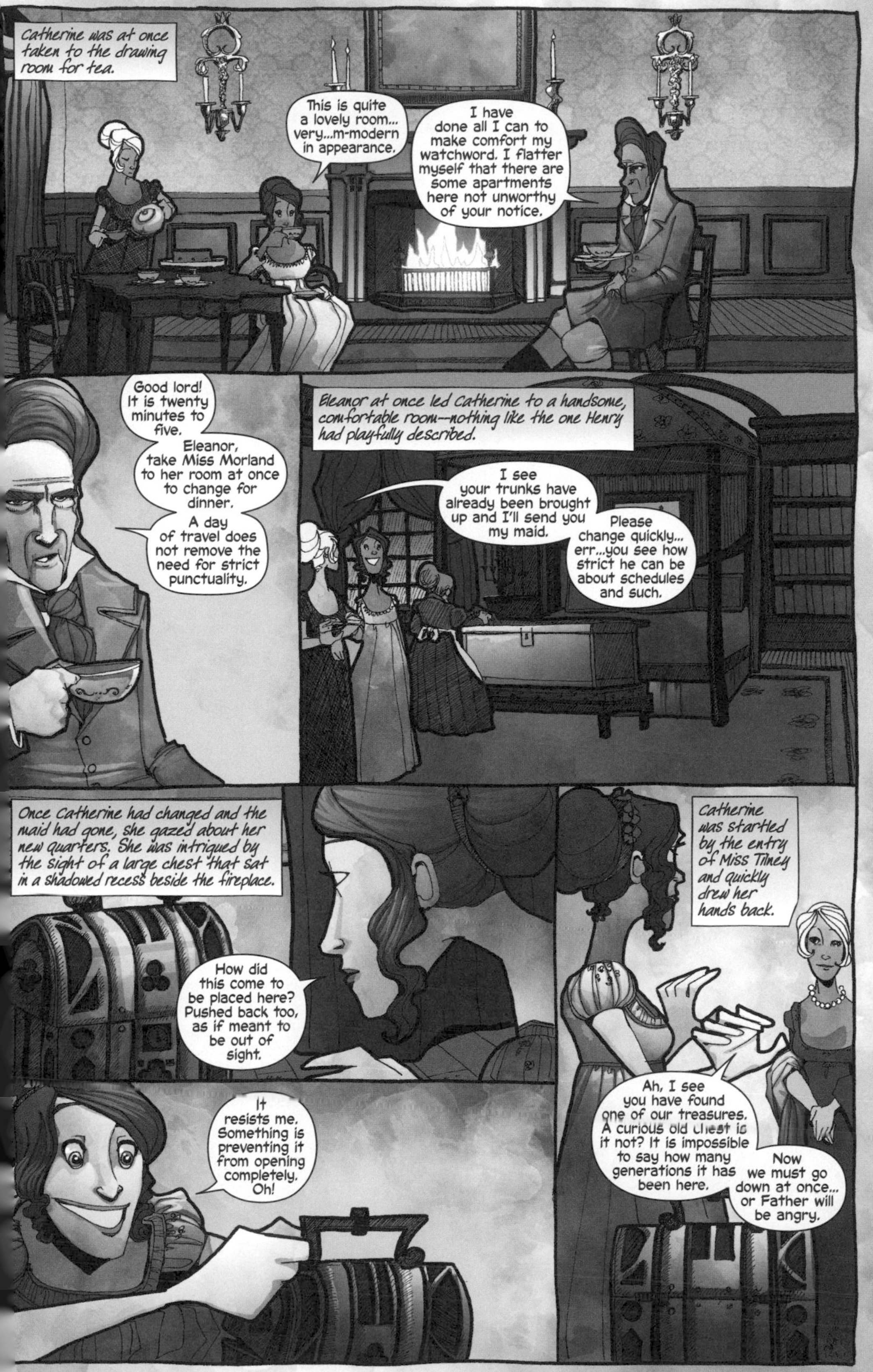
Catherine was at once taken to the drawing room for tea.
This is quite a lovely room... very...m-modern in appearance.
I have done all I can to make comfort my watchword. I flatter myself that there are some apartments here not unworthy of your notice.
Good lord! It is twenty minutes to five.
Eleanor, take Miss Morland to her room at once to change for dinner.
A day of travel does not remove the need for strict punctuality.
Eleanor at once led Catherine to a handsome, comfortable room--nothing like the one Henry had playfully described.
I see your trunks have already been brought up and I'll send you my maid.
Please change quickly... err...you see how strict he can be about schedules and such.
Once Catherine had changed and the maid had gone, she gazed about her new quarters. She was intrigued by the sight of a large chest that sat in a shadowed recess beside the fireplace.
How did this come to be placed here? Pushed back too, as if meant to be out of sight.
It resists me. Something is preventing it from opening completely. Oh!
Catherine was startled by the entry of Miss Tilney and quickly drew her hands back.
Ah, I see you have found one of our treasures. A curious old chest is it not? It is impossible to say how many generations it has been here.
Now we must go down at once... or Father will be angry.

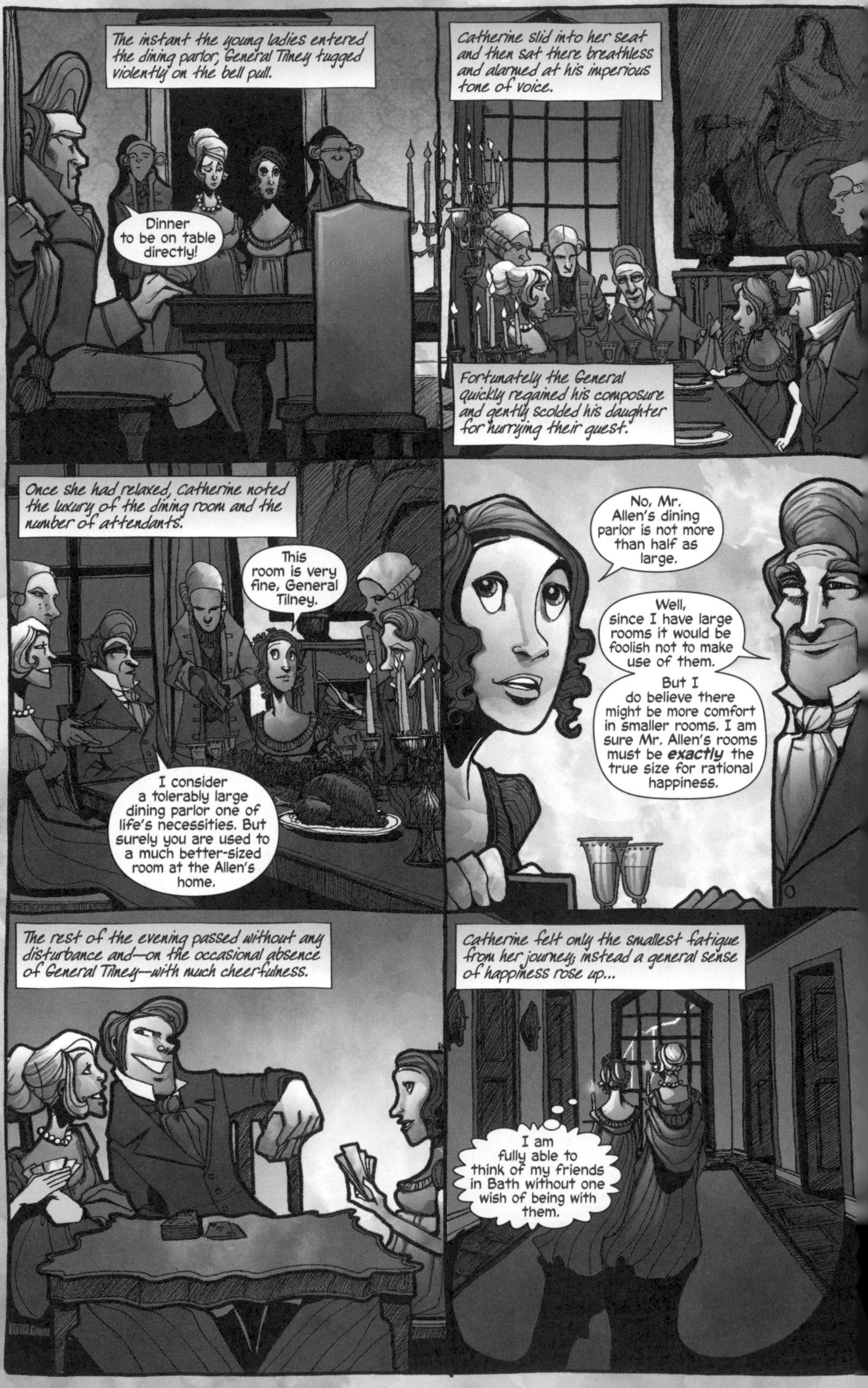
The instant the young ladies entered the dining parlor, General Tilney tugged violently on the bell pull.
Dinner to be on table directly!
Catherine slid into her seat and then sat there breathless and alarmed at his imperious tone of voice.
Fortunately the General quickly regained his composure and gently scolded his daughter for hurrying their guest.
Once she had relaxed, Catherine noted the luxury of the dining room and the number of attendants.
This room is very fine, General Tilney.
I consider a tolerably large dining parlor one of life's necessities. But surely you are used to a much better-sized room at the Allen's home.
No, Mr. Allen's dining parlor is not more than half as large.
Well, since I have large rooms it would be foolish not to make use of them.
But I do believe there might be more comfort in smaller rooms. I am sure Mr. Allen's rooms must be exactly the true size for rational happiness.
The rest of the evening passed without any disturbance and--on the occasional absence of General Tilney--with much cheerfulness.
Catherine felt only the smallest fatigue from her journey; instead a general sense of happiness rose up...
I am fully able to think of my friends in Bath without one wish of being with them.

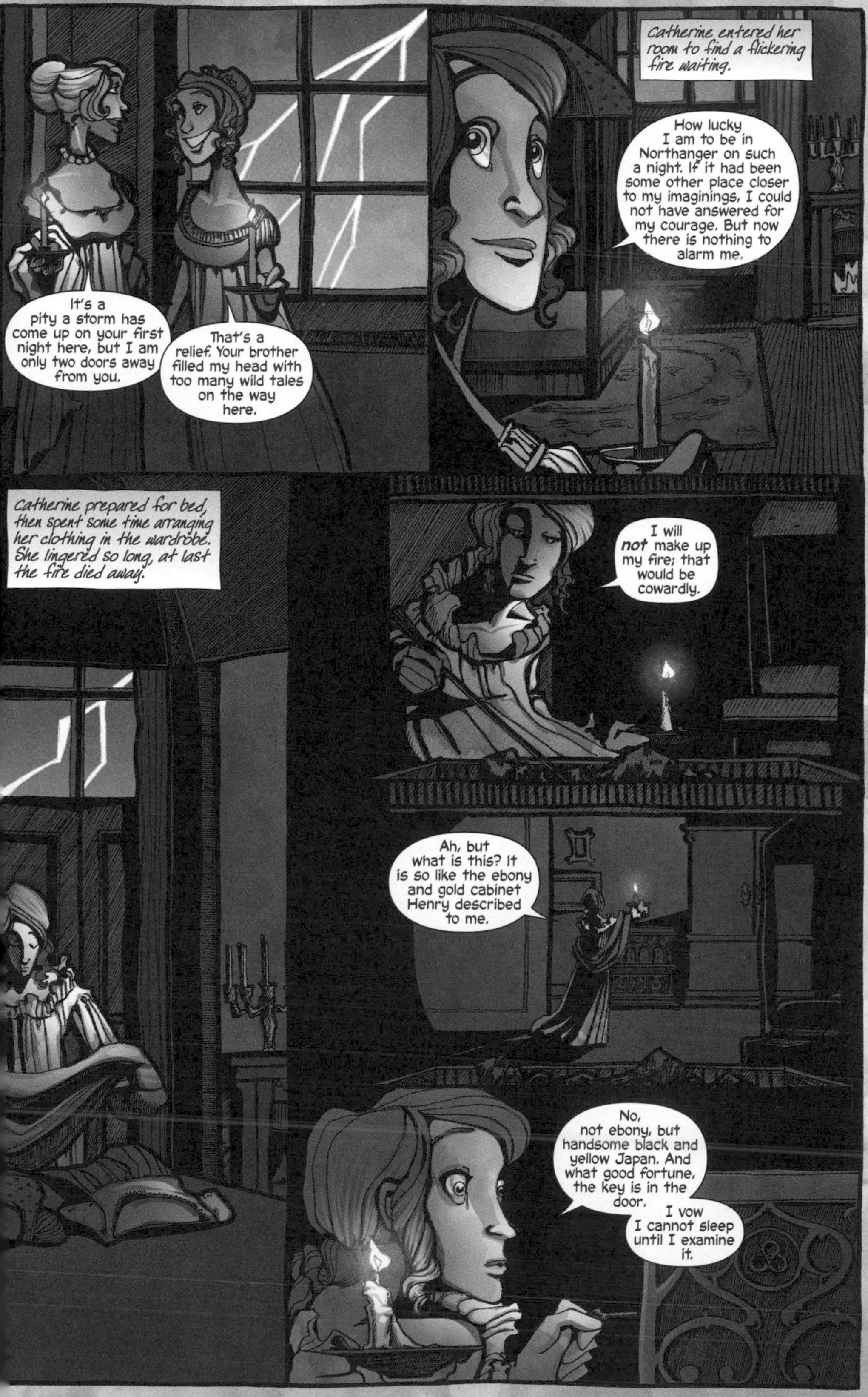
It's a pity a storm has come up on your first night here, but I am only two doors away from you.
That's a relief. Your brother filled my head with too many wild tales on the way here.
Catherine entered her room to find a flickering fire waiting.
How lucky I am to be in Northanger on such a night. If it had been some other place closer to my imaginings, I could not have answered for my courage. But now there is nothing to alarm me.
Catherine prepared for bed, then spent some time arranging her clothing in the wardrobe. She lingered so long, at last the fire died away.
I will *not* make up my fire; that would be cowardly.
Ah, but what is this? It is so like the ebony and gold cabinet Henry described to me.
No, not ebony, but handsome black and yellow Japan. And what good fortune, the key is in the door.
I vow I cannot sleep until I examine it.

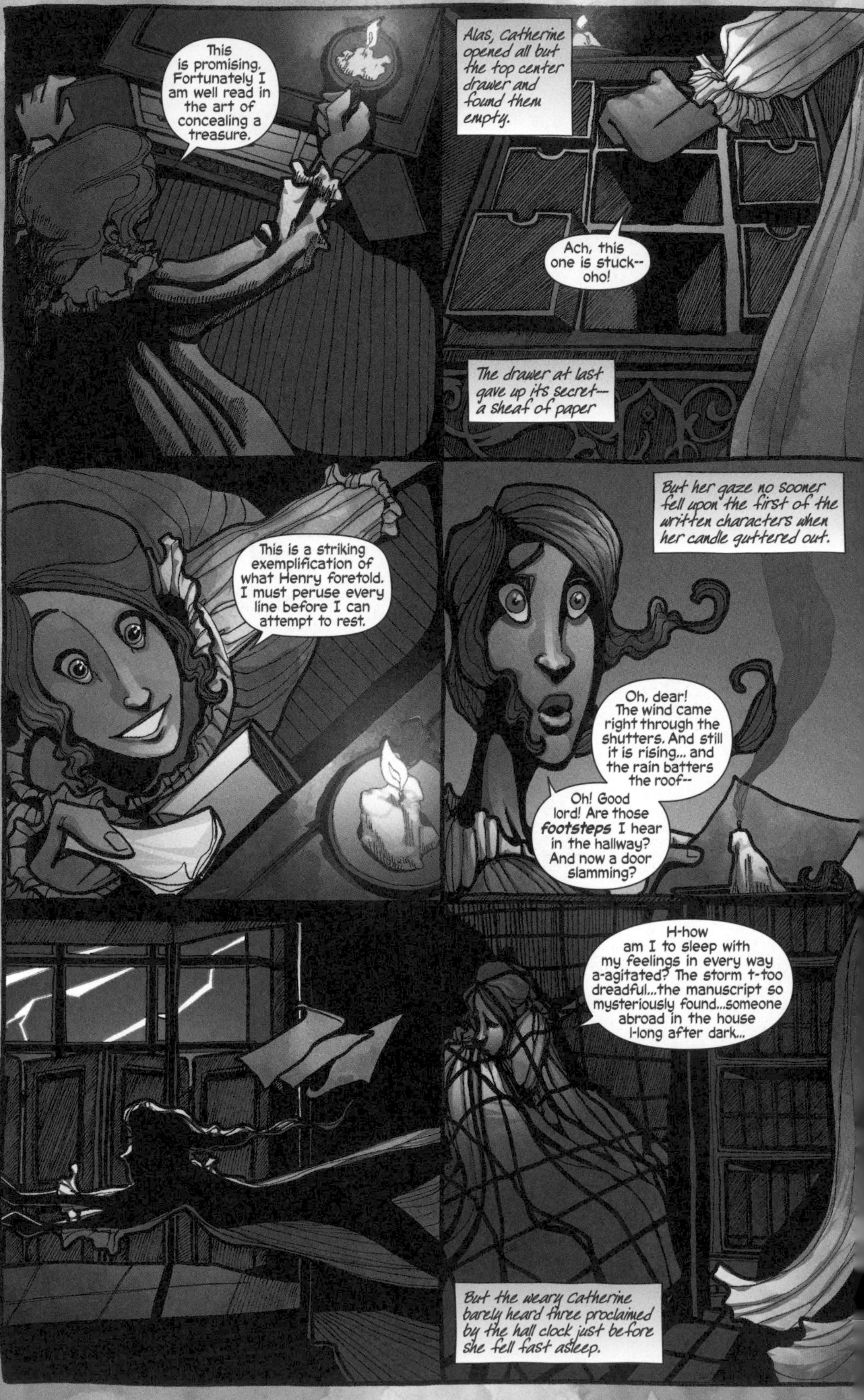
This is promising. Fortunately I am well read in the art of concealing a treasure.
Alas, Catherine opened all but the top center drawer and found them empty.
Ach, this one is stuck--oho!
The drawer at last gave up its secret--a sheaf of paper
This is a striking exemplification of what Henry foretold. I must peruse every line before I can attempt to rest.
But her gaze no sooner fell upon the first of the written characters when her candle guttered out.
Oh, dear! The wind came right through the shutters. And still it is rising... and the rain batters the roof--
Oh! Good lord! Are those footsteps I hear in the hallway? And now a door slamming?
H-how am I to sleep with my feelings in every way a-agitated? The storm t-too dreadful...the manuscript so mysteriously found...someone abroad in the house l-long after dark...
But the weary Catherine barely heard three proclaimed by the hall clock just before she fell fast asleep.

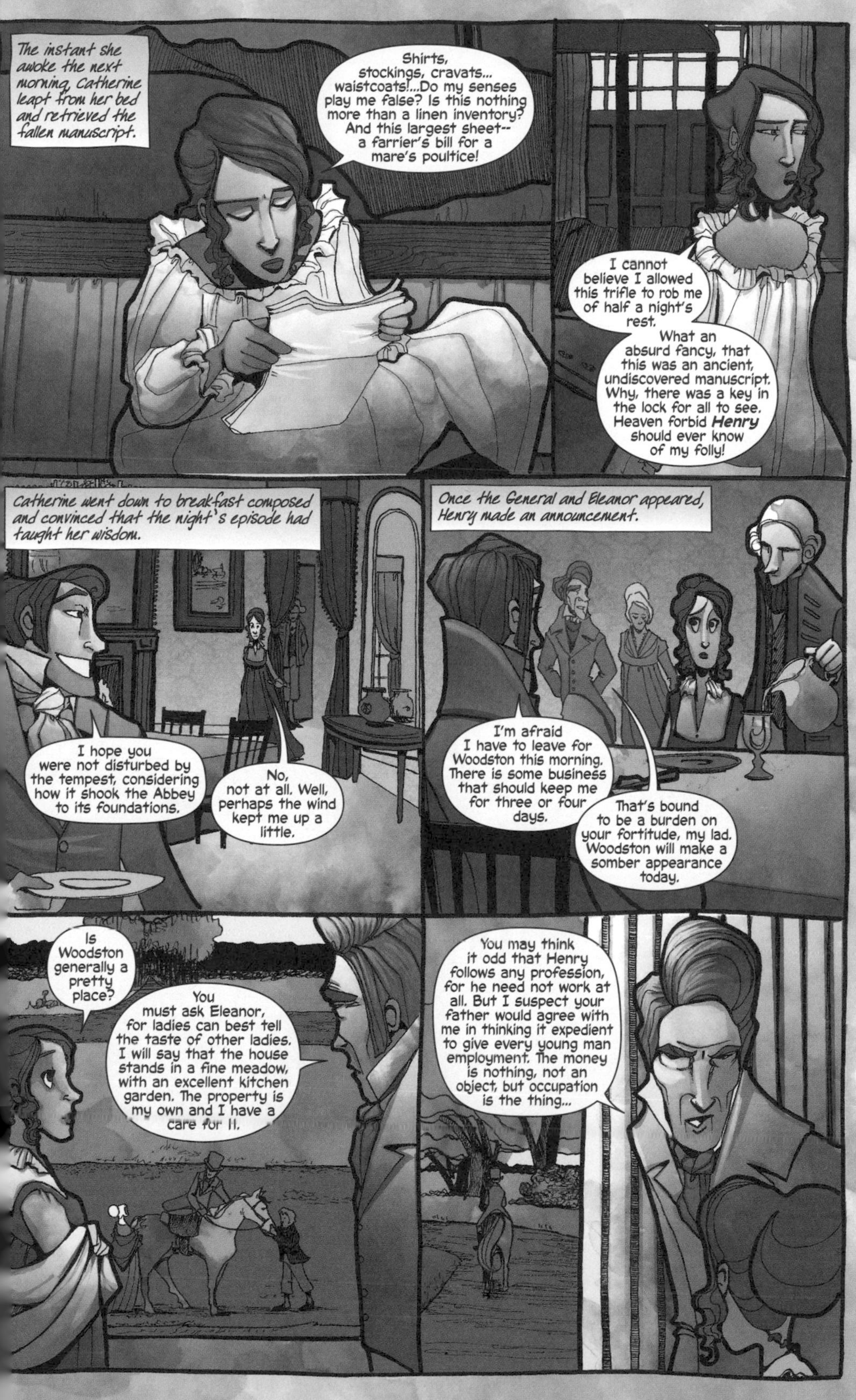
The instant she awoke the next morning, Catherine leapt from her bed and retrieved the fallen manuscript.
Shirts, stockings, cravats... waistcoats!...Do my senses play me false? Is this nothing more than a linen inventory? And this largest sheet-- a farrier's bill for a mare's poultice!
I cannot believe I allowed this trifle to rob me of half a night's rest.
What an absurd fancy, that this was an ancient, undiscovered manuscript. Why, there was a key in the lock for all to see. Heaven forbid **Henry** should ever know of my folly!
Catherine went down to breakfast composed and convinced that the night's episode had taught her wisdom.
I hope you were not disturbed by the tempest, considering how it shook the Abbey to its foundations.
No, not at all. Well, perhaps the wind kept me up a little.
Once the General and Eleanor appeared, Henry made an announcement.
I'm afraid I have to leave for Woodston this morning. There is some business that should keep me for three or four days.
That's bound to be a burden on your fortitude, my lad. Woodston will make a somber appearance today.
Is Woodston generally a pretty place?
You must ask Eleanor, for ladies can best tell the taste of other ladies. I will say that the house stands in a fine meadow, with an excellent kitchen garden. The property is my own and I have a care for it.
You may think it odd that Henry follows any profession, for he need not work at all. But I suspect your father would agree with me in thinking it expedient to give every young man employment. The money is nothing, not an object, but occupation is the thing...

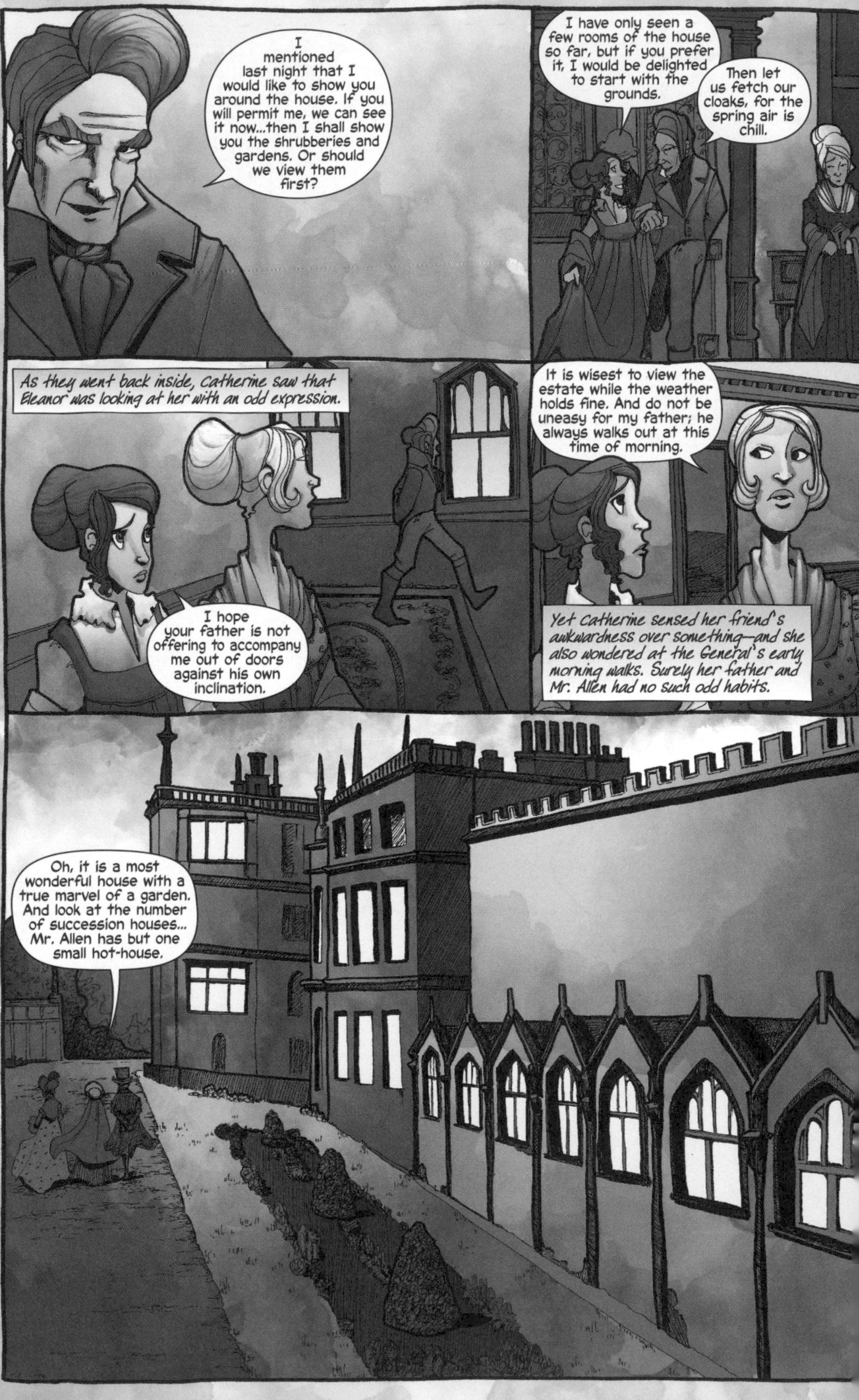

I mentioned last night that I would like to show you around the house. If you will permit me, we can see it now...then I shall show you the shrubberies and gardens. Or should we view them first?
I have only seen a few rooms of the house so far, but if you prefer it, I would be delighted to start with the grounds.
Then let us fetch our cloaks, for the spring air is chill.
As they went back inside, Catherine saw that Eleanor was looking at her with an odd expression.
I hope your father is not offering to accompany me out of doors against his own inclination.
It is wisest to view the estate while the weather holds fine. And do not be uneasy for my father; he always walks out at this time of morning.
Yet Catherine sensed her friend's awkwardness over something—and she also wondered at the General's early morning walks. Surely her father and Mr. Allen had no such odd habits.
Oh, it is a most wonderful house with a true marvel of a garden. And look at the number of succession houses... Mr. Allen has but one small hot-house.

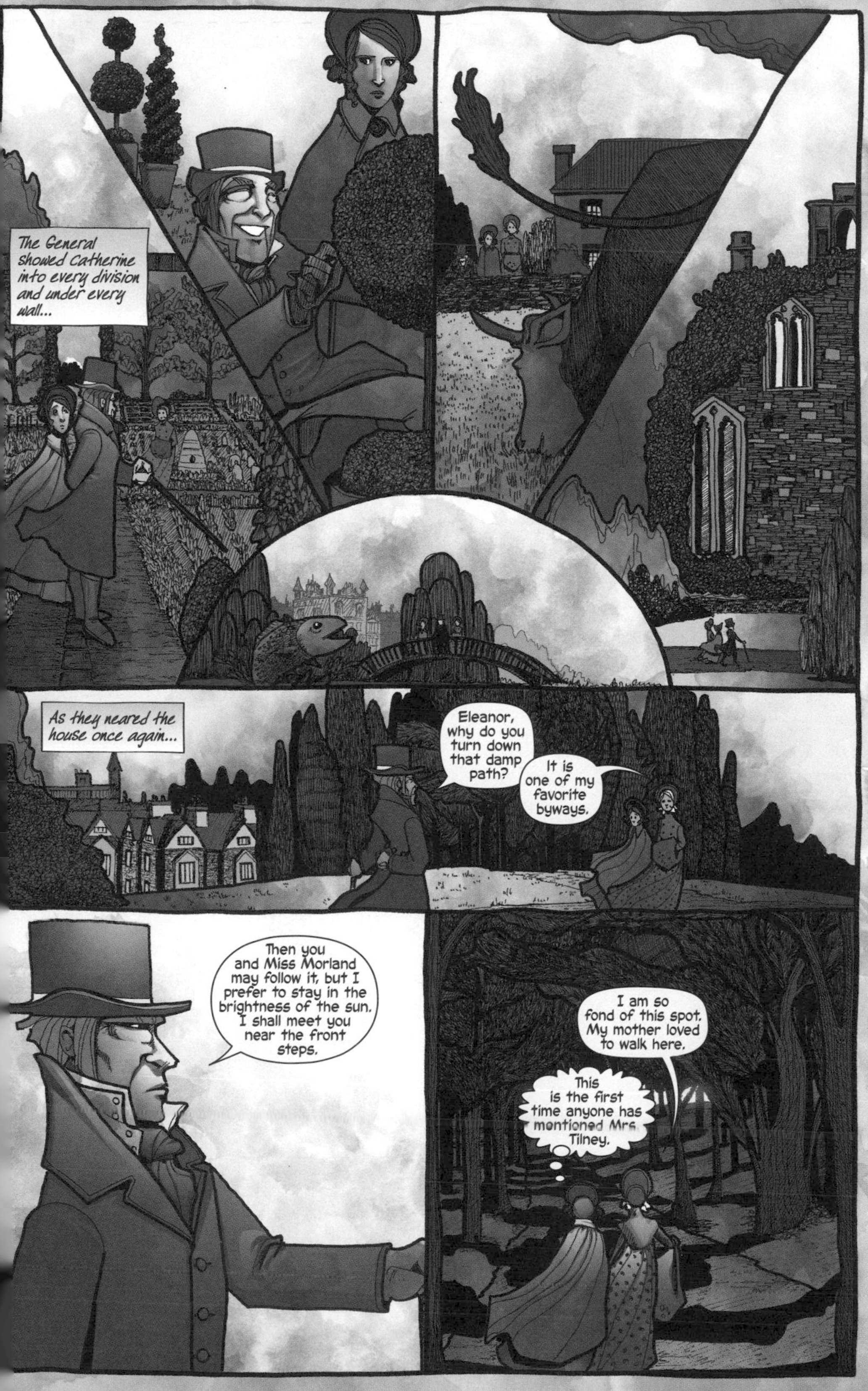

The General showed Catherine into every division and under every wall...
As they neared the house once again...
Eleanor, why do you turn down that damp path?
It is one of my favorite byways.
Then you and Miss Morland may follow it, but I prefer to stay in the brightness of the sun. I shall meet you near the front steps.
I am so fond of this spot. My mother loved to walk here.
This is the first time anyone has mentioned Mrs. Tilney.

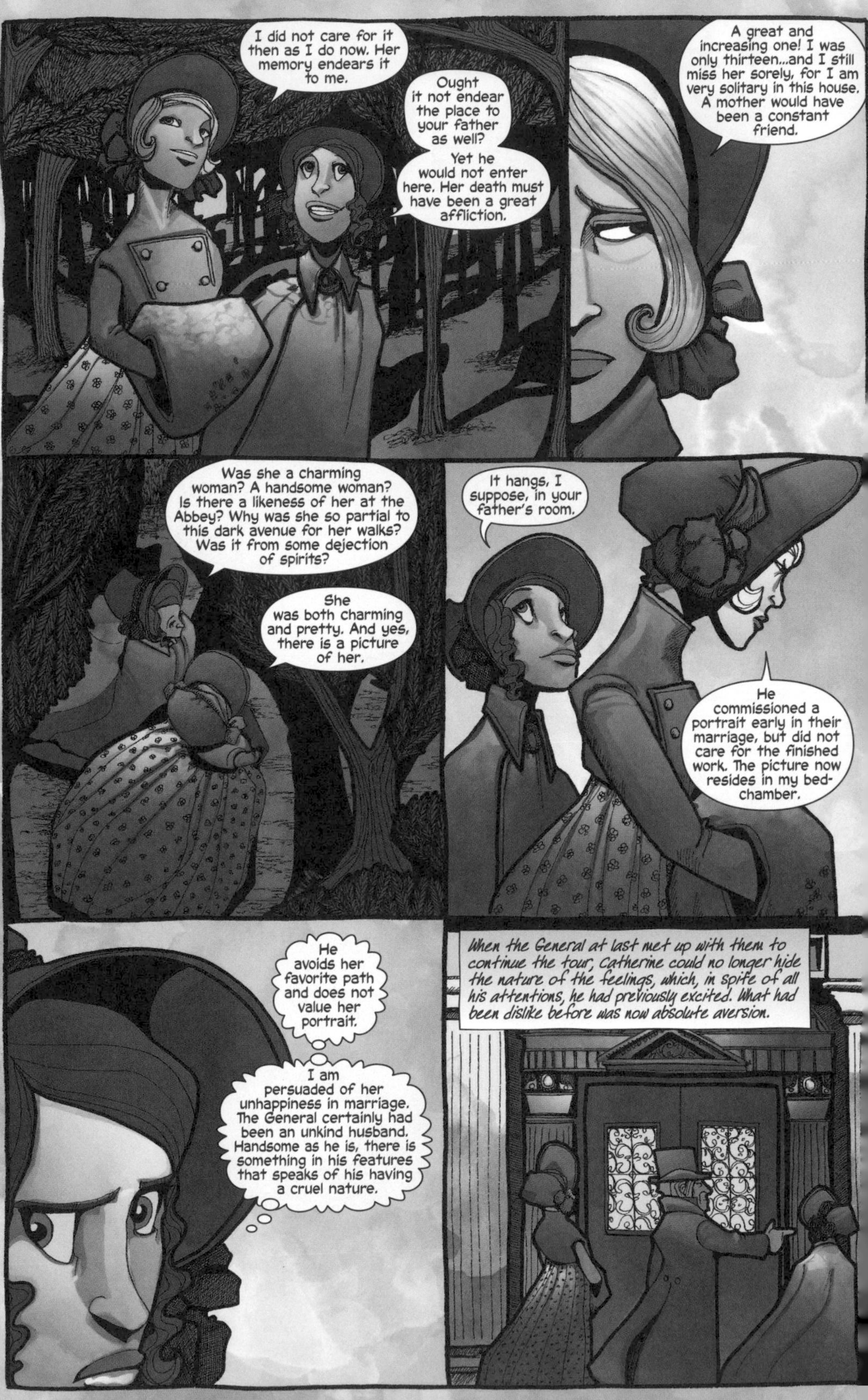
I did not care for it then as I do now. Her memory endears it to me.
Ought it not endear the place to your father as well?
Yet he would not enter here. Her death must have been a great affliction.
A great and increasing one! I was only thirteen...and I still miss her sorely, for I am very solitary in this house. A mother would have been a constant friend.
Was she a charming woman? A handsome woman? Is there a likeness of her at the Abbey? Why was she so partial to this dark avenue for her walks? Was it from some dejection of spirits?
She was both charming and pretty. And yes, there is a picture of her.
It hangs, I suppose, in your father's room.
He commissioned a portrait early in their marriage, but did not care for the finished work. The picture now resides in my bed-chamber.
He avoids her favorite path and does not value her portrait.
I am persuaded of her unhappiness in marriage. The General certainly had been an unkind husband. Handsome as he is, there is something in his features that speaks of his having a cruel nature.
When the General at last met up with them to continue the tour, Catherine could no longer hide the nature of the feelings, which, in spite of all his attentions, he had previously excited. What had been dislike before was now absolute aversion.

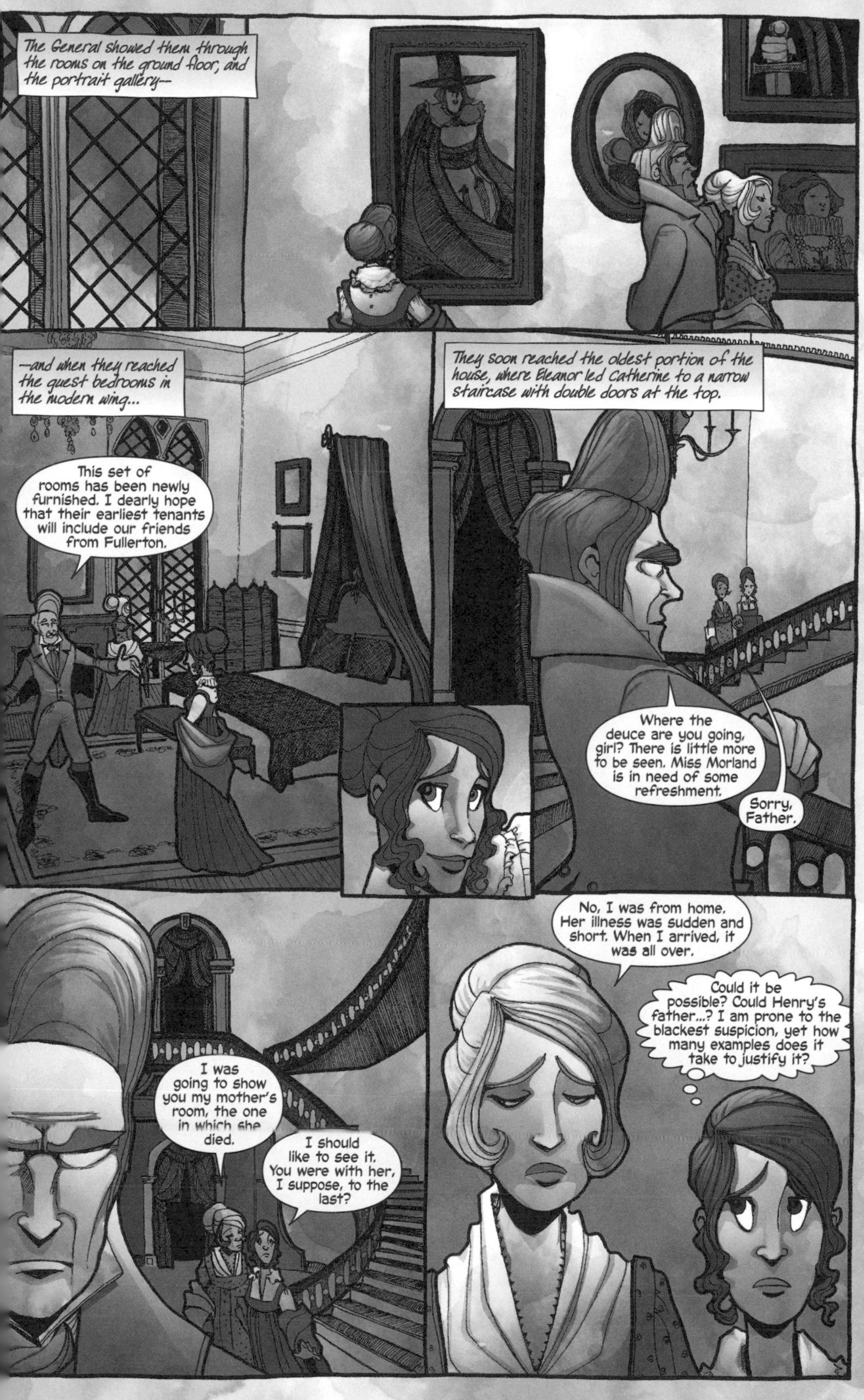

The General showed them through the rooms on the ground floor, and the portrait gallery--
--and when they reached the guest bedrooms in the modern wing...
This set of rooms has been newly furnished. I dearly hope that their earliest tenants will include our friends from Fullerton.
They soon reached the oldest portion of the house, where Eleanor led Catherine to a narrow staircase with double doors at the top.
Where the deuce are you going, girl? There is little more to be seen. Miss Morland is in need of some refreshment.
Sorry, Father.
I was going to show you my mother's room, the one in which she died.
I should like to see it. You were with her, I suppose, to the last?
No, I was from home. Her illness was sudden and short. When I arrived, it was all over.
Could it be possible? Could Henry's father...? I am prone to the blackest suspicion, yet how many examples does it take to justify it?

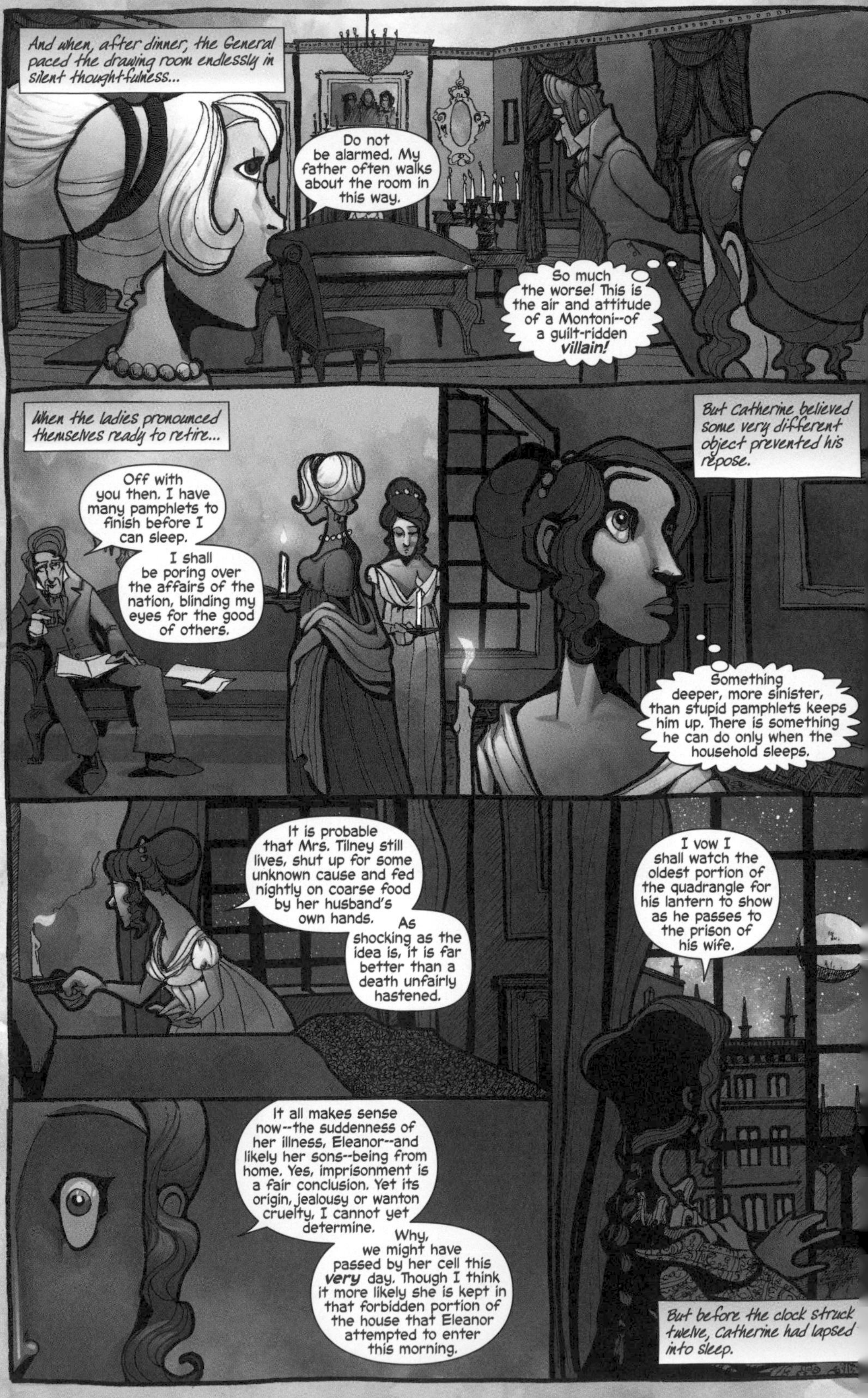
And when, after dinner, the General paced the drawing room endlessly in silent thought-fulness...
Do not be alarmed. My father often walks about the room in this way.
So much the worse! This is the air and attitude of a Montoni--of a guilt-ridden villain!
When the ladies pronounced themselves ready to retire...
Off with you then. I have many pamphlets to finish before I can sleep.
I shall be poring over the affairs of the nation, blinding my eyes for the good of others.
But Catherine believed some very different object prevented his repose.
Something deeper, more sinister, than stupid pamphlets keeps him up. There is something he can do only when the household sleeps.
It is probable that Mrs. Tilney still lives, shut up for some unknown cause and fed nightly on coarse food by her husband's own hands.
As shocking as the idea is, it is far better than a death unfairly hastened.
I vow I shall watch the oldest portion of the quadrangle for his lantern to show as he passes to the prison of his wife.
It all makes sense now--the suddenness of her illness, Eleanor--and likely her sons--being from home. Yes, imprisonment is a fair conclusion. Yet its origin, jealousy or wanton cruelty, I cannot yet determine.
Why, we might have passed by her cell this very day. Though I think it more likely she is kept in that forbidden portion of the house that Eleanor attempted to enter this morning.
But before the clock struck twelve, Catherine had lapsed into sleep.

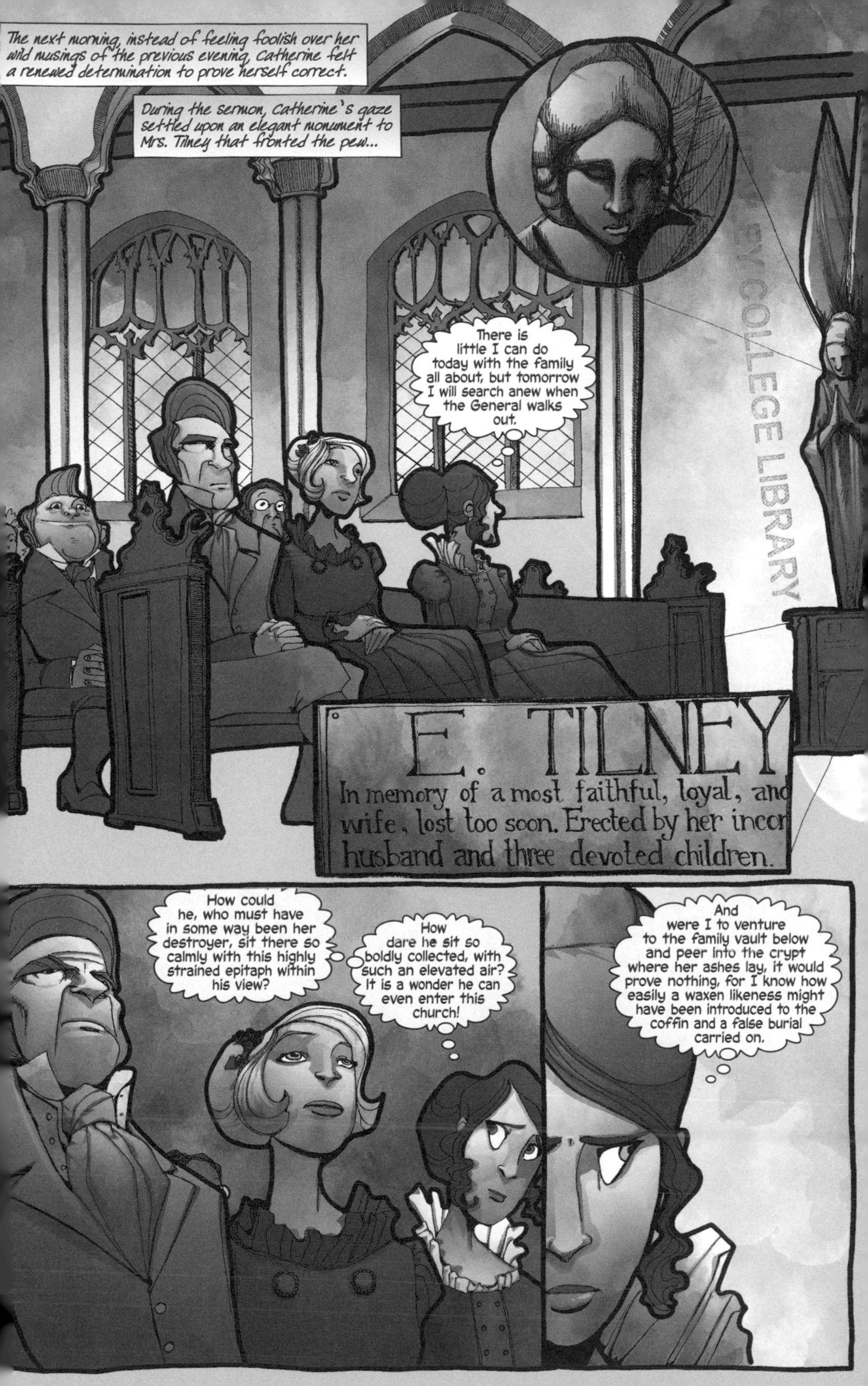
The next morning, instead of feeling foolish over her wild musings of the previous evening, Catherine felt a renewed determination to prove herself correct.
During the sermon, Catherine's gaze settled upon an elegant monument to Mrs. Tilney that fronted the pew...
There is little I can do today with the family all about, but tomorrow I will search anew when the General walks out.
E. TILNEY
In memory of a most faithful, loyal, an
wife, lost too soon. Erected by her incor
husband and three devoted children.
How could he, who must have in some way been her destroyer, sit there so calmly with this highly strained epitaph within his view?
How dare he sit so boldly collected, with such an elevated air? It is a wonder he can even enter this church!
And were I to venture to the family vault below and peer into the crypt where her ashes lay, it would prove nothing, for I know how easily a waxen likeness might have been introduced to the coffin and a false burial carried on.

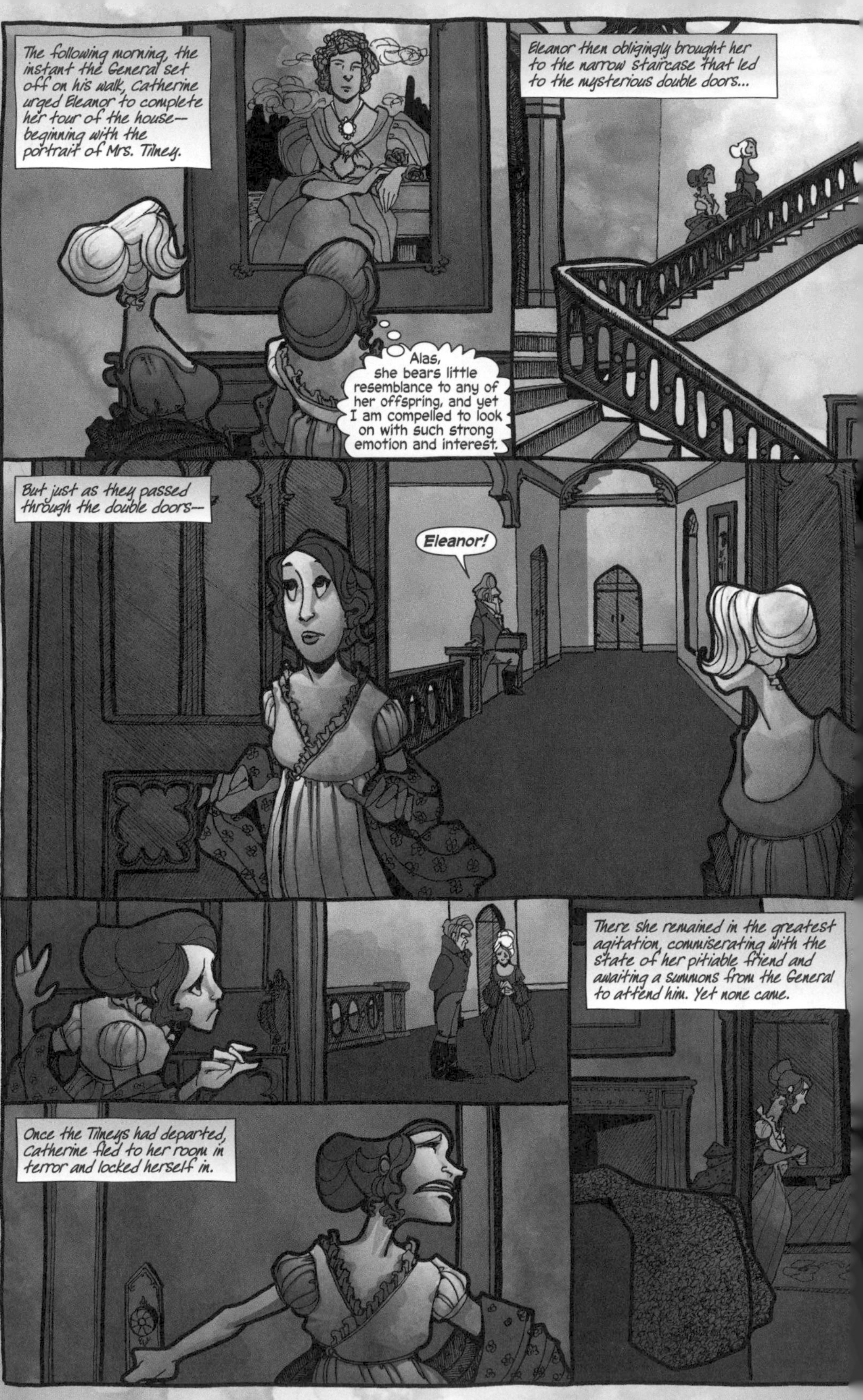
The following morning, the instant the General set off on his walk, Catherine urged Eleanor to complete her tour of the house—beginning with the portrait of Mrs. Tilney.
Alas, she bears little resemblance to any of her offspring, and yet I am compelled to look on with such strong emotion and interest.
Eleanor then obligingly brought her to the narrow staircase that led to the mysterious double doors...
But just as they passed through the double doors—
Eleanor!
Once the Tilneys had departed, Catherine fled to her room in terror and locked herself in.
There she remained in the greatest agitation, commiserating with the state of her pitiable friend and awaiting a summons from the General to attend him. Yet none came.

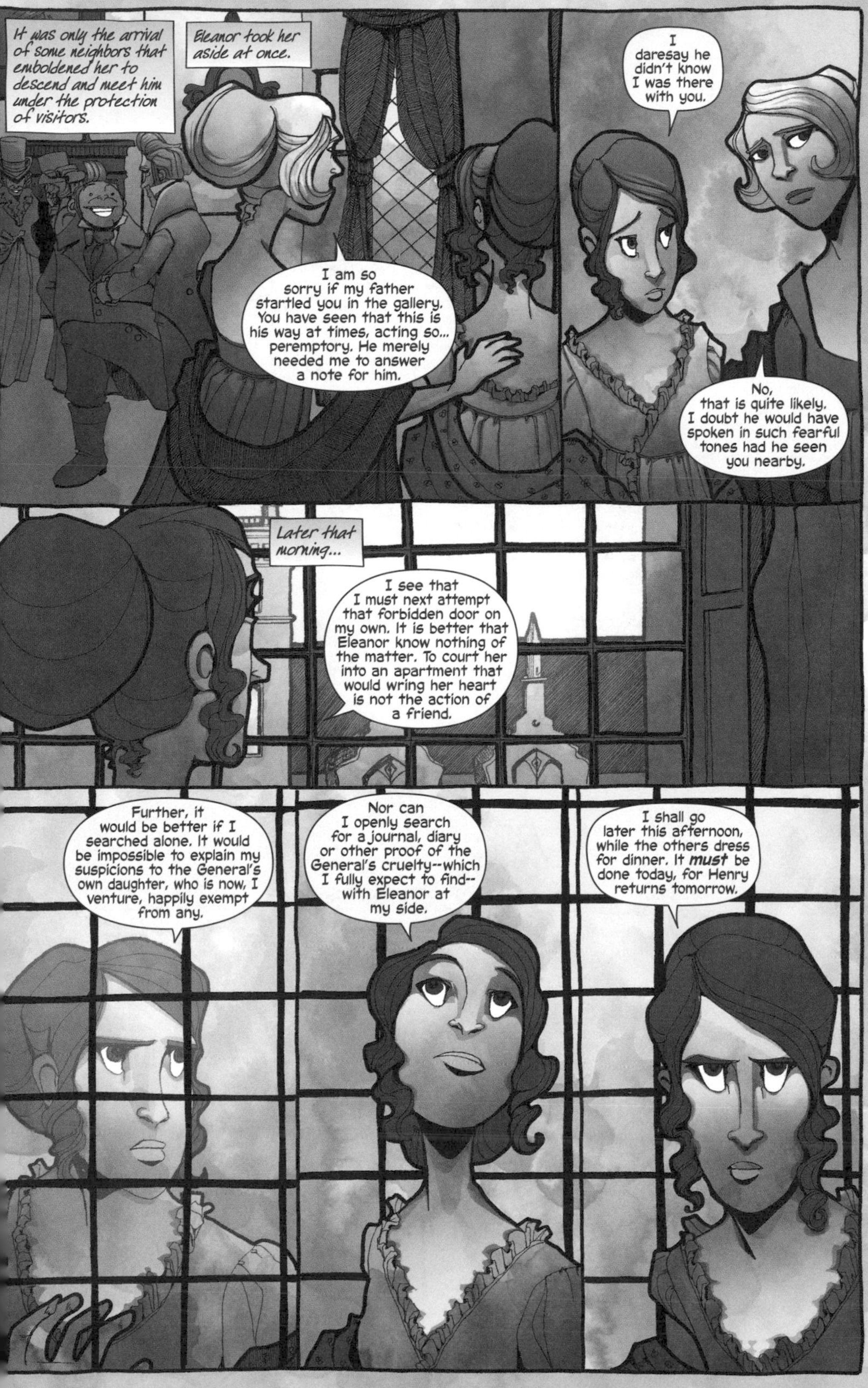
It was only the arrival of some neighbors that emboldened her to descend and meet him under the protection of visitors.
Eleanor took her aside at once.
I am so sorry if my father startled you in the gallery. You have seen that this is his way at times, acting so... peremptory. He merely needed me to answer a note for him.
I daresay he didn't know I was there with you.
No, that is quite likely. I doubt he would have spoken in such fearful tones had he seen you nearby.
Later that morning...
I see that I must next attempt that forbidden door on my own. It is better that Eleanor know nothing of the matter. To court her into an apartment that would wring her heart is not the action of a friend.
Further, it would be better if I searched alone. It would be impossible to explain my suspicions to the General's own daughter, who is now, I venture, happily exempt from any.
Nor can I openly search for a journal, diary or other proof of the General's cruelty--which I fully expect to find--with Eleanor at my side.
I shall go later this afternoon, while the others dress for dinner. It must be done today, for Henry returns tomorrow.

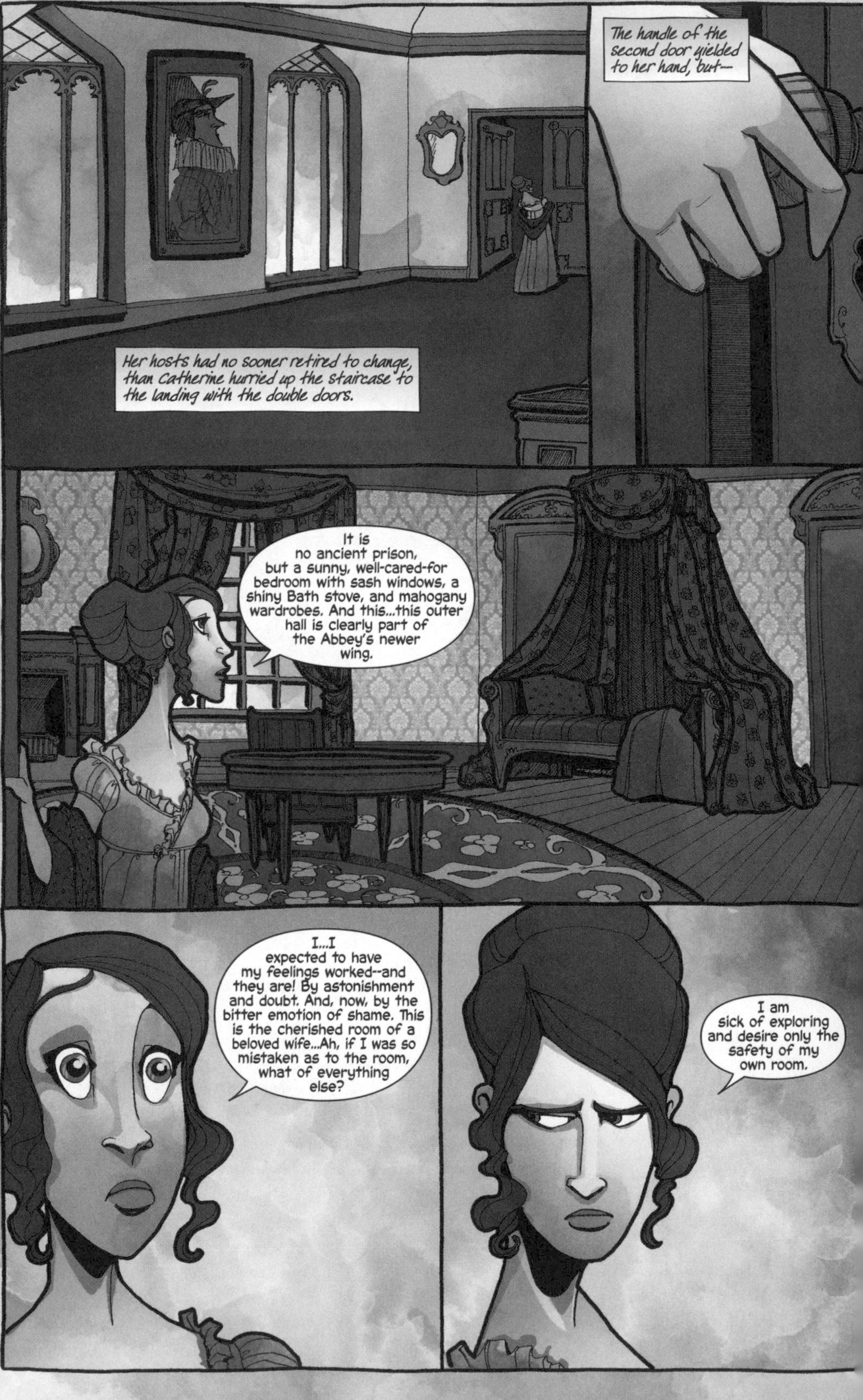
Her hosts had no sooner retired to change, than Catherine hurried up the staircase to the landing with the double doors.
The handle of the second door yielded to her hand, but--
It is no ancient prison, but a sunny, well-cared-for bedroom with sash windows, a shiny Bath stove, and mahogany wardrobes. And this...this outer hall is clearly part of the Abbey's newer wing.
I...I expected to have my feelings worked--and they are! By astonishment and doubt. And, now, by the bitter emotion of shame. This is the cherished room of a beloved wife...Ah, if I was so mistaken as to the room, what of everything else?
I am sick of exploring and desire only the safety of my own room.

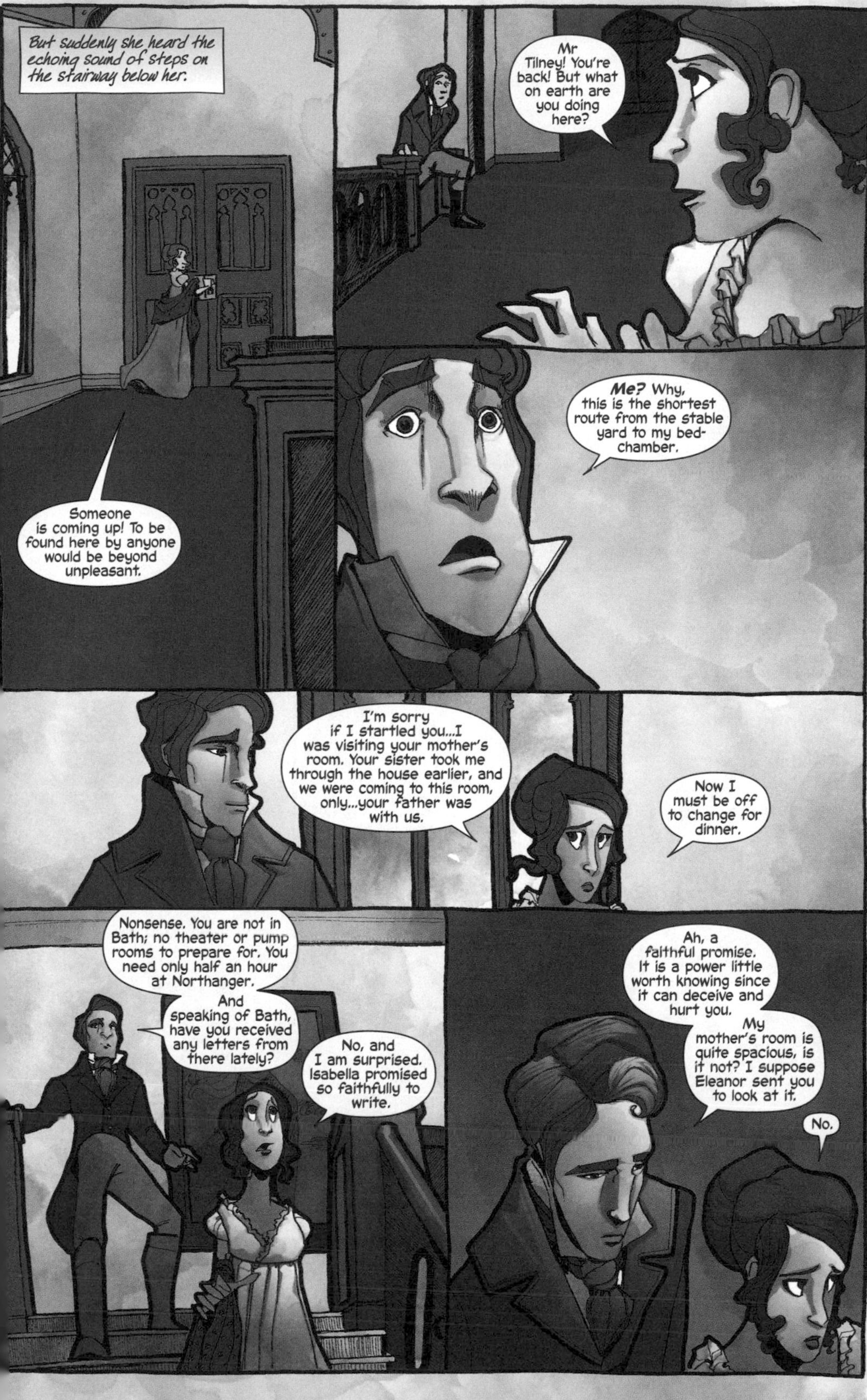

But suddenly she heard the echoing sound of steps on the stairway below her.
Someone is coming up! To be found here by anyone would be beyond unpleasant.
Mr Tilney! You're back! But what on earth are you doing here?
Me? Why, this is the shortest route from the stable yard to my bed-chamber.
I'm sorry if I startled you...I was visiting your mother's room. Your sister took me through the house earlier, and we were coming to this room, only...your father was with us.
Now I must be off to change for dinner.
Nonsense. You are not in Bath; no theater or pump rooms to prepare for. You need only half an hour at Northanger.
And speaking of Bath, have you received any letters from there lately?
No, and I am surprised. Isabella promised so faithfully to write.
Ah, a faithful promise. It is a power little worth knowing since it can deceive and hurt you.
My mother's room is quite spacious, is it not? I suppose Eleanor sent you to look at it.
No.

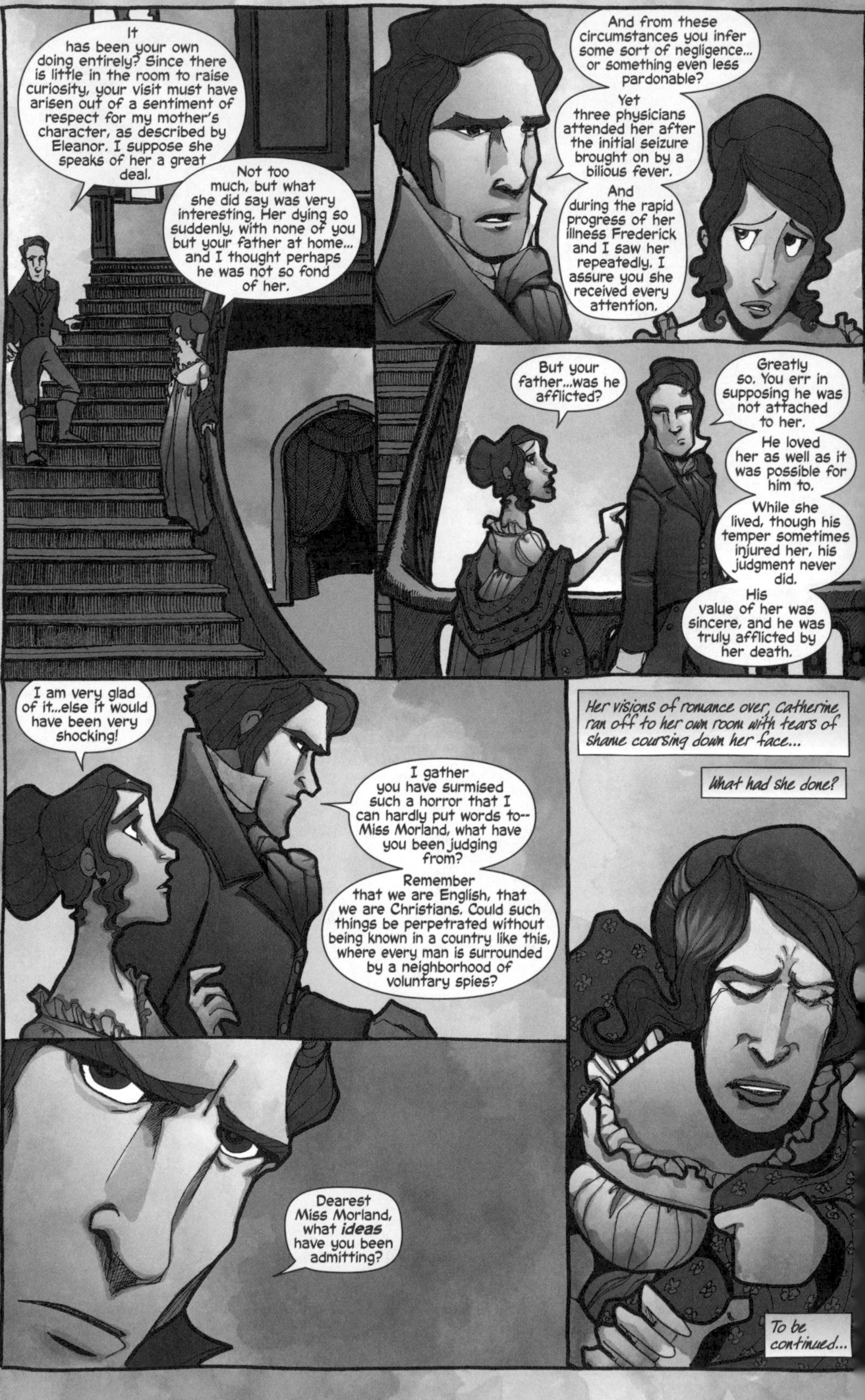
It has been your own doing entirely? Since there is little in the room to raise curiosity, your visit must have arisen out of a sentiment of respect for my mother's character, as described by Eleanor. I suppose she speaks of her a great deal.
Not too much, but what she did say was very interesting. Her dying so suddenly, with none of you but your father at home... and I thought perhaps he was not so fond of her.
And from these circumstances you infer some sort of negligence... or something even less pardonable?
Yet three physicians attended her after the initial seizure brought on by a bilious fever.
And during the rapid progress of her illness Frederick and I saw her repeatedly. I assure you she received every attention.
But your father...was he afflicted?
Greatly so. You err in supposing he was not attached to her.
He loved her as well as it was possible for him to.
While she lived, though his temper sometimes injured her, his judgment never did.
His value of her was sincere, and he was truly afflicted by her death.
I am very glad of it...else it would have been very shocking!
I gather you have surmised such a horror that I can hardly put words to--Miss Morland, what have you been judging from?
Remember that we are English, that we are Christians. Could such things be perpetrated without being known in a country like this, where every man is surrounded by a neighborhood of voluntary spies?
Dearest Miss Morland, what *ideas* have you been admitting?
Her visions of romance over, Catherine ran off to her own room with tears of shame coursing down her face...
What had she done?
To be continued...

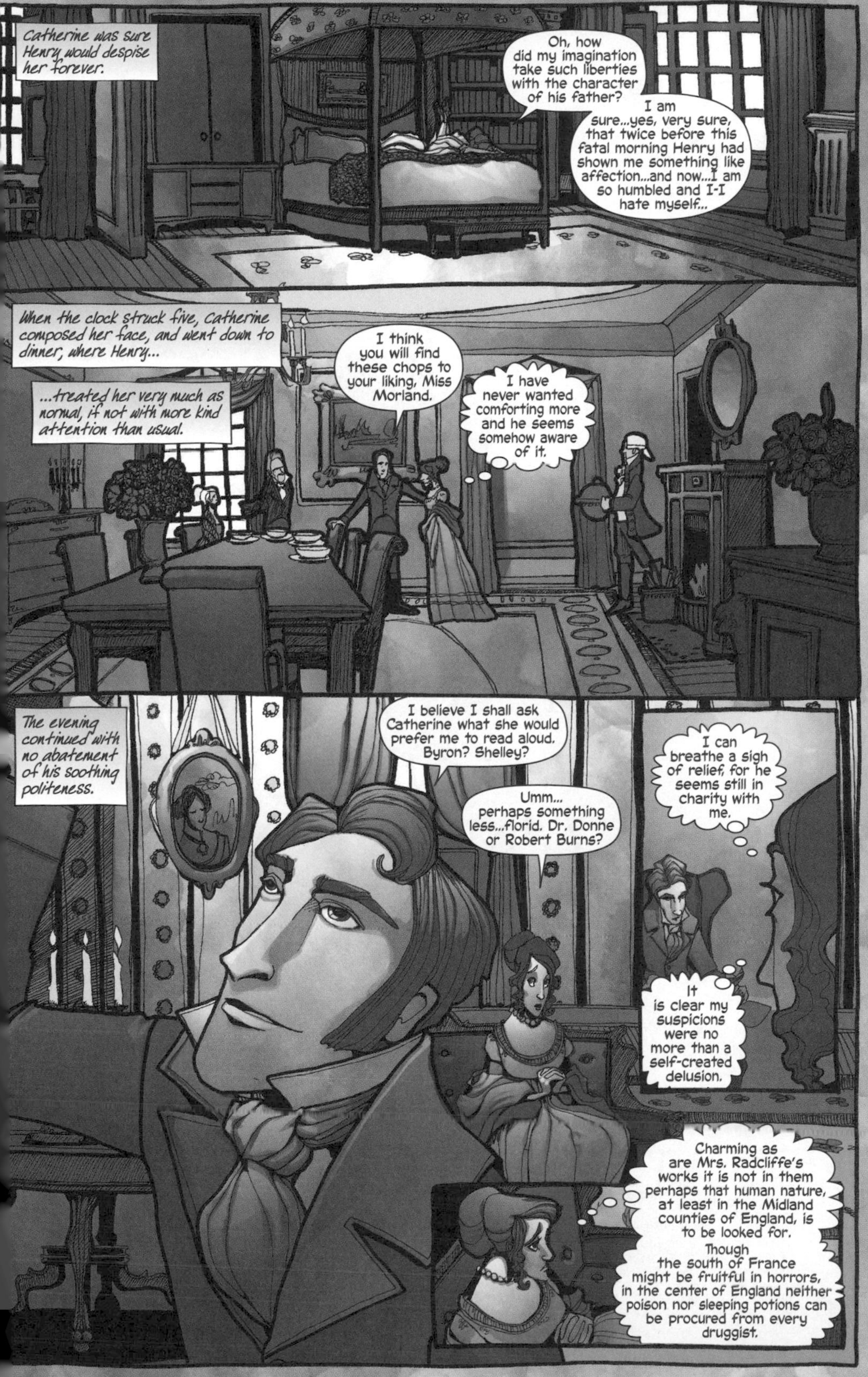
Catherine was sure Henry would despise her forever.
Oh, how did my imagination take such liberties with the character of his father?
I am sure...yes, very sure, that twice before this fatal morning Henry had shown me something like affection...and now...I am so humbled and I-I hate myself...
When the clock struck five, Catherine composed her face, and went down to dinner, where Henry...
...treated her very much as normal, if not with more kind attention than usual.
I think you will find these chops to your liking, Miss Morland.
I have never wanted comforting more and he seems somehow aware of it.
The evening continued with no abatement of his soothing politeness.
I believe I shall ask Catherine what she would prefer me to read aloud. Byron? Shelley?
Umm... perhaps something less...florid. Dr. Donne or Robert Burns?
I can breathe a sigh of relief, for he seems still in charity with me.
It is clear my suspicions were no more than a self-created delusion.
Charming as are Mrs. Radcliffe's works it is not in them perhaps that human nature, at least in the Midland counties of England, is to be looked for.
Though the south of France might be fruitful in horrors, in the center of England neither poison nor sleeping potions can be procured from every druggist.

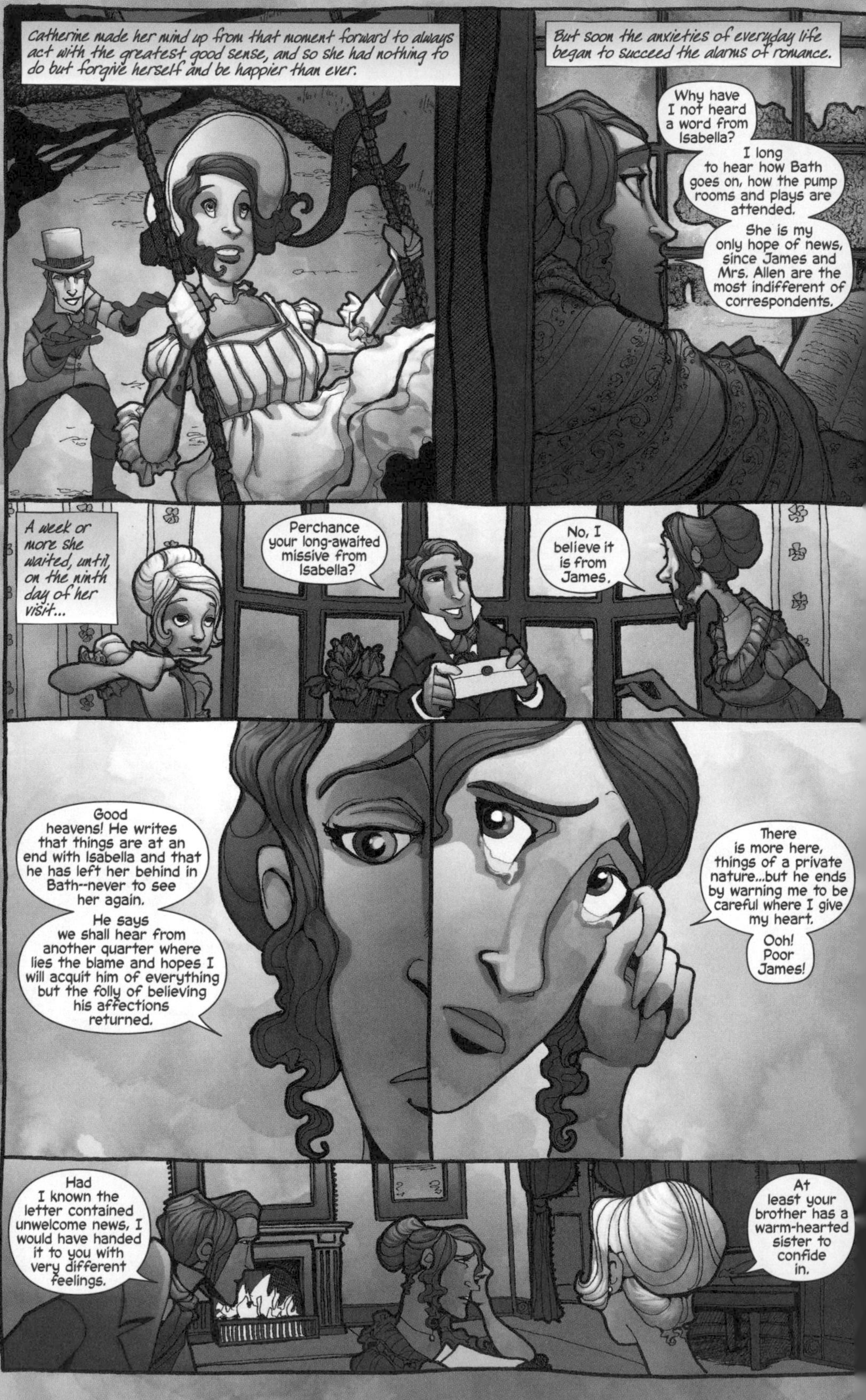
Catherine made her mind up from that moment forward to always act with the greatest good sense, and so she had nothing to do but forgive herself and be happier than ever.
But soon the anxieties of everyday life began to succeed the alarms of romance.
Why have I not heard a word from Isabella?
I long to hear how Bath goes on, how the pump rooms and plays are attended.
She is my only hope of news, since James and Mrs. Allen are the most indifferent of correspondents.
A week or more she waited, until, on the ninth day of her visit...
Perchance your long-awaited missive from Isabella?
No, I believe it is from James.
Good heavens! He writes that things are at an end with Isabella and that he has left her behind in Bath--never to see her again.
He says we shall hear from another quarter where lies the blame and hopes I will acquit him of everything but the folly of believing his affections returned.
There is more here, things of a private nature...but he ends by warning me to be careful where I give my heart.
Ooh! Poor James!
Had I known the letter contained unwelcome news, I would have handed it to you with very different feelings.
At least your brother has a warm-hearted sister to confide in.

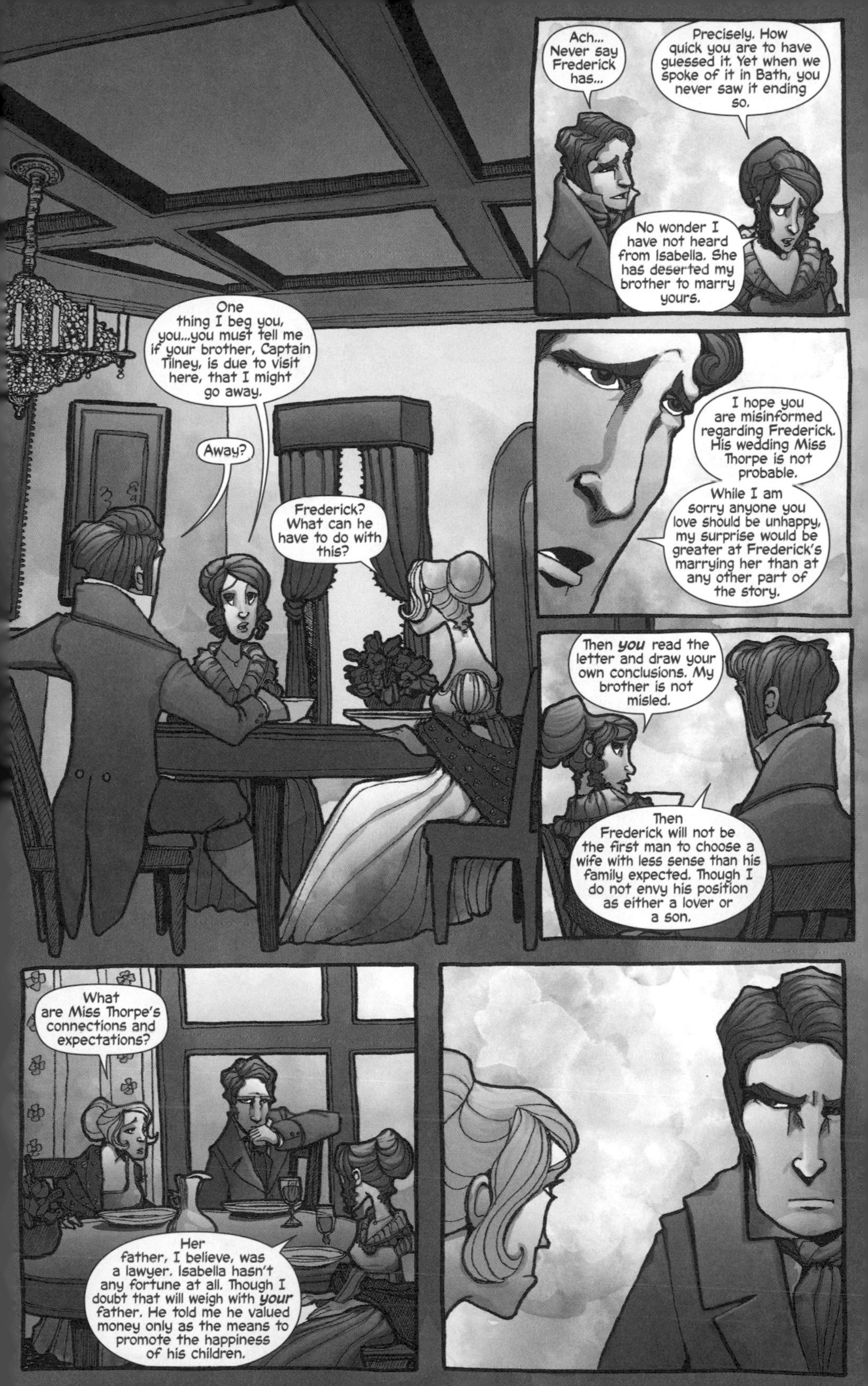
Ach... Never say Frederick has...
Precisely. How quick you are to have guessed it. Yet when we spoke of it in Bath, you never saw it ending so.
No wonder I have not heard from Isabella. She has deserted my brother to marry yours.
One thing I beg you, you...you must tell me if your brother, Captain Tilney, is due to visit here, that I might go away.
Away?
Frederick? What can he have to do with this?
I hope you are misinformed regarding Frederick. His wedding Miss Thorpe is not probable.
While I am sorry anyone you love should be unhappy, my surprise would be greater at Frederick's marrying her than at any other part of the story.
Then you read the letter and draw your own conclusions. My brother is not misled.
Then Frederick will not be the first man to choose a wife with less sense than his family expected. Though I do not envy his position as either a lover or a son.
What are Miss Thorpe's connections and expectations?
Her father, I believe, was a lawyer. Isabella hasn't any fortune at all. Though I doubt that will weigh with your father. He told me he valued money only as the means to promote the happiness of his children.

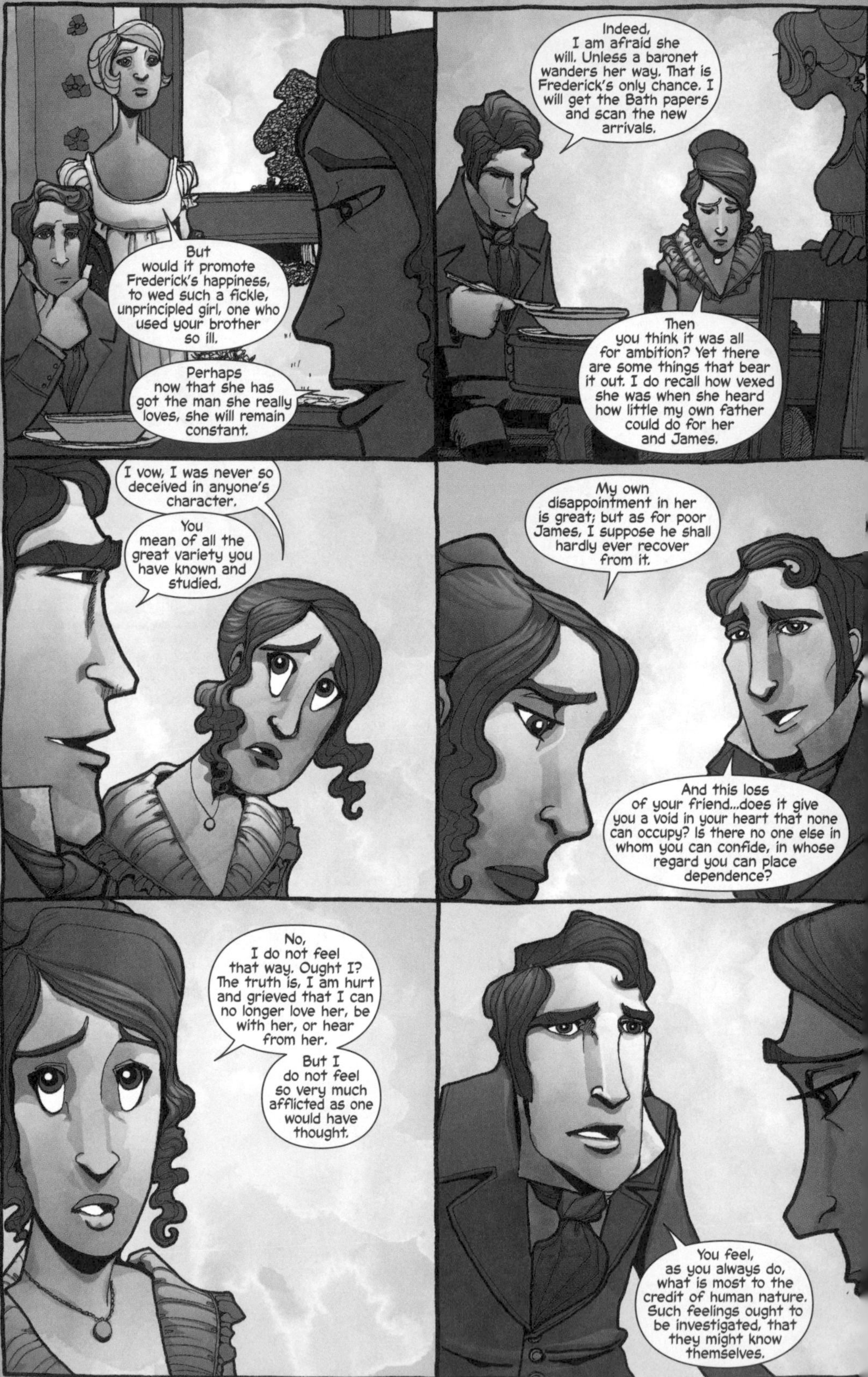
But would it promote Frederick's happiness, to wed such a fickle, unprincipled girl, one who used your brother so ill.
Perhaps now that she has got the man she really loves, she will remain constant.
Indeed, I am afraid she will. Unless a baronet wanders her way. That is Frederick's only chance. I will get the Bath papers and scan the new arrivals.
Then you think it was all for ambition? Yet there are some things that bear it out. I do recall how vexed she was when she heard how little my own father could do for her and James.
I vow, I was never so deceived in anyone's character.
You mean of all the great variety you have known and studied.
My own disappointment in her is great; but as for poor James, I suppose he shall hardly ever recover from it.
And this loss of your friend...does it give you a void in your heart that none can occupy? Is there no one else in whom you can confide, in whose regard you can place dependence?
No, I do not feel that way. Ought I? The truth is, I am hurt and grieved that I can no longer love her, be with her, or hear from her.
But I do not feel so very much afflicted as one would have thought.
You feel, as you always do, what is most to the credit of human nature. Such feelings ought to be investigated, that they might know themselves.

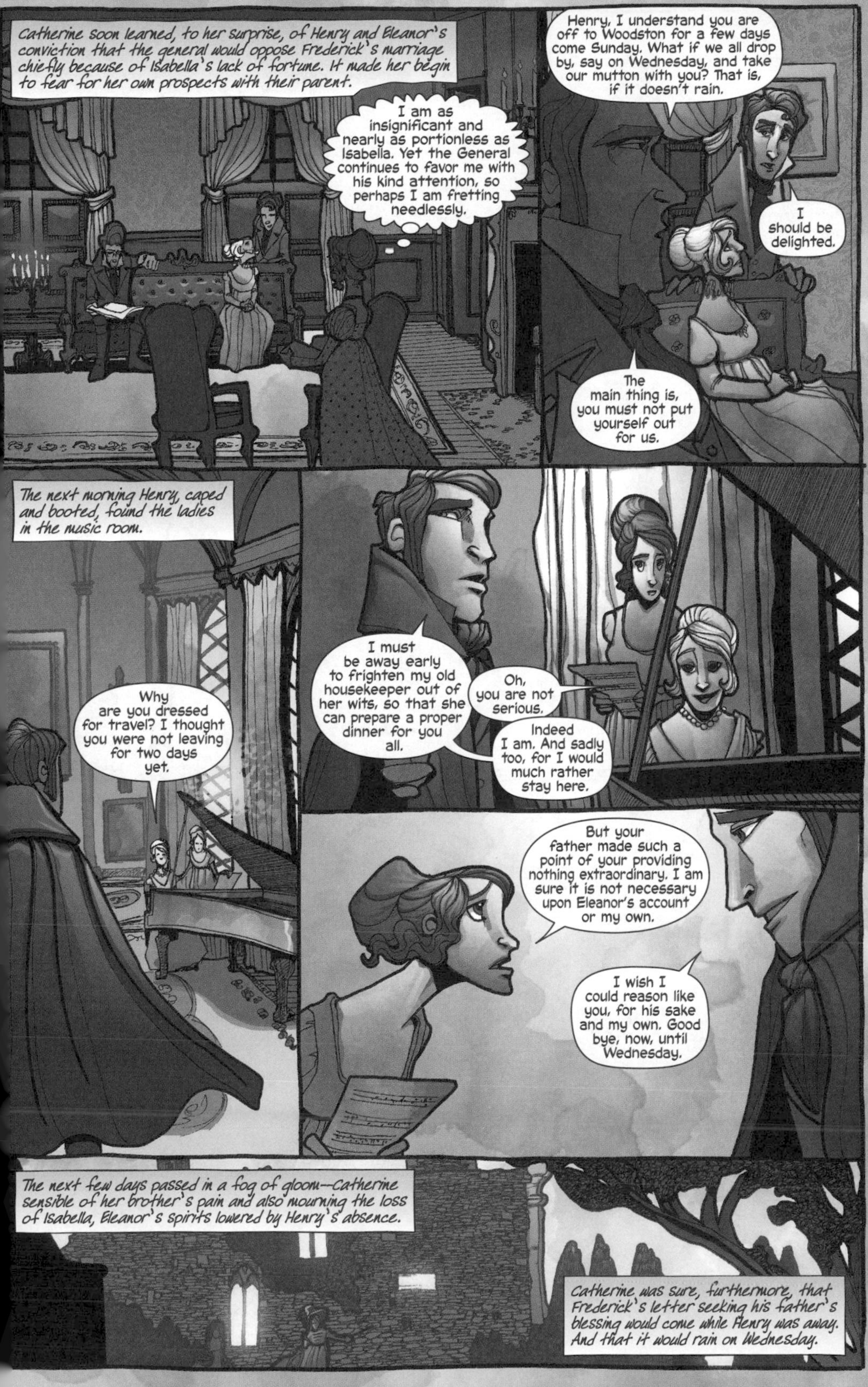
Catherine soon learned, to her surprise, of Henry and Eleanor's conviction that the general would oppose Frederick's marriage chiefly because of Isabella's lack of fortune. It made her begin to fear for her own prospects with their parent.
I am as insignificant and nearly as portionless as Isabella. Yet the General continues to favor me with his kind attention, so perhaps I am fretting needlessly.
Henry, I understand you are off to Woodston for a few days come Sunday. What if we all drop by, say on Wednesday, and take our mutton with you? That is, if it doesn't rain.
I should be delighted.
The main thing is, you must not put yourself out for us.
The next morning Henry, caped and booted, found the ladies in the music room.
Why are you dressed for travel? I thought you were not leaving for two days yet.
I must be away early to frighten my old housekeeper out of her wits, so that she can prepare a proper dinner for you all.
Oh, you are not serious.
Indeed I am. And sadly too, for I would much rather stay here.
But your father made such a point of your providing nothing extraordinary. I am sure it is not necessary upon Eleanor's account or my own.
I wish I could reason like you, for his sake and my own. Good bye, now, until Wednesday.
The next few days passed in a fog of gloom—Catherine sensible of her brother's pain and also mourning the loss of Isabella, Eleanor's spirits lowered by Henry's absence.
Catherine was sure, furthermore, that Frederick's letter seeking his father's blessing would come while Henry was away. And that it would rain on Wednesday.

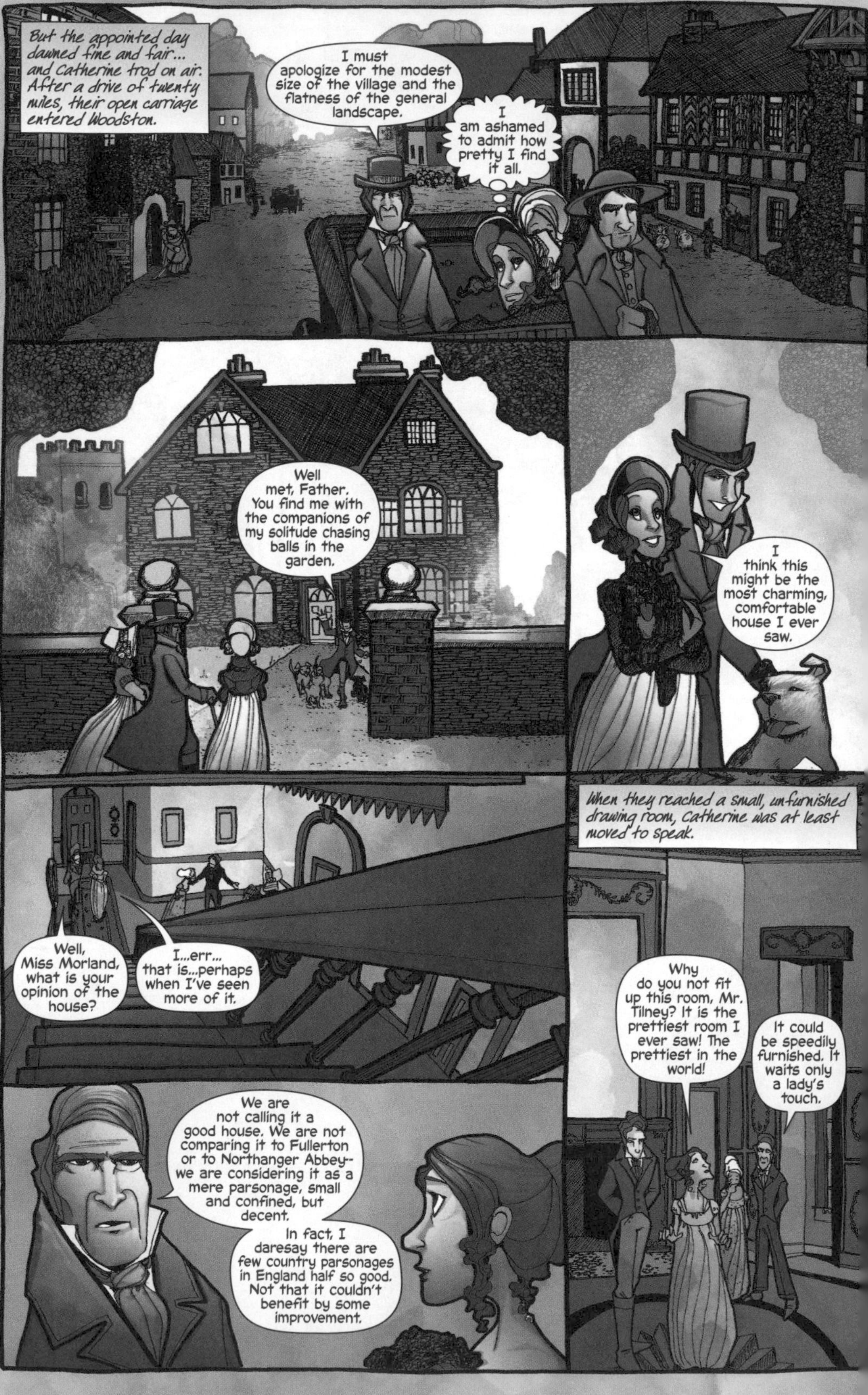
But the appointed day dawned fine and fair... and Catherine trod on air. After a drive of twenty miles, their open carriage entered Woodston.
I must apologize for the modest size of the village and the flatness of the general landscape.
I am ashamed to admit how pretty I find it all.
Well met, Father. You find me with the companions of my solitude chasing balls in the garden.
I think this might be the most charming, comfortable house I ever saw.
Well, Miss Morland, what is your opinion of the house?
I...err... that is...perhaps when I've seen more of it.
We are not calling it a good house. We are not comparing it to Fullerton or to Northanger Abbey-we are considering it as a mere parsonage, small and confined, but decent.
In fact, I daresay there are few country parsonages in England half so good. Not that it couldn't benefit by some improvement.
When they reached a small, unfurnished drawing room, Catherine was at least moved to speak.
Why do you not fit up this room, Mr. Tilney? It is the prettiest room I ever saw! The prettiest in the world!
It could be speedily furnished. It waits only a lady's touch.

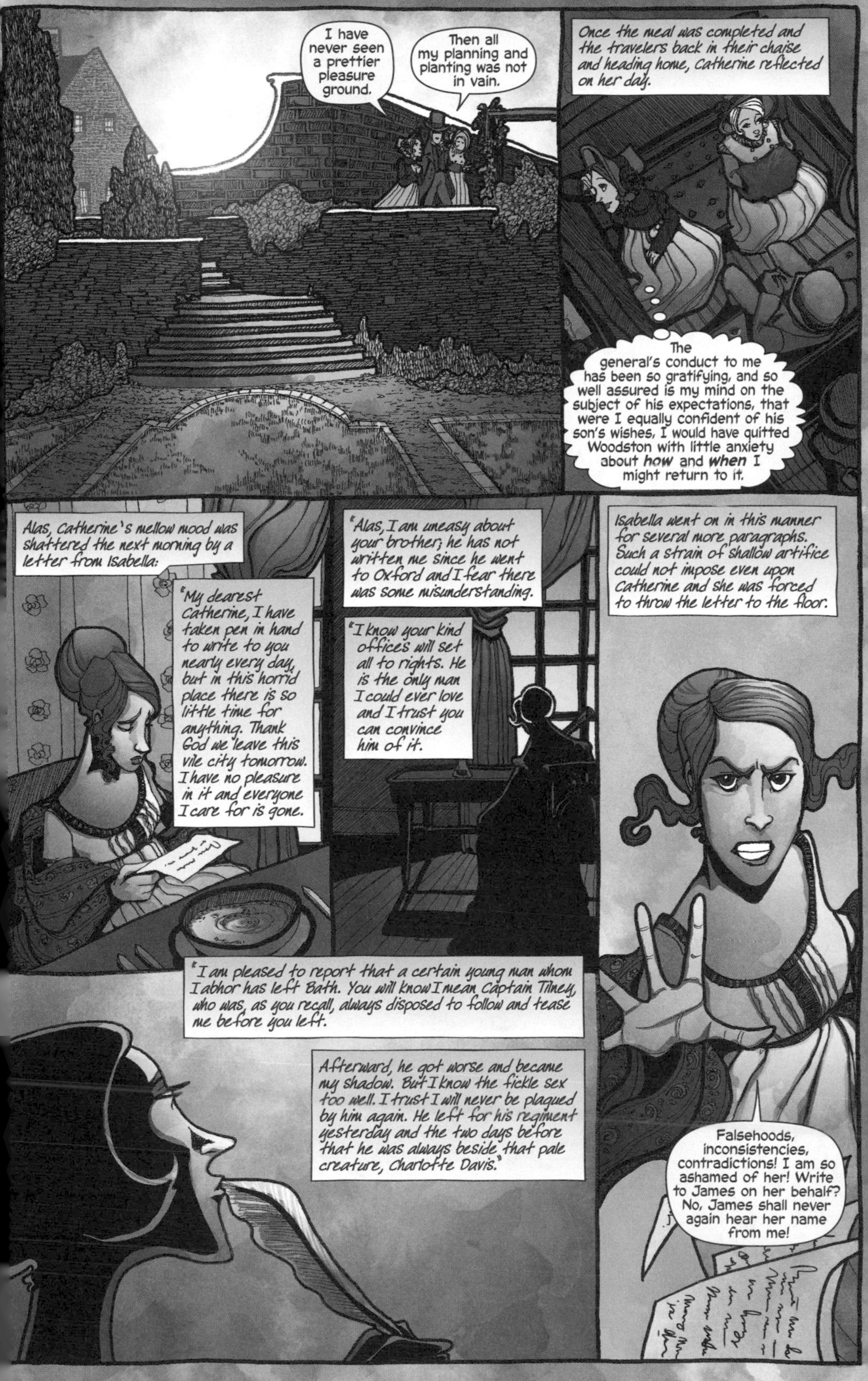
I have never seen a prettier pleasure ground.
Then all my planning and planting was not in vain.
Once the meal was completed and the travelers back in their chaise and heading home, Catherine reflected on her day.
The general's conduct to me has been so gratifying, and so well assured is my mind on the subject of his expectations, that were I equally confident of his son's wishes, I would have quitted Woodston with little anxiety about **how** and **when** I might return to it.
Alas, Catherine's mellow mood was shattered the next morning by a letter from Isabella:
"My dearest Catherine, I have taken pen in hand to write to you nearly every day, but in this horrid place there is so little time for anything. Thank God we leave this vile city tomorrow. I have no pleasure in it and everyone I care for is gone.
"Alas, I am uneasy about your brother; he has not written me since he went to Oxford and I fear there was some misunderstanding.
"I know your kind offices will set all to rights. He is the only man I could ever love and I trust you can convince him of it.
"I am pleased to report that a certain young man whom I abhor has left Bath. You will know I mean Captain Tilney, who was, as you recall, always disposed to follow and tease me before you left.
Afterward, he got worse and became my shadow. But I know the fickle sex too well. I trust I will never be plagued by him again. He left for his regiment yesterday and the two days before that he was always beside that pale creature, Charlotte Davis."
Isabella went on in this manner for several more paragraphs. Such a strain of shallow artifice could not impose even upon Catherine and she was forced to throw the letter to the floor.
Falsehoods, inconsistencies, contradictions! I am so ashamed of her! Write to James on her behalf? No, James shall never again hear her name from me!

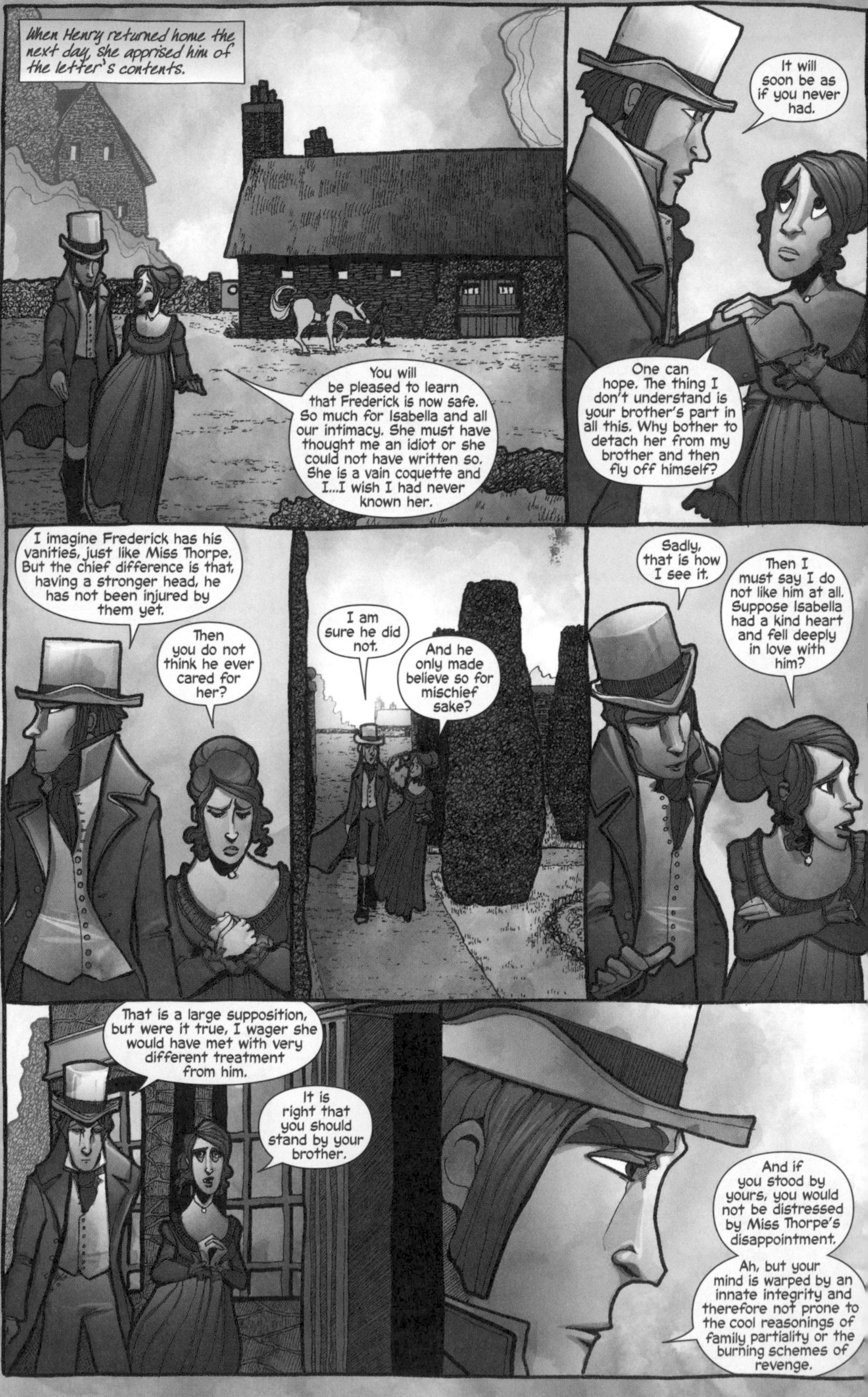
When Henry returned home the next day, she apprised him of the letter's contents.
You will be pleased to learn that Frederick is now safe. So much for Isabella and all our intimacy. She must have thought me an idiot or she could not have written so. She is a vain coquette and I...I wish I had never known her.
It will soon be as if you never had.
One can hope. The thing I don't understand is your brother's part in all this. Why bother to detach her from my brother and then fly off himself?
I imagine Frederick has his vanities, just like Miss Thorpe. But the chief difference is that, having a stronger head, he has not been injured by them yet.
Then you do not think he ever cared for her?
I am sure he did not.
And he only made believe so for mischief sake?
Sadly, that is how I see it.
Then I must say I do not like him at all. Suppose Isabella had a kind heart and fell deeply in love with him?
That is a large supposition, but were it true, I wager she would have met with very different treatment from him.
It is right that you should stand by your brother.
And if you stood by yours, you would not be distressed by Miss Thorpe's disappointment.
Ah, but your mind is warped by an innate integrity and therefore not prone to the cool reasonings of family partiality or the burning schemes of revenge.

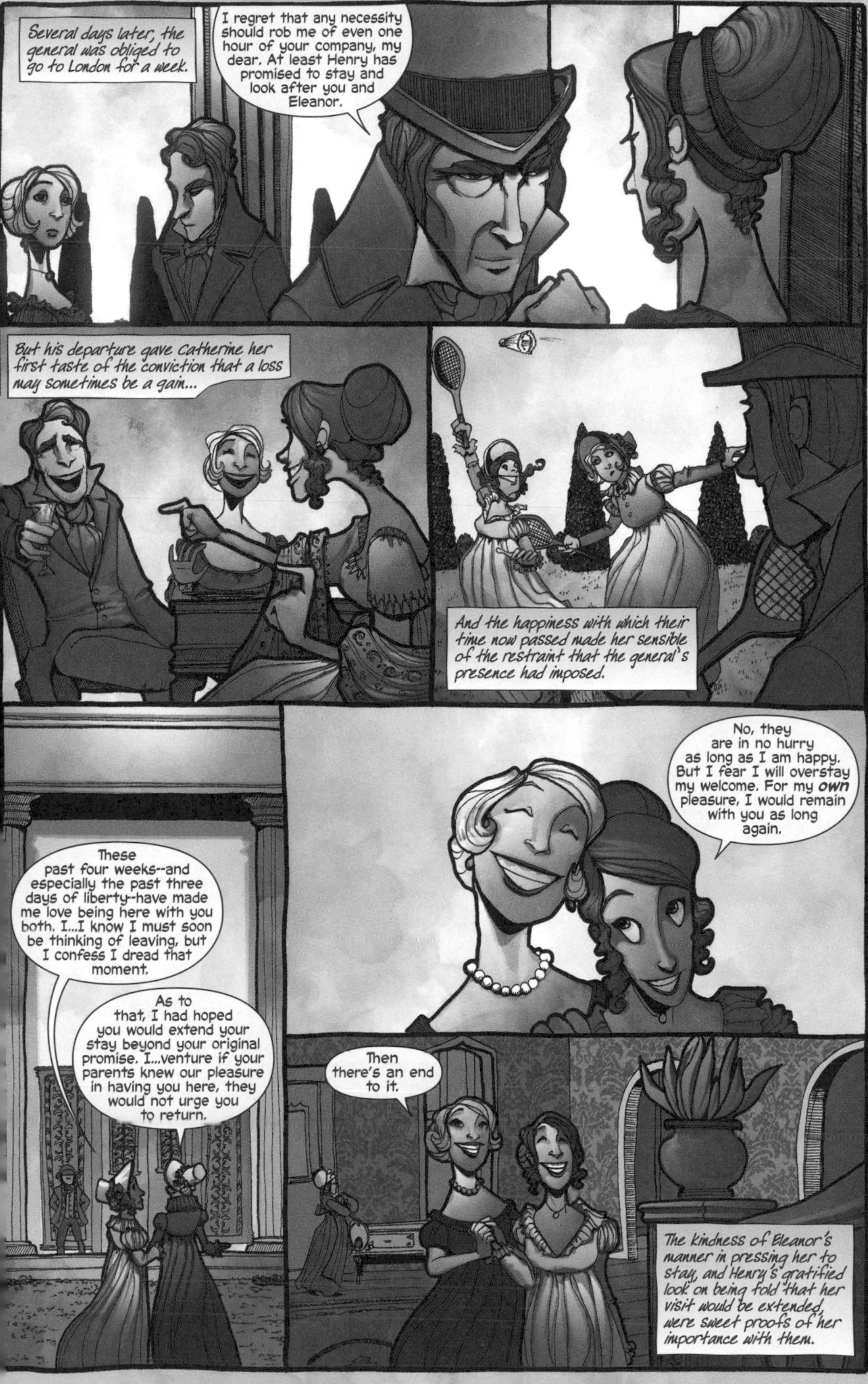

Several days later, the general was obliged to go to London for a week.
I regret that any necessity should rob me of even one hour of your company, my dear. At least Henry has promised to stay and look after you and Eleanor.
But his departure gave Catherine her first taste of the conviction that a loss may sometimes be a gain...
And the happiness with which their time now passed made her sensible of the restraint that the general's presence had imposed.
These past four weeks--and especially the past three days of liberty--have made me love being here with you both. I...I know I must soon be thinking of leaving, but I confess I dread that moment.
As to that, I had hoped you would extend your stay beyond your original promise. I...venture if your parents knew our pleasure in having you here, they would not urge you to return.
No, they are in no hurry as long as I am happy. But I fear I will overstay my welcome. For my own pleasure, I would remain with you as long again.
Then there's an end to it.
The kindness of Eleanor's manner in pressing her to stay, and Henry's gratified look on being told that her visit would be extended, were sweet proofs of her importance with them.

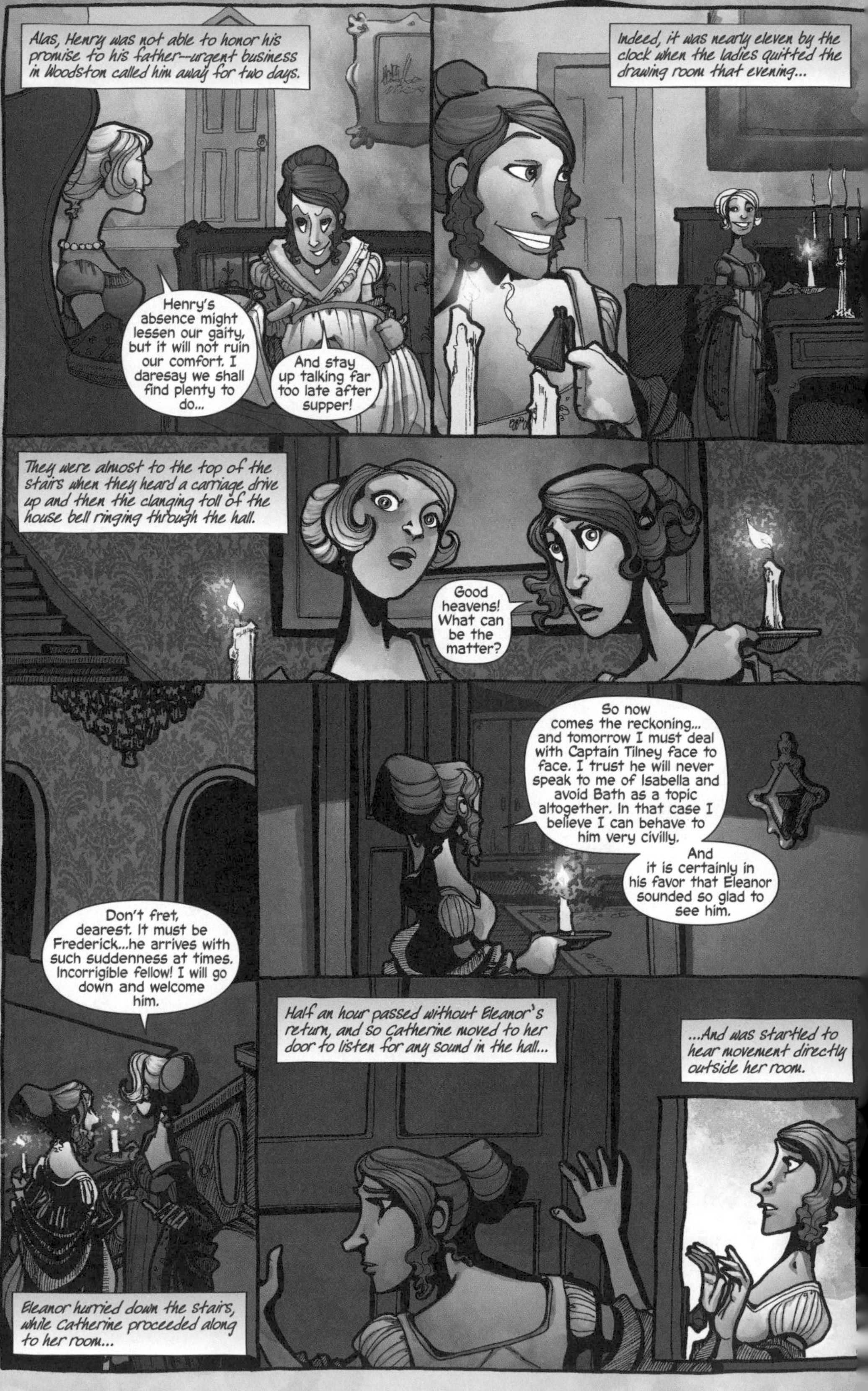

Alas, Henry was not able to honor his promise to his father--urgent business in Woodston called him away for two days.
Henry's absence might lessen our gaity, but it will not ruin our comfort. I daresay we shall find plenty to do...
And stay up talking far too late after supper!
Indeed, it was nearly eleven by the clock when the ladies quitted the drawing room that evening...
They were almost to the top of the stairs when they heard a carriage drive up and then the clanging toll of the house bell ringing through the hall.
Good heavens! What can be the matter?
Don't fret, dearest. It must be Frederick...he arrives with such suddenness at times. Incorrigible fellow! I will go down and welcome him.
Eleanor hurried down the stairs, while Catherine proceeded along to her room...
So now comes the reckoning... and tomorrow I must deal with Captain Tilney face to face. I trust he will never speak to me of Isabella and avoid Bath as a topic altogether. In that case I believe I can behave to him very civilly.
And it is certainly in his favor that Eleanor sounded so glad to see him.
Half an hour passed without Eleanor's return, and so Catherine moved to her door to listen for any sound in the hall...
...And was startled to hear movement directly outside her room.

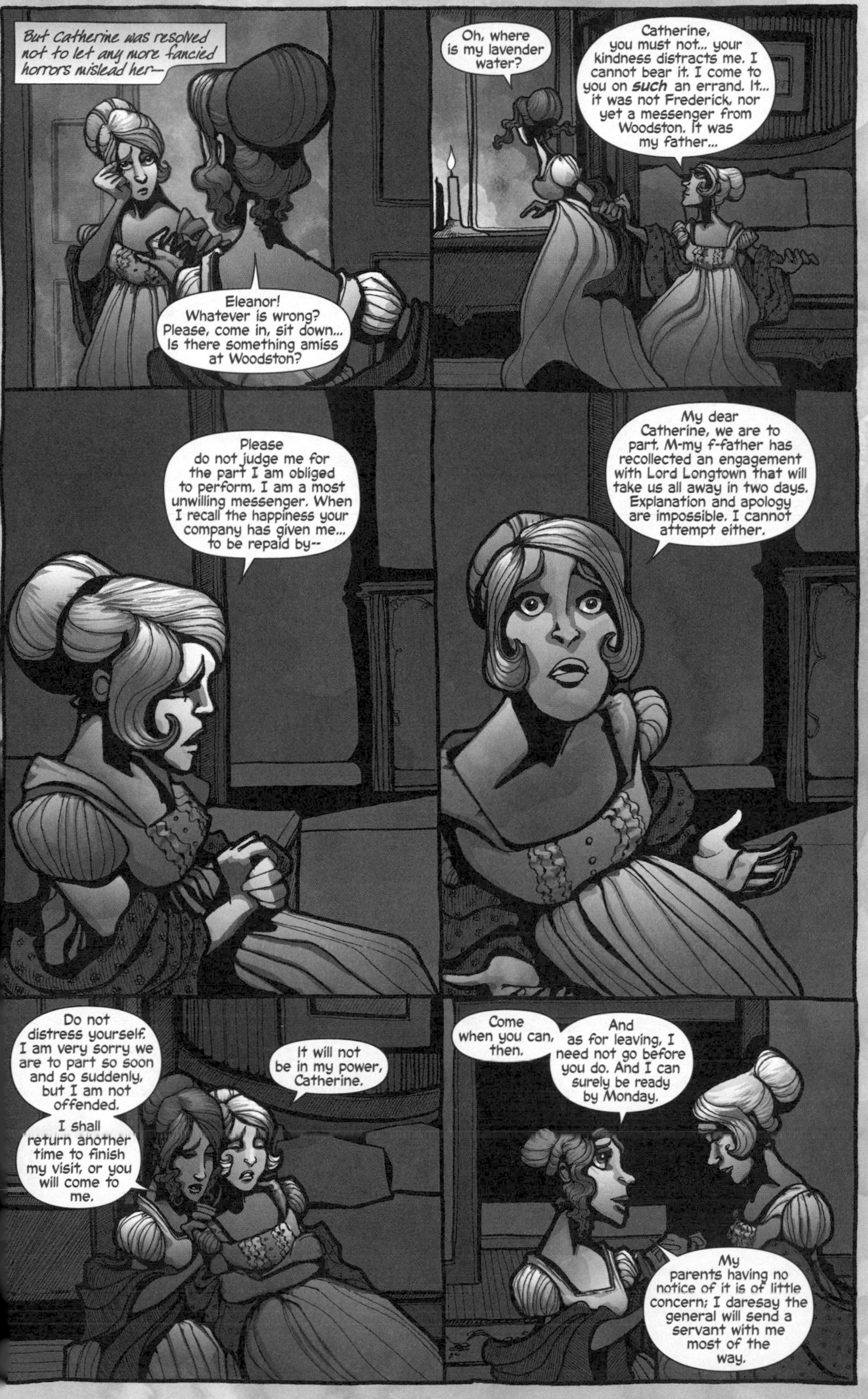
But Catherine was resolved not to let any more fancied horrors mislead her--
Eleanor! Whatever is wrong? Please, come in, sit down... Is there something amiss at Woodston?
Oh, where is my lavender water?
Catherine, you must not... your kindness distracts me. I cannot bear it. I come to you on *such* an errand. It... it was not Frederick, nor yet a messenger from Woodston. It was my father...
Please do not judge me for the part I am obliged to perform. I am a most unwilling messenger. When I recall the happiness your company has given me... to be repaid by--
My dear Catherine, we are to part. M-my f-father has recollected an engagement with Lord Longtown that will take us all away in two days. Explanation and apology are impossible. I cannot attempt either.
Do not distress yourself. I am very sorry we are to part so soon and so suddenly, but I am not offended.
I shall return another time to finish my visit, or you will come to me.
It will not be in my power, Catherine.
Come when you can, then.
And as for leaving, I need not go before you do. And I can surely be ready by Monday.
My parents having no notice of it is of little concern; I daresay the general will send a servant with me most of the way.

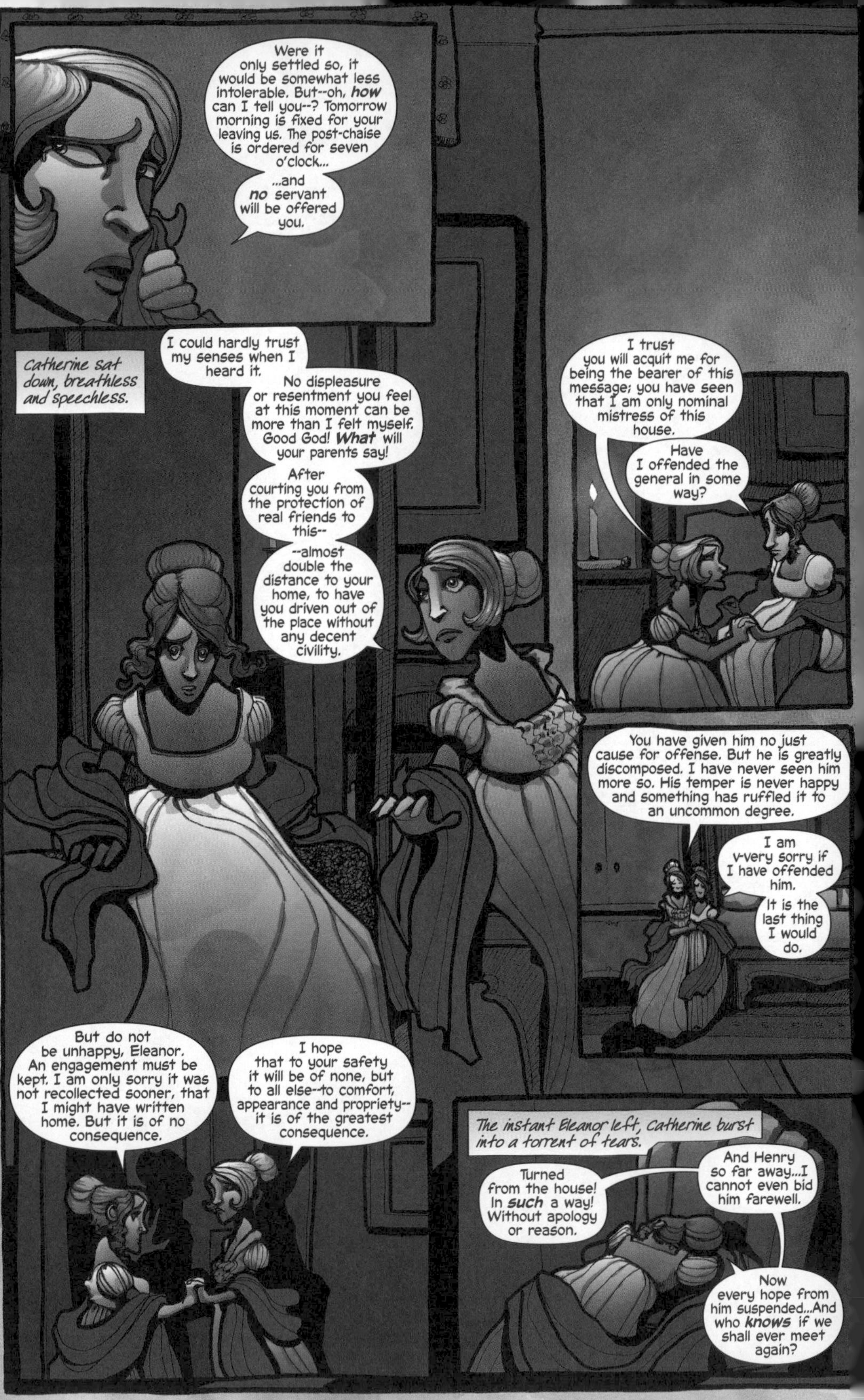
Were it only settled so, it would be somewhat less intolerable. But--oh, how can I tell you--? Tomorrow morning is fixed for your leaving us. The post-chaise is ordered for seven o'clock...
...and no servant will be offered you.
Catherine sat down, breathless and speechless.
I could hardly trust my senses when I heard it.
No displeasure or resentment you feel at this moment can be more than I felt myself. Good God! What will your parents say!
After courting you from the protection of real friends to this--
--almost double the distance to your home, to have you driven out of the place without any decent civility.
I trust you will acquit me for being the bearer of this message; you have seen that I am only nominal mistress of this house.
Have I offended the general in some way?
You have given him no just cause for offense. But he is greatly discomposed. I have never seen him more so. His temper is never happy and something has ruffled it to an uncommon degree.
I am v-very sorry if I have offended him.
It is the last thing I would do.
But do not be unhappy, Eleanor. An engagement must be kept. I am only sorry it was not recollected sooner, that I might have written home. But it is of no consequence.
I hope that to your safety it will be of none, but to all else--to comfort, appearance and propriety--it is of the greatest consequence.
The instant Eleanor left, Catherine burst into a torrent of tears.
Turned from the house! In such a way! Without apology or reason.
And Henry so far away...I cannot even bid him farewell.
Now every hope from him suspended...And who knows if we shall ever meet again?

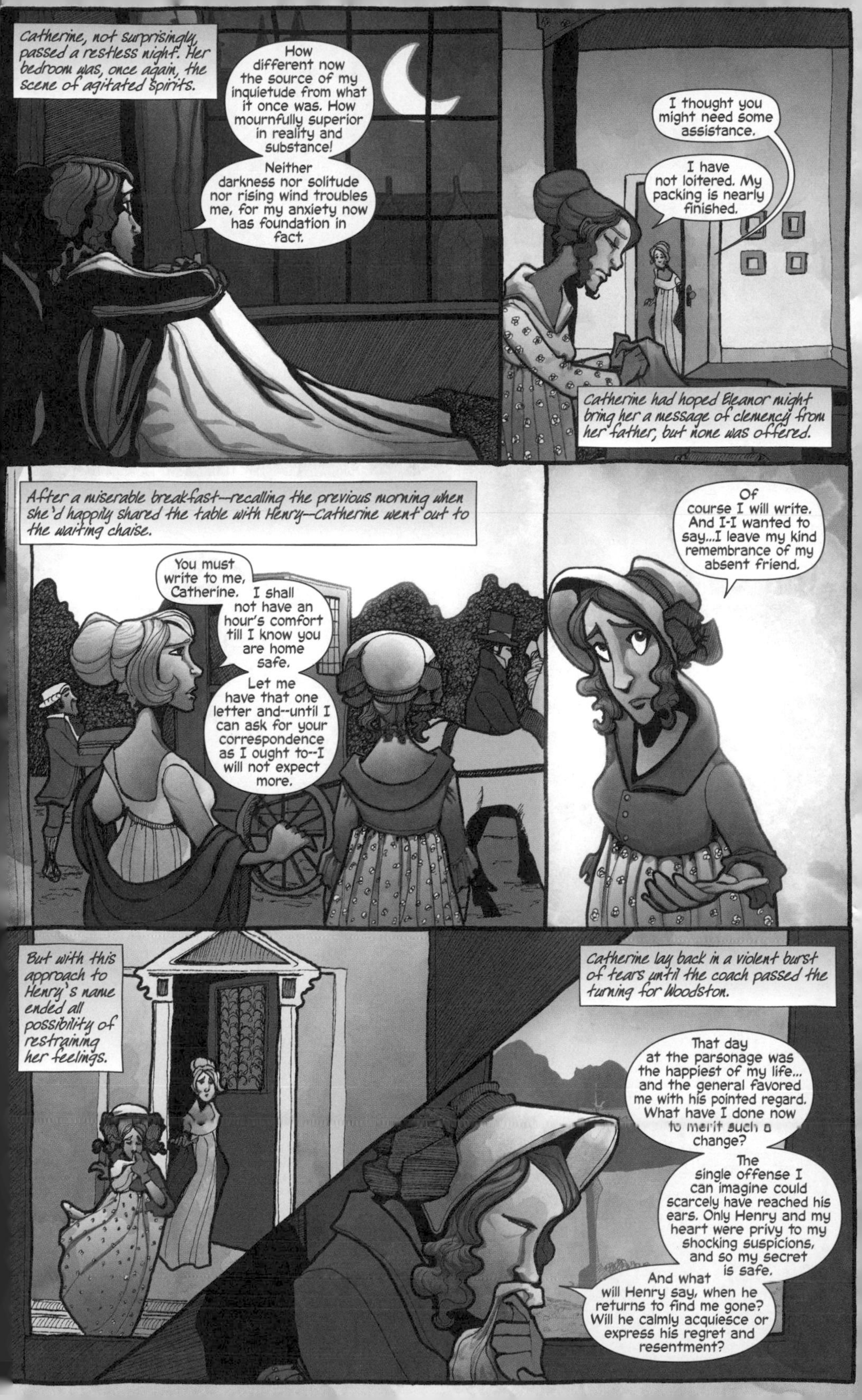
Catherine, not surprisingly, passed a restless night. Her bedroom was, once again, the scene of agitated spirits.
How different now the source of my inquietude from what it once was. How mournfully superior in reality and substance!
Neither darkness nor solitude nor rising wind troubles me, for my anxiety now has foundation in fact.
I thought you might need some assistance.
I have not loitered. My packing is nearly finished.
Catherine had hoped Eleanor might bring her a message of clemency from her father, but none was offered.
After a miserable breakfast--recalling the previous morning when she'd happily shared the table with Henry--Catherine went out to the waiting chaise.
You must write to me, Catherine.
I shall not have an hour's comfort till I know you are home safe.
Let me have that one letter and--until I can ask for your correspondence as I ought to--I will not expect more.
Of course I will write. And I-I wanted to say...I leave my kind remembrance of my absent friend.
But with this approach to Henry's name ended all possibility of restraining her feelings.
Catherine lay back in a violent burst of tears until the coach passed the turning for Woodston.
That day at the parsonage was the happiest of my life... and the general favored me with his pointed regard. What have I done now to merit such a change?
The single offense I can imagine could scarcely have reached his ears. Only Henry and my heart were privy to my shocking suspicions, and so my secret is safe.
And what will Henry say, when he returns to find me gone? Will he calmly acquiesce or express his regret and resentment?

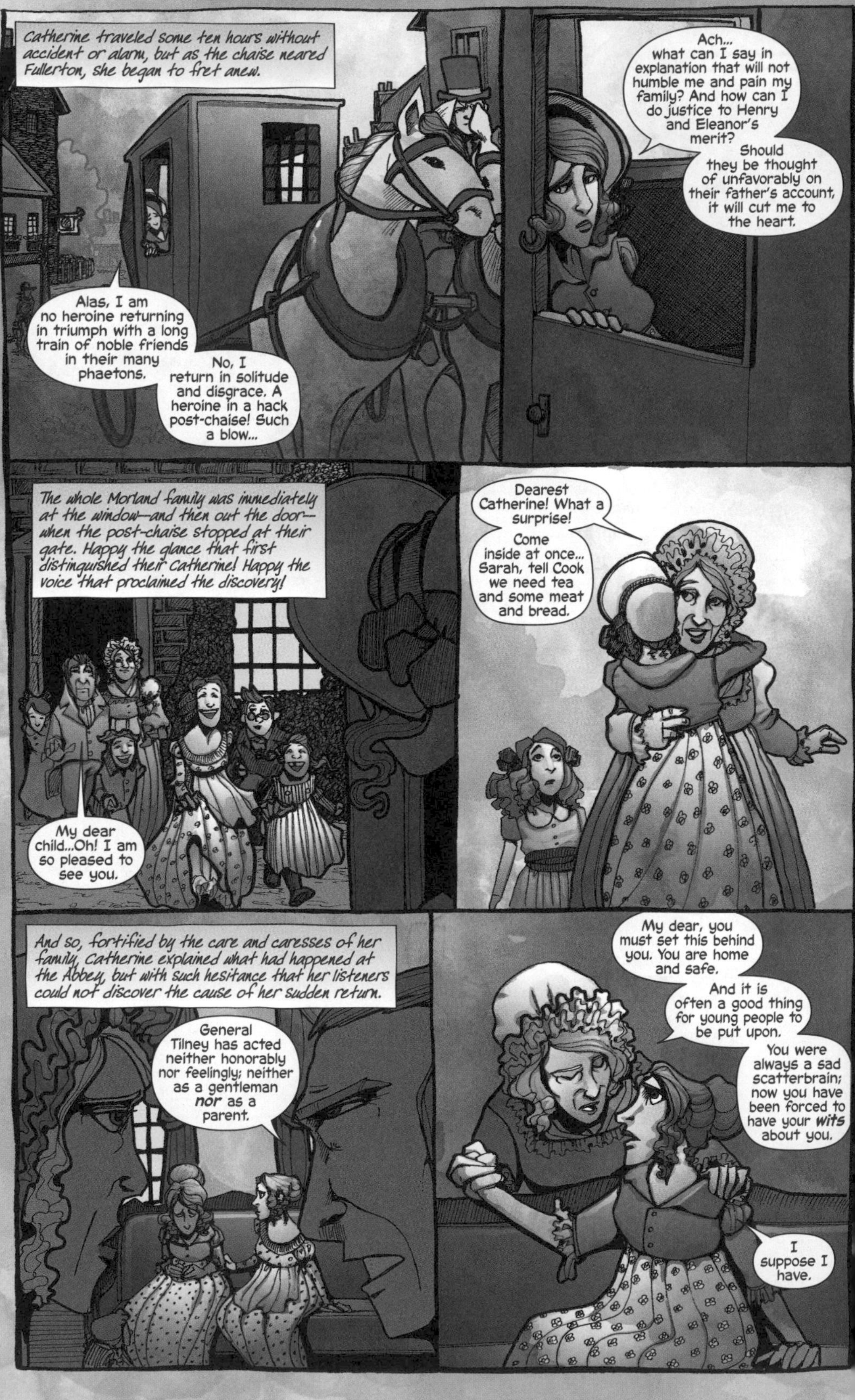

Catherine traveled some ten hours without accident or alarm, but as the chaise neared Fullerton, she began to fret anew.
Alas, I am no heroine returning in triumph with a long train of noble friends in their many phaetons.
No, I return in solitude and disgrace. A heroine in a hack post-chaise! Such a blow...
Ach... what can I say in explanation that will not humble me and pain my family? And how can I do justice to Henry and Eleanor's merit?
Should they be thought of unfavorably on their father's account, it will cut me to the heart.
The whole Morland family was immediately at the window—and then out the door—when the post-chaise stopped at their gate. Happy the glance that first distinguished their Catherine! Happy the voice that proclaimed the discovery!
My dear child...Oh! I am so pleased to see you.
Dearest Catherine! What a surprise!
Come inside at once... Sarah, tell Cook we need tea and some meat and bread.
And so, fortified by the care and caresses of her family, Catherine explained what had happened at the Abbey, but with such hesitance that her listeners could not discover the cause of her sudden return.
General Tilney has acted neither honorably nor feelingly; neither as a gentleman nor as a parent.
My dear, you must set this behind you. You are home and safe.
And it is often a good thing for young people to be put upon.
You were always a sad scatterbrain; now you have been forced to have your wits about you.
I suppose I have.

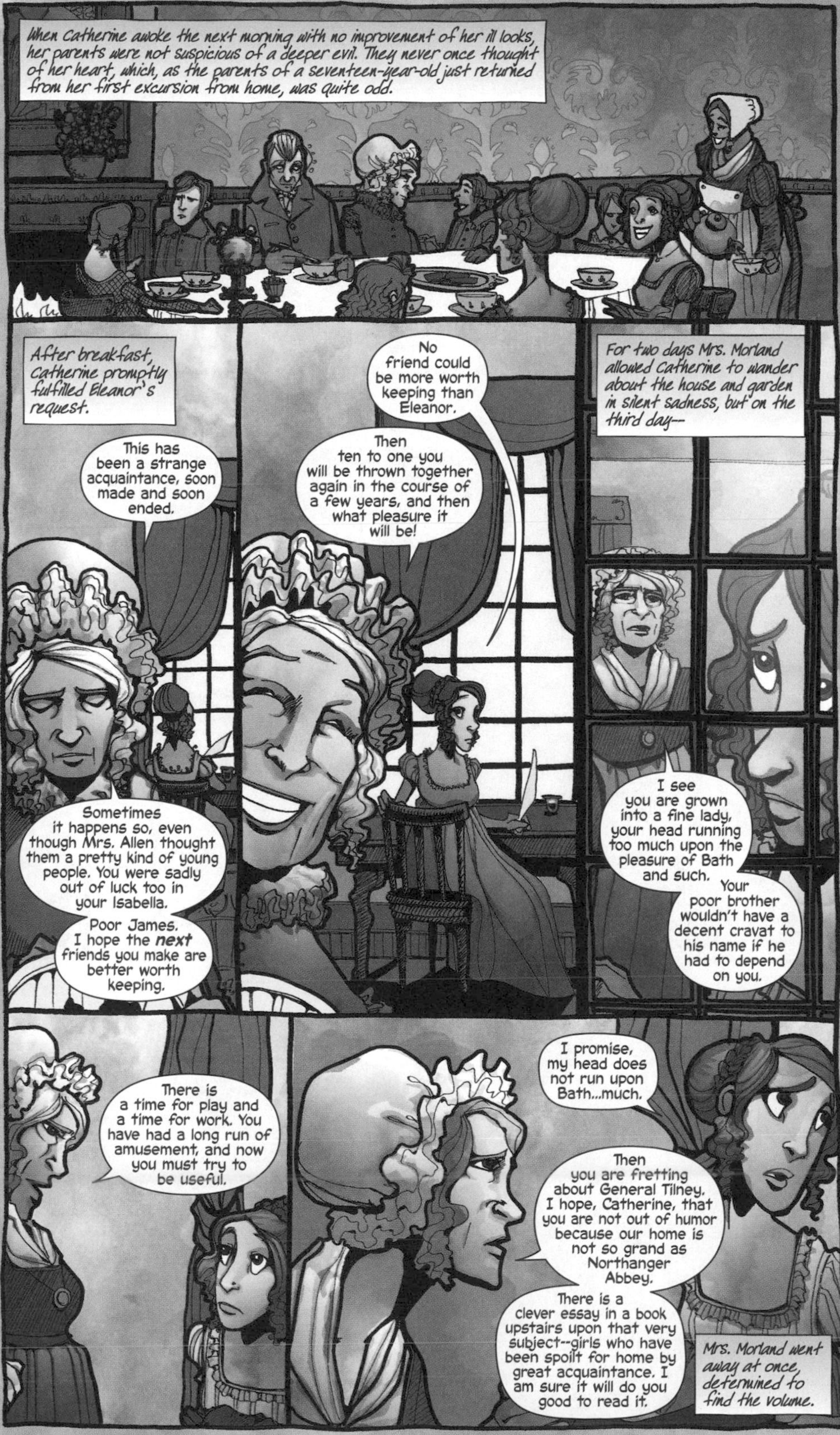
When Catherine awoke the next morning with no improvement of her ill looks, her parents were not suspicious of a deeper evil. They never once thought of her heart, which, as the parents of a seventeen-year-old just returned from her first excursion from home, was quite odd.
After breakfast, Catherine promptly fulfilled Eleanor's request.
This has been a strange acquaintance, soon made and soon ended.
Sometimes it happens so, even though Mrs. Allen thought them a pretty kind of young people. You were sadly out of luck too in your Isabella.
Poor James. I hope the ***next*** friends you make are better worth keeping.
No friend could be more worth keeping than Eleanor.
Then ten to one you will be thrown together again in the course of a few years, and then what pleasure it will be!
For two days Mrs. Morland allowed Catherine to wander about the house and garden in silent sadness, but on the third day--
I see you are grown into a fine lady, your head running too much upon the pleasure of Bath and such.
Your poor brother wouldn't have a decent cravat to his name if he had to depend on you.
There is a time for play and a time for work. You have had a long run of amusement, and now you must try to be useful.
I promise, my head does not run upon Bath...much.
Then you are fretting about General Tilney. I hope, Catherine, that you are not out of humor because our home is not so grand as Northanger Abbey.
There is a clever essay in a book upstairs upon that very subject--girls who have been spoilt for home by great acquaintance. I am sure it will do you good to read it.
Mrs. Morland went away at once, determined to find the volume.

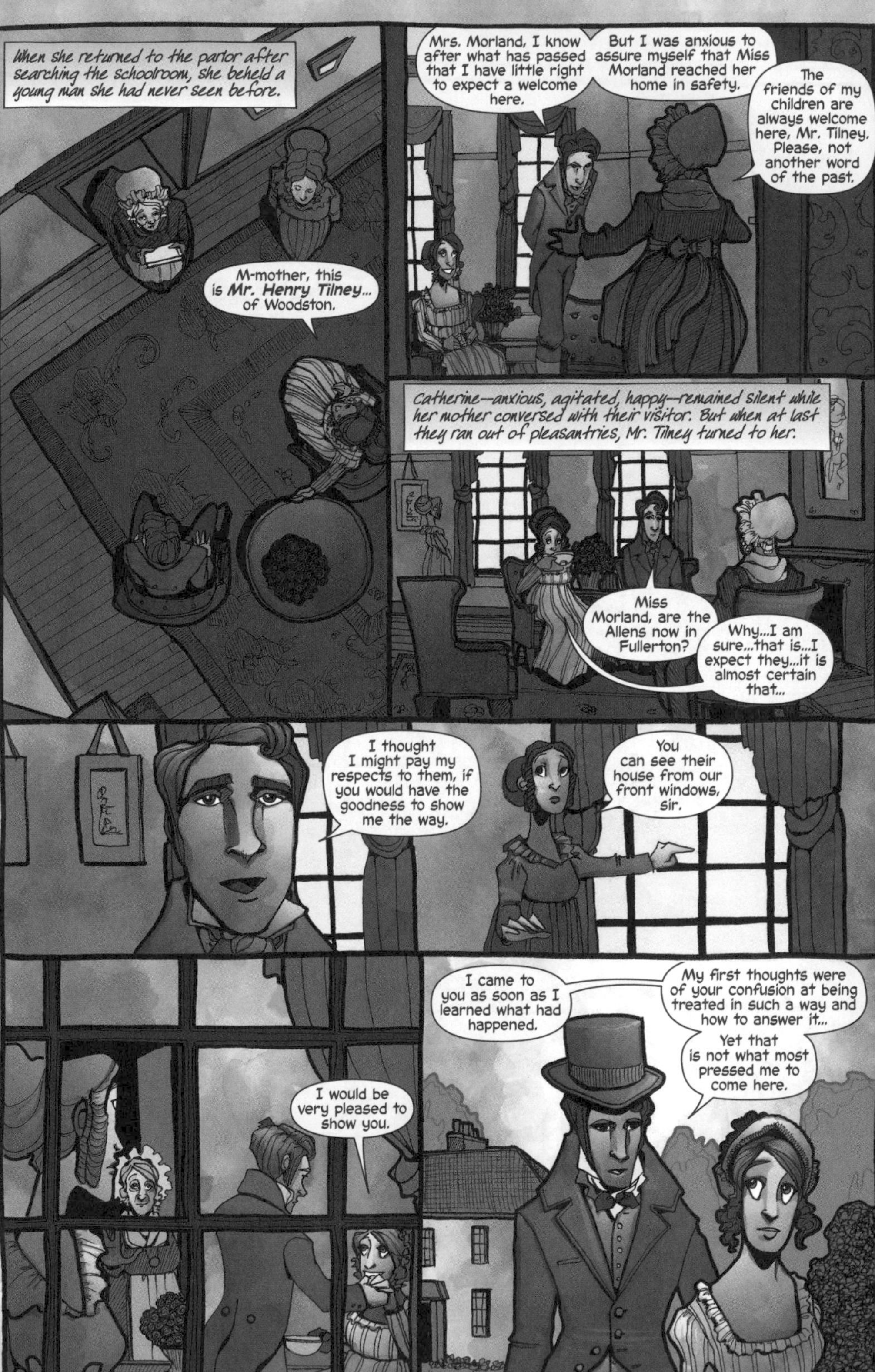
When she returned to the parlor after searching the schoolroom, she beheld a young man she had never seen before.
M-mother, this is Mr. Henry Tilney... of Woodston.
Mrs. Morland, I know after what has passed that I have little right to expect a welcome here.
But I was anxious to assure myself that Miss Morland reached her home in safety.
The friends of my children are always welcome here, Mr. Tilney. Please, not another word of the past.
Catherine—anxious, agitated, happy—remained silent while her mother conversed with their visitor. But when at last they ran out of pleasantries, Mr. Tilney turned to her.
Miss Morland, are the Allens now in Fullerton?
Why...I am sure...that is...I expect they...it is almost certain that...
I thought I might pay my respects to them, if you would have the goodness to show me the way.
You can see their house from our front windows, sir.
I would be very pleased to show you.
I came to you as soon as I learned what had happened.
My first thoughts were of your confusion at being treated in such a way and how to answer it...
Yet that is not what most pressed me to come here.

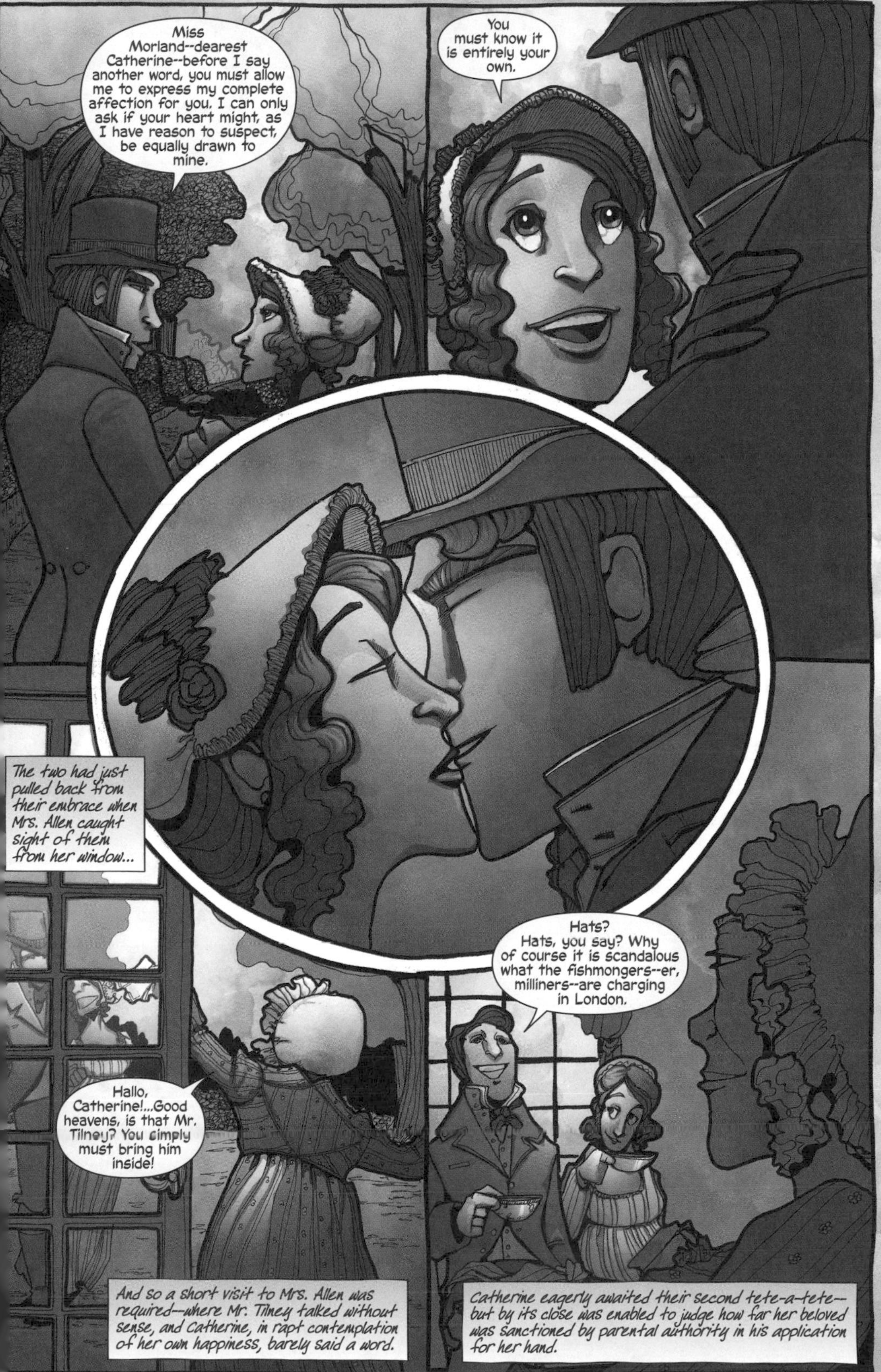
Miss Morland--dearest Catherine--before I say another word, you must allow me to express my complete affection for you. I can only ask if your heart might, as I have reason to suspect, be equally drawn to mine.
You must know it is entirely your own.
The two had just pulled back from their embrace when Mrs. Allen caught sight of them from her window...
Hallo, Catherine!...Good heavens, is that Mr. Tilney? You simply must bring him inside!
Hats? Hats, you say? Why of course it is scandalous what the fishmongers--er, milliners--are charging in London.
And so a short visit to Mrs. Allen was required--where Mr. Tilney talked without sense, and Catherine, in rapt contemplation of her own happiness, barely said a word.
Catherine eagerly awaited their second tete-a-tete--but by its close was enabled to judge how far her beloved was sanctioned by parental authority in his application for her hand.

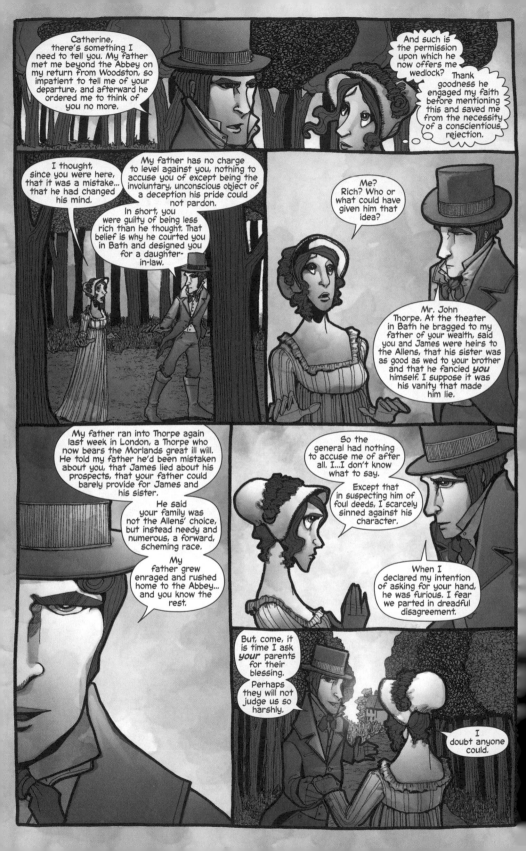

Catherine, there's something I need to tell you. My father met me beyond the Abbey on my return from Woodston, so impatient to tell me of your departure, and afterward he ordered me to think of you no more.

And such is the permission upon which he now offers me wedlock? Thank goodness he engaged my faith before mentioning this and saved me from the necessity of a conscientious rejection.

I thought, since you were here, that it was a mistake... that he had changed his mind.

My father has no charge to level against you, nothing to accuse you of except being the involuntary, unconscious object of a deception his pride could not pardon.

In short, you were guilty of being less rich than he thought. That belief is why he courted you in Bath and designed you for a daughter-in-law.

Me? Rich? Who or what could have given him that idea?

Mr. John Thorpe. At the theater in Bath he bragged to my father of your wealth, said you and James were heirs to the Allens, that his sister was as good as wed to your brother and that he fancied you himself. I suppose it was his vanity that made him lie.

My father ran into Thorpe again last week in London, a Thorpe who now bears the Morlands great ill will. He told my father he'd been mistaken about you, that James lied about his prospects, that your father could barely provide for James and his sister.

He said your family was not the Allens' choice, but instead needy and numerous, a forward, scheming race.

My father grew enraged and rushed home to the Abbey... and you know the rest.

So the general had nothing to accuse me of after all. I...I don't know what to say.

Except that in suspecting him of foul deeds, I scarcely sinned against his character.

When I declared my intention of asking for your hand, he was furious. I fear we parted in dreadful disagreement.

But, come, it is time I ask your parents for their blessing.

Perhaps they will not judge us so harshly.

I doubt anyone could.

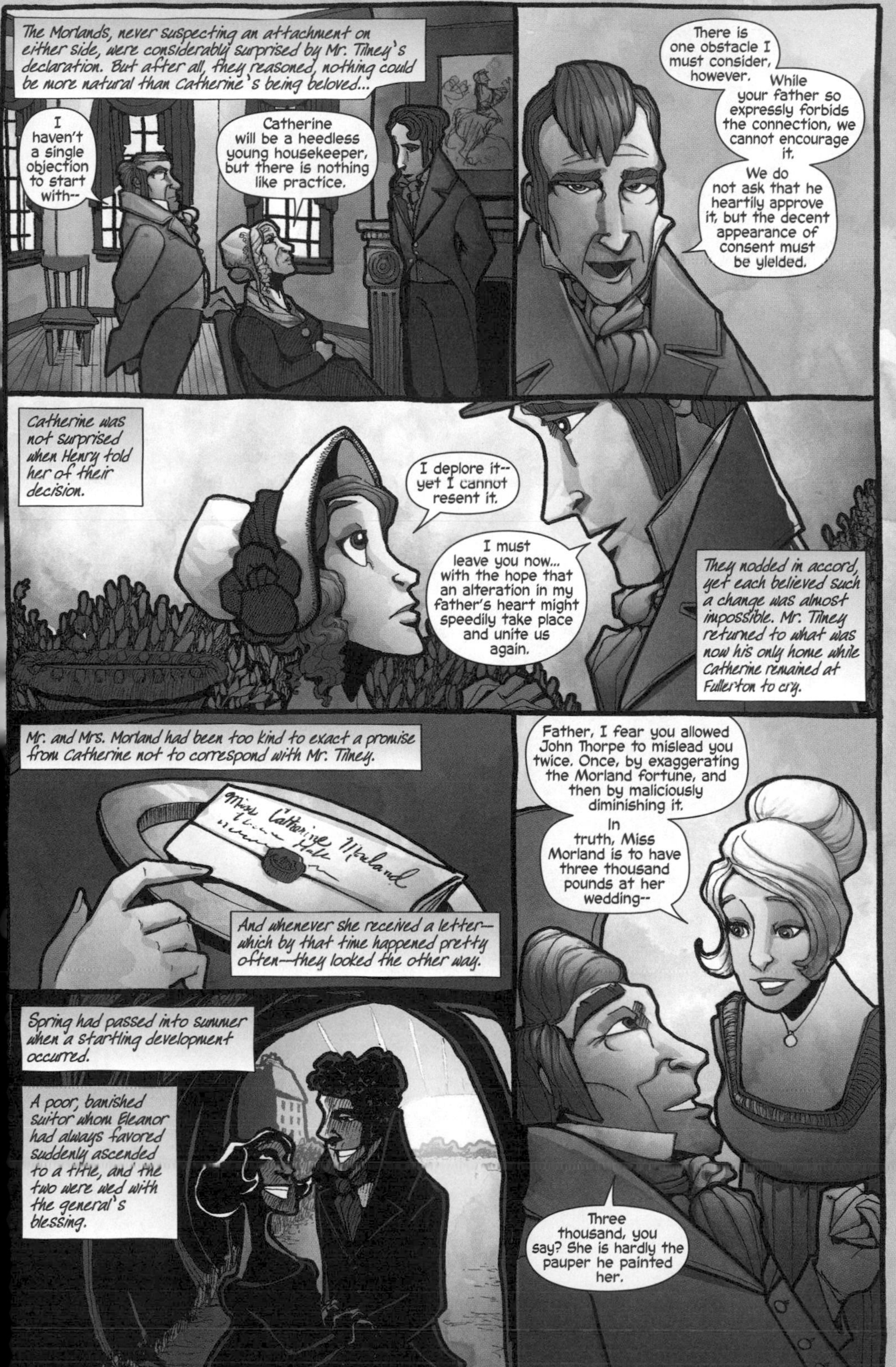

The Morlands, never suspecting an attachment on either side, were considerably surprised by Mr. Tilney's declaration. But after all, they reasoned, nothing could be more natural than Catherine's being beloved...
I haven't a single objection to start with--
Catherine will be a heedless young housekeeper, but there is nothing like practice.
There is one obstacle I must consider, however.
While your father so expressly forbids the connection, we cannot encourage it.
We do not ask that he heartily approve it, but the decent appearance of consent must be yielded.
Catherine was not surprised when Henry told her of their decision.
I deplore it-- yet I cannot resent it.
I must leave you now... with the hope that an alteration in my father's heart might speedily take place and unite us again.
They nodded in accord, yet each believed such a change was almost impossible. Mr. Tilney returned to what was now his only home while Catherine remained at Fullerton to cry.
Mr. and Mrs. Morland had been too kind to exact a promise from Catherine not to correspond with Mr. Tilney.
Miss Catherine Morland
And whenever she received a letter-- which by that time happened pretty often--they looked the other way.
Father, I fear you allowed John Thorpe to mislead you twice. Once, by exaggerating the Morland fortune, and then by maliciously diminishing it.
In truth, Miss Morland is to have three thousand pounds at her wedding--
Three thousand, you say? She is hardly the pauper he painted her.
Spring had passed into summer when a startling development occurred.
A poor, banished suitor whom Eleanor had always favored suddenly ascended to a title, and the two were wed with the general's blessing.

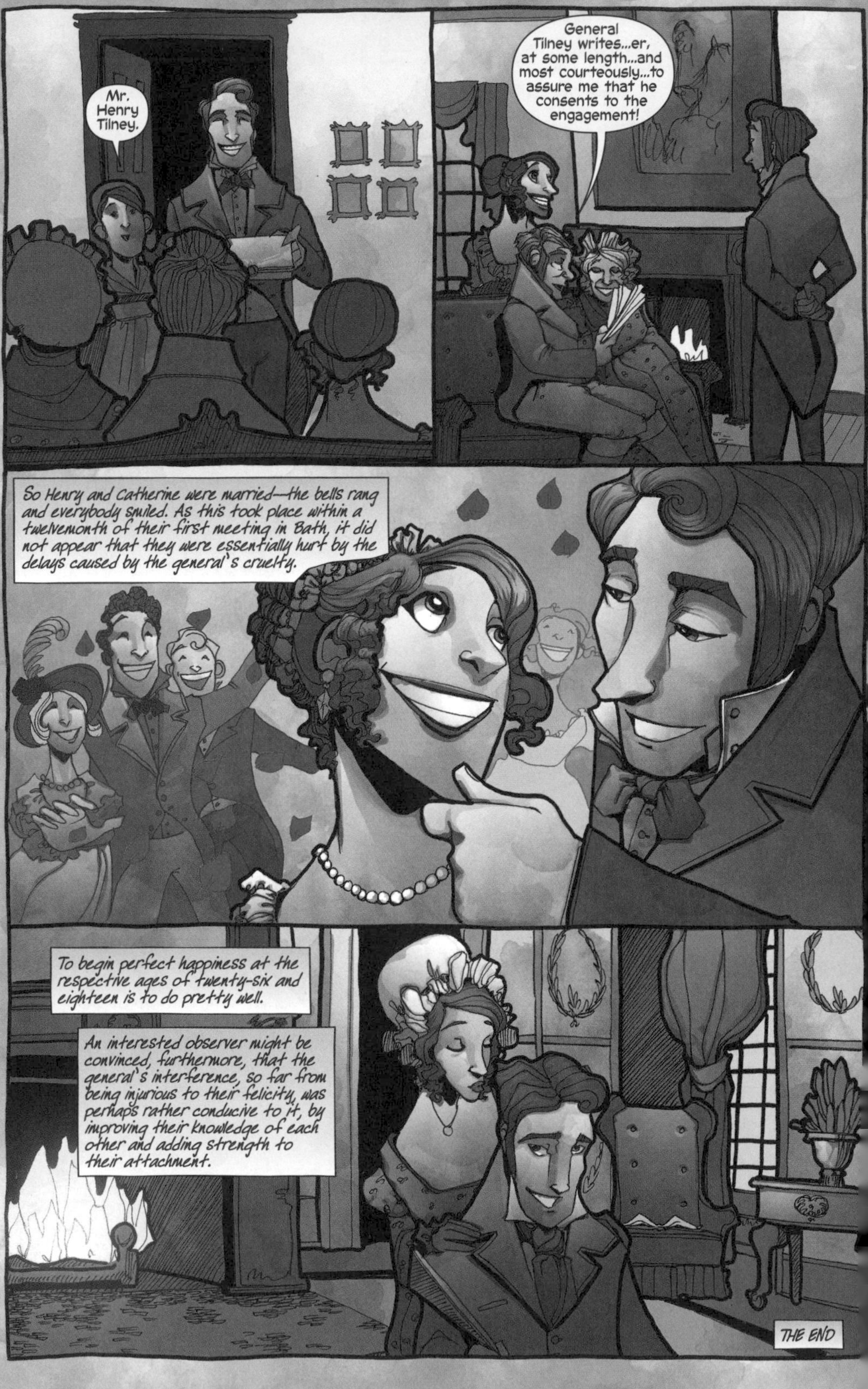
Mr. Henry Tilney.
General Tilney writes...er, at some length...and most courteously...to assure me that he consents to the engagement!
So Henry and Catherine were married--the bells rang and everybody smiled. As this took place within a twelvemonth of their first meeting in Bath, it did not appear that they were essentially hurt by the delays caused by the general's cruelty.
To begin perfect happiness at the respective ages of twenty-six and eighteen is to do pretty well.
An interested observer might be convinced, furthermore, that the general's interference, so far from being injurious to their felicity, was perhaps rather conducive to it, by improving their knowledge of each other and adding strength to their attachment.
THE END

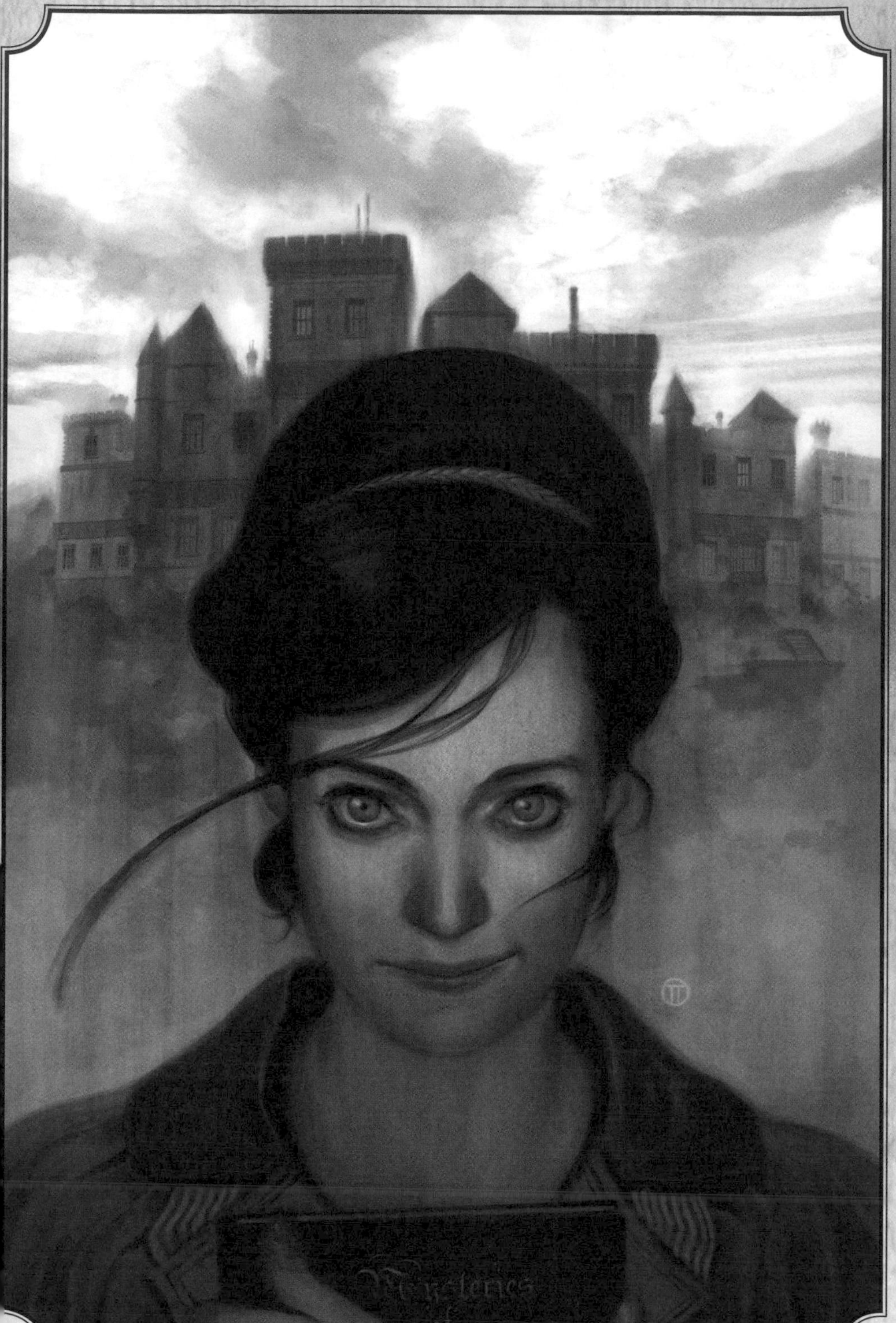
Mysteries
of

ONE

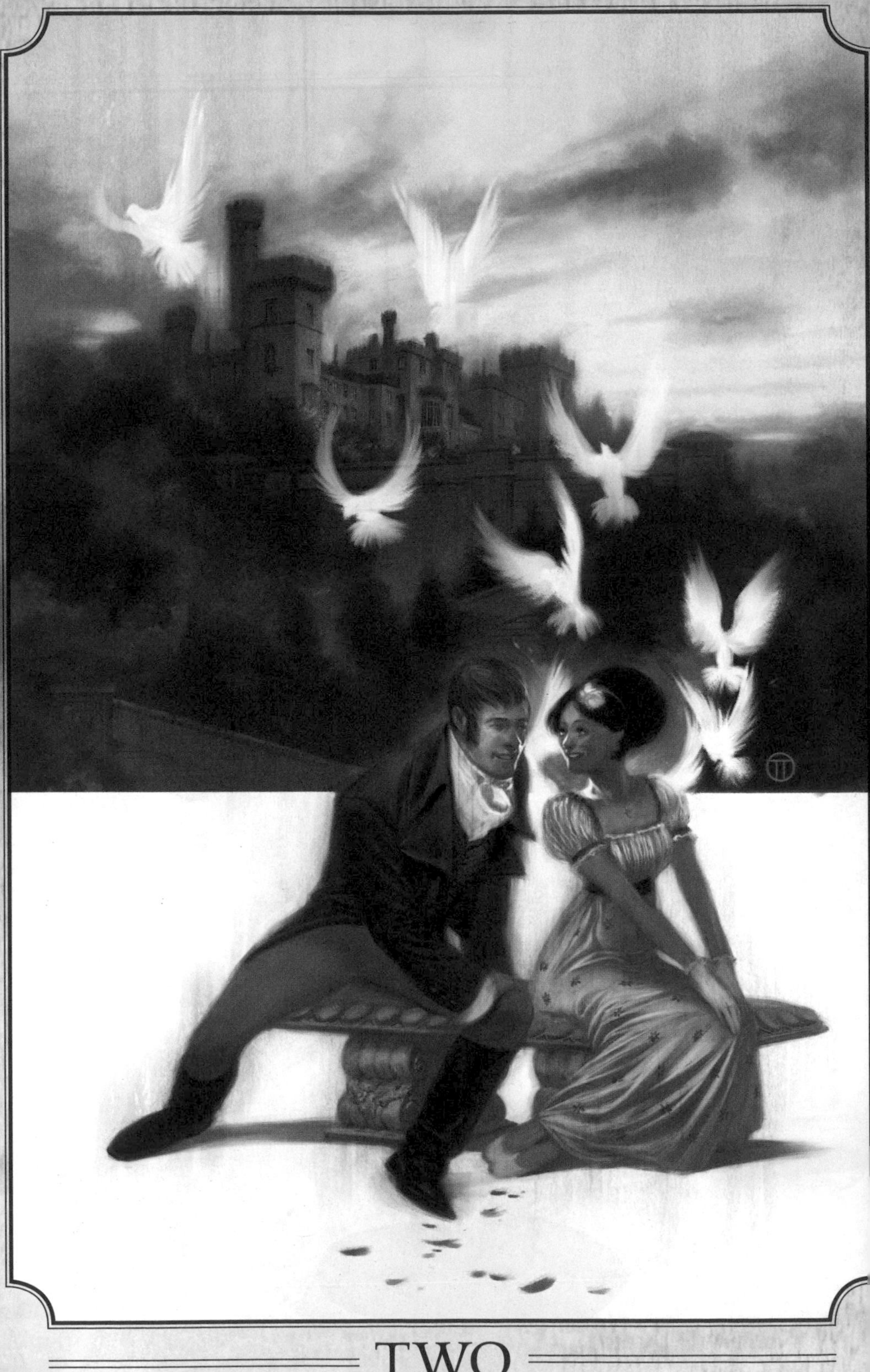

TWO

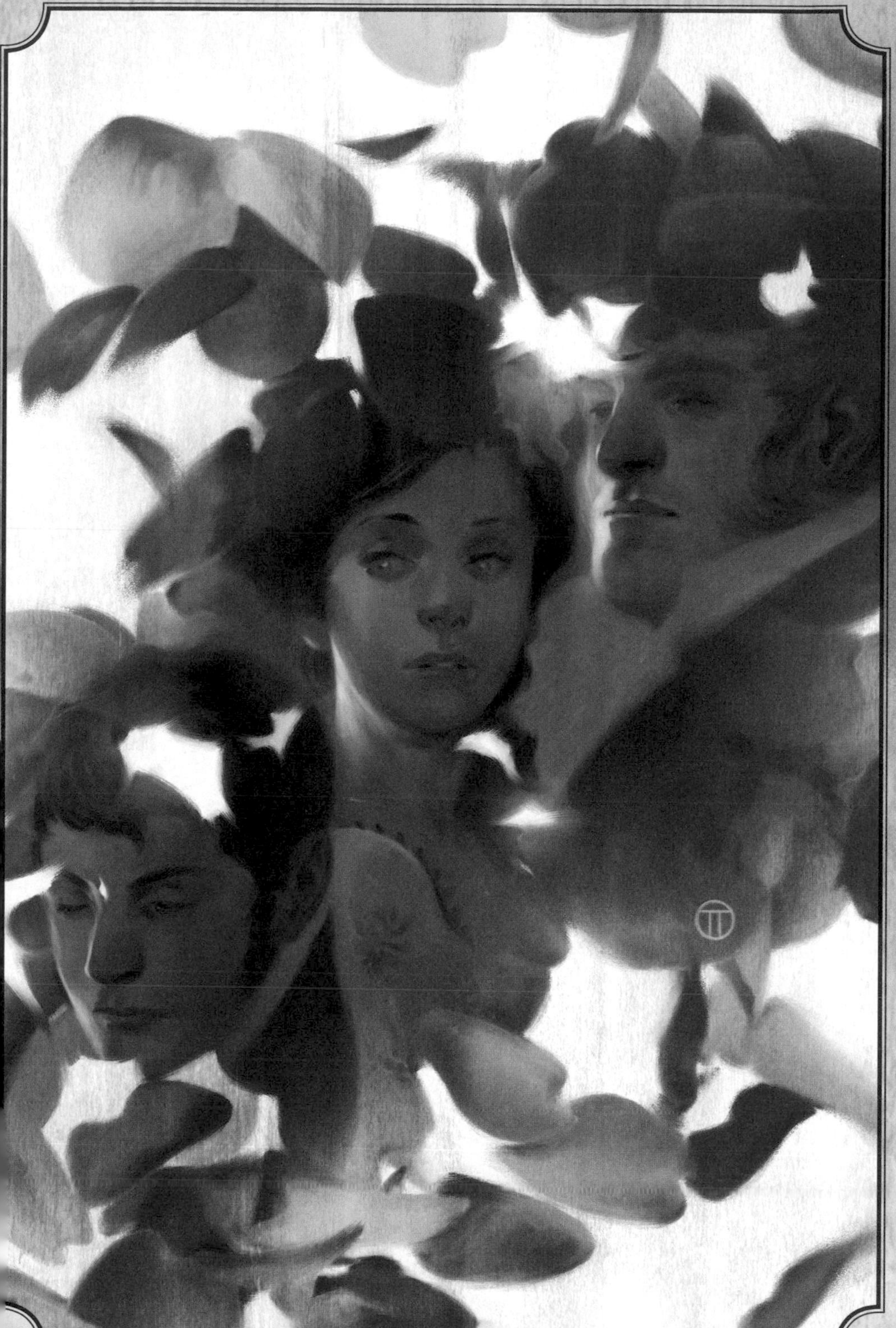

THREE

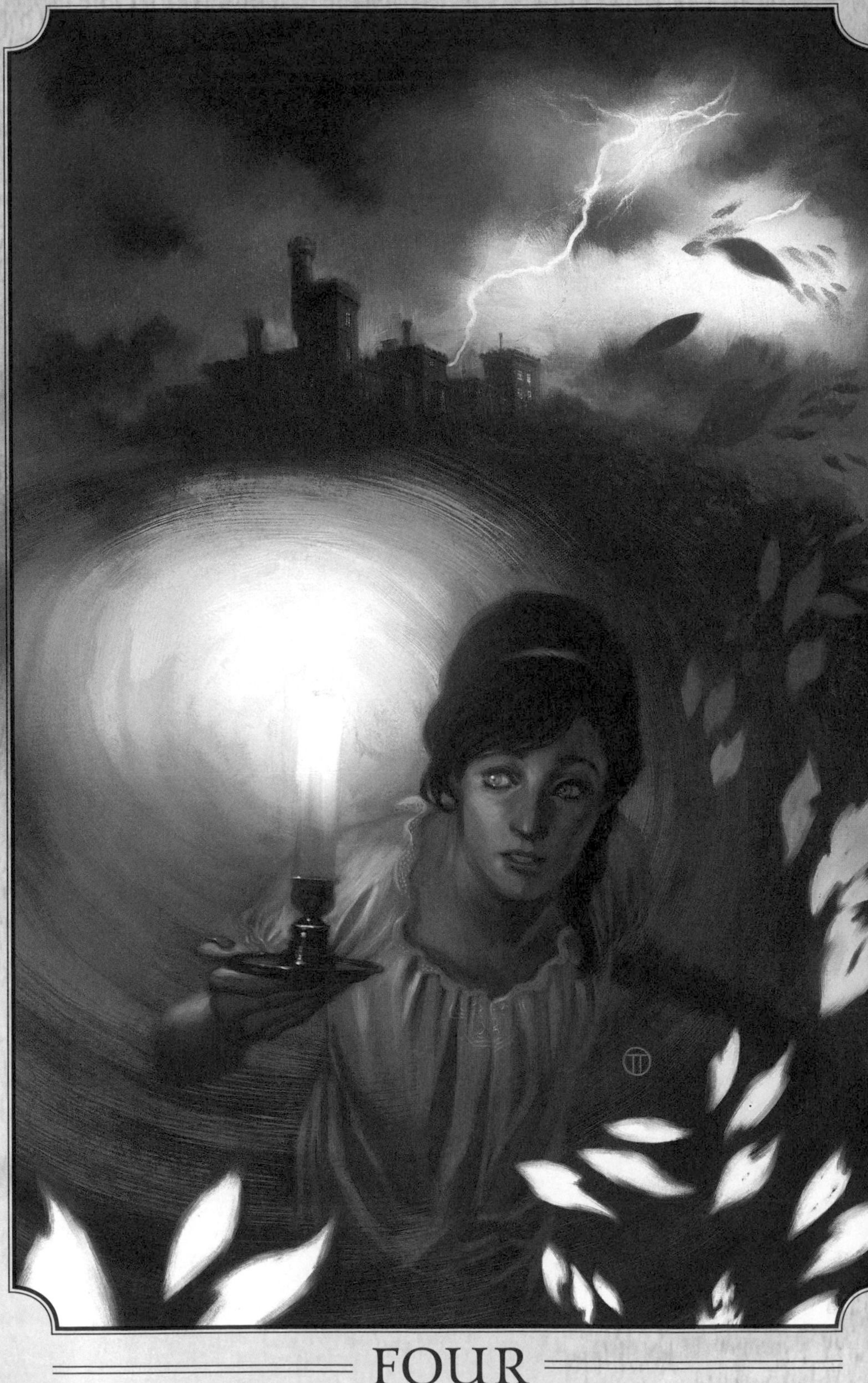

FOUR

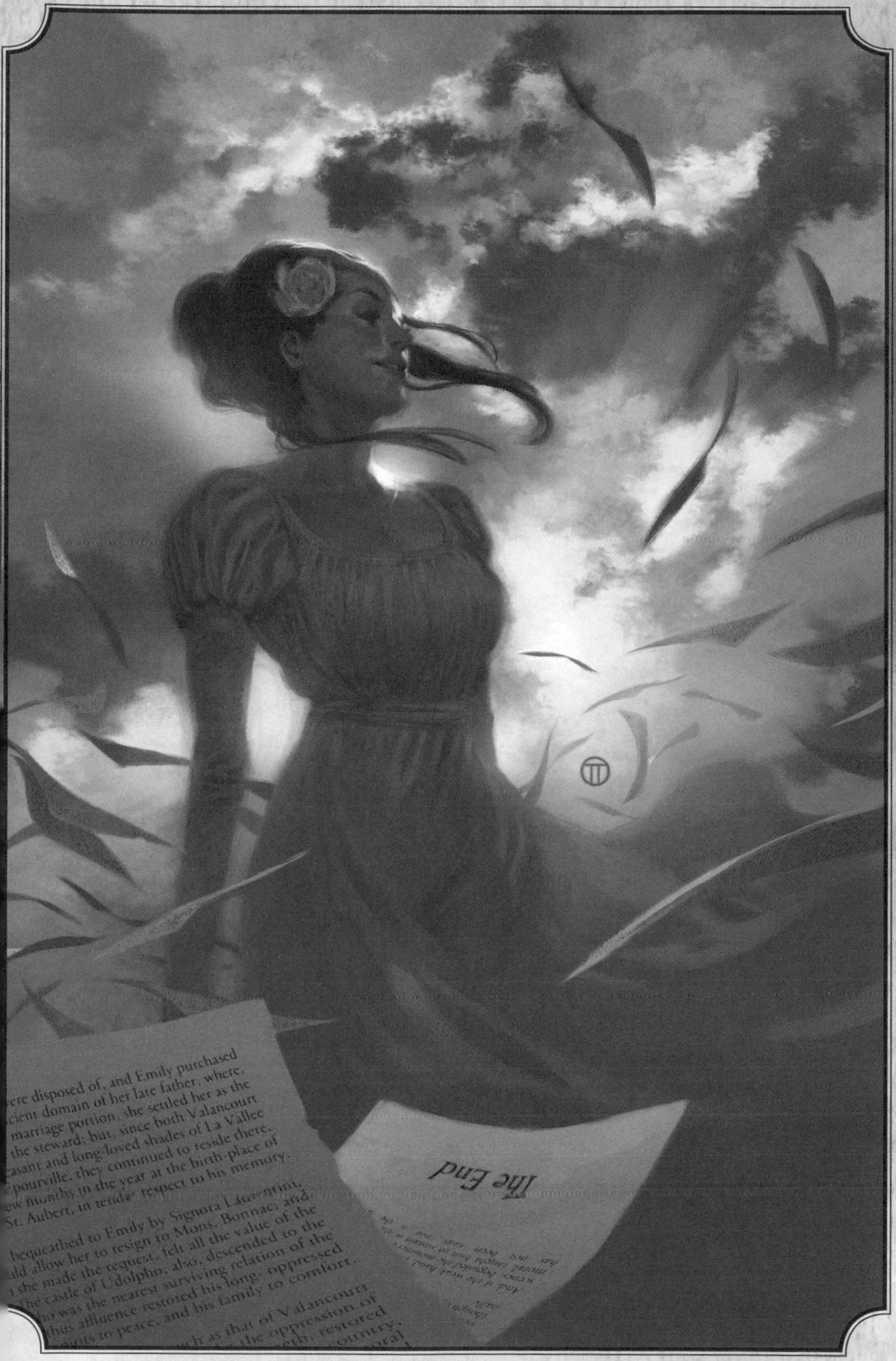
ere disposed of, and Emily purchased
cient domain of her late father, where,
marriage portion, she settled her as the
the steward; but, since both Valancourt
easant and long-loved shades of La Vallee
epourville, they continued to reside there,
ew months in the year at the birth-place of
St. Aubert, in tender respect to his memory.
bequeathed to Emily by Signora Laurentini,
ild allow her to resign to Mons. Bonnac; and
she made the request, felt all the value of the
he castle of Udolpho, also, descended to the
ho was the nearest surviving relation of the
hus affluence restored his long- oppressed
to peace, and his family to comfort.
as that of Valancourt
the oppression of
restored
The End

FIVE